Marketing Performance Assessment

Thomas V. Bonoma

Bruce H. Clark

Harvard Business School

Harvard Business School Press   **Boston, Massachusetts**

92 91 90 89 88   5 4 3 2 1

Library of Congress Cataloging-in-Publication Data

Bonoma, Thomas V.
  Marketing performance assessment / Thomas V. Bonoma,
Bruce H. Clark.
    p.   cm.
  Bibliography: p. 185
  Includes index.
  ISBN 0-87584-203-8 (alk. paper)
  1. Marketing—Evaluation.   I. Clark, Bruce H., 1958–
II. Title.
HF5415.B5243 1988   88-21428
658.8′007′23—dc 19   CIP

Contents

List of Tables

List of Figures

Preface

This book is the result of more than two years' effort to understand the determinants of assessing marketing performance. That effort, in turn, could not have been made without six previous years of research devoted to understanding marketing implementation, or the rules of good marketing practice. In this sense, this book is profoundly overdue, for a lot has gone into it. In another, more important way, this work is premature, for we have only started on the path of data collection which lies ahead and cannot yet assert with confidence that our views on assessing marketing performance are as empirically valid as they appear theoretically sensible.

The purpose of this book is simple, though it may turn out to be unattainable. It is to offer a method for assessing marketing performance that is applicable both within and between firms, that generates sound norms by which managers may compare themselves and their programs, and that instructs managers in the steps they can take to improve program performance. The reason the goal may turn out to be unattainable is not so much because it is grand, or even because many others have thrown themselves on the rocks of assessing marketing performance in the last fifty years with mixed, but always bloody, results. Rather, this project never can be complete, regardless of what data we have or go on to collect, but will remain only a series of increasingly interesting "confirmatory instances" in which the model works. It was a small succession of these instances which now leads us to offer this preliminary statement of our thinking about marketing performance assessment. A future book will present the results from a national sample on an instrument (presented here) embodying the model we offer.

What is unique in this book, and about the way in which it encourages readers to think about marketing performance, is that we combine relevant psychological thought with useful marketing knowledge to offer a model of marketing performance which explicitly re-includes judgments of marketing quality by the managers doing or supervising the marketing job. Furthermore, the model is based on several years' study of the elements and structure of marketing execution, which gives it a well-grounded starting place.

We hope the book will be useful both to academics and managers. Though we have written it primarily for researchers, it has much managerial relevance. The interested manager might do well to skip Chapters 2–5, and should read Chapter 7 only if he or she has the time or interest. For managers, then, the most productive reading path is Chapters 1, 6, and 8–10. The three case studies presented in Appendix A will be useful to both sorts of readers, but perhaps in different ways. Similarly, the marketing performance assessment questionnaire given in Appendix B should be useful to academics and to managers, but again, differently: the former may wish to modify it, while the latter may wish to fill it out for programs of interest. Finally, the annotated bibliography in Appendix C, which compiles more than fifty years of research into marketing productivity, will be, we suspect, of interest primarily to academics, but we have written it to be a useful management reading list as well.

The academic reader can, of course, read the book in chapter order, but may wish to take a quick look at the model in Chapters 5 and 6 to determine whether there is interest in tracing the flow of previous work. Chapter 7 should be thoroughly examined, perhaps in conjunction with Appendix B. And the early data points in Appendix A, while wholly clinical, offer some interesting insights when read in conjunction with Chapter 8.

We are grateful to a number of parties for their help during this project. The Division of Research at the Harvard Business School is one of them. The School is one of the few places in the world where researchers can contemplate and engage in projects of the magnitude that we propose and partially execute here.

So many of our HBS colleagues have given us so much help during the last several years that we hesitate to identify individuals. Still, Professors Benson Shapiro and Melvyn Menezes must be singled out as important influences on our work; Professor Menezes has in fact contributed to it directly in the LifeSpan case given in Appendix A. A number of managers—some depicted in the case studies, others attending one or another of Harvard Business School's executive programs—and some clients, the victims of an impromptu lecturette on marketing performance, were valuable contributors and critics throughout the project. An early opportunity to present the model to managers and academics on the Marketing Science Institute's Visiting Committee helped as well. These parties, along with many others, improved the manuscript materially. We of course are responsible for any remaining shortcomings.

Boston, Massachusetts   Thomas V. Bonoma
April 1988   Bruce H. Clark

Marketing Performance Assessment

Chapter 1

Introduction: The Philosopher's Stone

Introduction

The assessment of <u>marketing performance</u>, often called <u>mar-keting productivity analysis</u>, remains a seductive but elusive concept for scholars and practitioners alike. It is seductive because agreed-upon or accepted measures of marketing productivity hold the promise of opening scholarly doors heretofore locked, and of clarifying muddy pools of managerial performance. It is elusive because for as long as marketers have practiced their craft, both they and the general managers who supervise them have looked unsuccessfully for clear, present, and reliable signals of performance by which marketing merit could be judged (e.g., Oxenfeldt, 1959; Webster, 1981). More than any other concept in the marketing discipline, the notion of a general measure of marketing performance represents both the allure and continual disappointment of the "philosopher's stone." If it could only be found, much could be evaluated and much would become clear.

While much work has gone into researching the inputs to the marketing equation (see below), achieving a coherent view of the output or performance measures of marketing has remained a difficult and generally unrewarding business (cf., e.g., Feder, 1965; Mehrotra, 1984; Heskett, 1965; Miller, 1967). Indeed, perhaps no other concept in marketing's short history has proven as stubbornly resistant to conceptualization, definition, or application as that of <u>marketing performance</u>. The <u>reasons</u> for this are many, but prominent among them are that:

• Marketing as a discipline (cf., Bonoma, 1985a; Drucker, 1974) intertwines not only with many other functions internal to the corporation, like production, but also with external factions like the "trade" (distribution channels) and end-users themselves. It is thus complicated in its operation and effects, for its tentacles touch and are touched by important and uncontrolled parties external to the corporation. Any measure must take these complexities into account.

• Second, marketing is a "boundary role" function (e.g., Wind and Cardozo, 1974). Consequently, marketing operations constantly bob on the cross-cutting currents of the goals of the firm and the wants of customers. Marketing is expected to mediate intelligently between these currents. This makes marketing's outputs lagged, multivocal, and subject to so many influences that establishing cause-and-effect linkages is difficult. For example, the effects of just a single low-level action in marketing, doubling the advertising budget, may not be determinable for some time, if ever (Feder, 1965).

• Third, as we noted above, marketing as a discipline has always focused much more on inputs than on outputs (cf., Bonoma, 1985a). For at least the last two decades, marketing research has largely been concerned with correct specification of the independent variable side of marketing practice, detailing the elements or variables available for manipulation to the marketer (Borden, 1964), the nature and composition of "good" strategy (e.g., Abell and Hammond, 1979), and variables that can be entered either into a regression equation (e.g., PIMS; see Schoeffler, Buzzell, and Heany, 1974) or into some causal modeling scheme (e.g., Bagozzi, 1980) in order to predict share or sales results. The nature of those results, and the meaning of "results" itself, has been treated either as obvious (e.g., market share; but see Oxenfeldt, 1959, for an exception) or as a matter for later inquiry.

Much of the promised later inquiry on marketing performance, however, has never appeared. A computer search of an electronic marketing database shows that over the past decade there have been more than sixteen thousand articles written on marketing and almost eleven thousand on the topic of productivity. A search for articles on marketing productivity, however, yields substantially less than one hundred citations—and 20 percent of *these* one hundred articles are papers calling for more work on marketing productivity!

As a consequence of these and other factors, marketing productivity has assumed the status of a concept that everyone endorses as useful and meaningful, but that seems to have little operational utility either to operating managers or to scholars. Following Theodore Beckman, we can say that "[j]ust as everyone is against sin, so everyone seems to be for productivity" (Beckman and Buzzell, 1958, p. 24).

With continued progress in two areas of marketing, it is timely to take a fresh look at marketing performance assessment. The first area of progress is marketing strategy itself, which over the last ten and especially five years has achieved a degree of sophistication that has clarified marketing's inputs to the point that its outputs may now legitimately be made a primary focus (read Mahajan et al., 1987, for a good and concise summary). The second area is the burgeoning interest in, and literature on, marketing implementation (e.g., Kotler, 1984; Bonoma, 1984, 1985a, 1985b; Stefflre, 1985), which has brought to bear a rudimentary but serviceable conceptual framework for marketing-in-practice. Work on marketing execution has made good progress in beginning to think about the determinants of marketing's outputs, though it has not concerned itself specifically with measuring marketing performance.

Purpose of the Book

The purpose of this work is to offer a novel perspective on and a testable model of what we call *marketing performance assessment*, or MPA. Distinct from the marketing productivity analyses of the past, marketing performance assessment denotes *the adjudged quality of marketing programs, directed by strategy, as these programs are executed in the marketplace.* To develop this model, the book explores lessons from the broad and deep literature concerning marketing performance and productivity. It also often goes beyond that literature to make forays into especially interesting allied areas.

Marketing Performance and Productivity: An Issues Tutorial

Most early work on performance assessment in marketing borrowed intellectually from scholarship in the manufacturing area. Seeking a measure of "marketing productivity," researchers examined manufacturing productivity. The evaluation of manufacturing productivity, in turn, borrowed heavily from elementary physics, where productivity equals force produced per unit energy expended (Sevin, 1965).

Both manufacturing and marketing productivity analyses have traditionally taken as their conceptual starting point an "output per unit input" equation, which stipulates that higher outputs or lower inputs are associated with higher productivity. In marketing, output per unit input has usually been translated into financial or competitive results measures factored by a proxy for effort, also often financial, thus meeting managerial needs for easy quantification. In this bald and skeletal sense, marketing productivity is a marvelously simple concept.

Problems arise, however, when we attempt to move away from broad theoretical agreement toward concrete specification of marketing's relevant inputs and outputs. Rayburn (1973), for example, despairing of making traditional accounting measures apply to marketing, lists four characteristics of marketing which make it more difficult to quantify than production. Among these characteristics are the facts that marketing's environment is more complex than that of production, that there are fewer repetitive marketing tasks than exist in the manufacturing operation, and that many of marketing's outcomes are heavily qualitative.

Nevertheless, a number of scholars have attempted to quantify marketing's inputs and outputs over the years. Table 1 gives a sampler of their efforts to show the diversity of views. These definitions are drawn from the later history of marketing productivity (i.e., since 1955), and will be reviewed in depth below.

As one examines the broadly flung literature, which loosely can be taken as attempting to specify and measure marketing's inputs and outputs, two cleavage points between the various approaches become apparent and thus allow a coherent, if not always unambiguous, classification of the literature. The first such cleavage point is that of effectiveness versus efficiency.

Effectiveness and Efficiency

The effectiveness versus efficiency distinction arose in management largely as a way of distinguishing means-related efforts from ends-related efforts. Efficiency measures, by our definition, record the relation between inputs and outputs, maximizing the latter relative to the former. Effectiveness measures, on the other hand, relate outputs to the ends or objectives of the organization. Peter Drucker (1974) makes a nice summary statement of the differences between effectiveness and efficiency:

> Effectiveness is the foundation of success— efficiency is the minimum condition for survival *after* success has been achieved. Efficiency is concerned with doing things right. Effectiveness is doing the right things. (p. 45)

The marketing literature contains curiously little discussion of what is right (effectiveness), and an almost total focus on how well marketing is done (efficiency). The reason that the effectiveness/efficiency cleavage remains powerful is that all discussions of efficiency presume at least implicit judgments on effectiveness, for no author who has yet written has seriously thought to suggest that marketers should become more efficient at ineffective actions. This presumption of effectiveness allows the literature as a whole to be nicely parceled into the

Table 1 Marketing Productivity Definitions

Author	Suggested Measure
Bucklin (1978)	$\dfrac{\text{Real marketing services produced}}{\text{Real inputs}}$
Sevin (1965)	$\dfrac{\text{Sales}}{\text{Marketing expense}}$ or $\dfrac{\text{Profit}}{\text{Marketing expense}}$
Mehrotra (1984)	Brand franchise = Relative price × relative market share
Barger (1955)	• Percentage of labor force in activity over time • Goods distributed per man-hour (in distribution)
Drucker (1985) (white-collar productivity in general)	• Units of output / employment • New product development time • Number of successful new products per time period • Number of staff members

great bulk of works on efficiency, a much smaller but conceptually more interesting set of pieces on effectiveness, and some few pieces that straddle these dimensions.

However, the failure of the literature to recognize the fundamentally different concerns of effectiveness and efficiency leads to odd confusions. As Cox, Goodman, and Fichandler (1965) explain the link between effectiveness and efficiency, "Tests of efficiency are based on comparisons of input and output. They take as given the objectives of the system under analysis" (p. 169). The presumption of effectiveness given a focus on efficiency means that the vast majority of marketing productivity measures and inquiries suffer from assumed, and often unexamined, goals. Sevin (1965) and his successors, for example, examine the problem of increasing profitability relative to marketing expenditures. Maximizing profit, however, is not always the right thing (the most effective action) for the organization, as when profits are consciously traded for market share in penetration pricing scenarios. We take special pains to examine the effectiveness goals of efficiency-driven inquiries below, for much can be learned from the exercise.

Though the great bulk of the marketing productivity literature has striven to describe or prescribe efficiency presuming effectiveness, a much smaller body of work has attacked the "what is right?" question directly. Though much of the work that we consider under the effectiveness label comes from outside marketing productivity's formal boundaries, and some even from sources outside marketing, the studies we examine raise provocative questions that logically precede inquiries about efficiency. We look at the literature through this efficiency/effectiveness glass below.

Macroeconomic versus Microeconomic Focus of Study

The second cleavage point in the literature is the level at which inquiries have been pitched. Figure 1 diagrams our classification scheme as a whole, with economic level of analysis on one axis and efficiency-effectiveness on the other. As the figure shows, there has been an interesting progression in work on marketing productivity from the macroeconomic, industry-wide studies of the 1930s, '40s, and '50s to the microeconomic, within-firm and sometimes

within-function inquiries of later decades. Almost all the early works on marketing performance (productivity works) focused on macroeconomic efficiency, either within a particular industry (usually wholesaling and retailing) or across industries. As macroeconomic understanding increased, so did frustration with findings so broad that they seemed inapplicable by any particular manager in any particular firm. This frustration was one of the driving forces behind much of the early microeconomic work. However, these macroeconomic and microeconomic researchers used measures that illuminated very different aspects of performance assessment; therefore, we categorize the literature on this dimension as well.

The MPA Model: A Preview

The model we propose is an explicit attempt to combine the effectiveness and efficiency strands in marketing performance assessment and thereby allow a composite statement to be made about overall marketing performance of a given program. In operationalizing this model, we draw heavily on our background in psychology. Unlike the many studies reviewed below, the MPA model explicitly incorporates the judgment of managers, making it a strongly behavioral and cognitive model of performance assessment. This stands in stark contrast to the many economics-oriented studies in the literature. We were surprised at how many studies weeded out the judgment and behaviors of the very managers they intended to aid. By integrating the knowledge of skilled managers in the MPA model, we believe we are much more likely to approximate performance assessment as managers really conduct it. We are hopeful this approach will prove as useful as it is novel.

In modeling "doing the right thing" (effectiveness), we compare program results to goals by weighing those results against management expectations. Expectations, in turn, arise from the goals of program and corporate strategy, and the sense of identity that the program and corporation have about what they do for a customer. We use management expectations precisely because they do incorporate the implicit identity of marketing theme and culture along with the explicit strategic goals a given program might have. We call the results-expectations comparison the measure of satisfaction.

Figure 1　Useful Cleavage Points in the Marketing Performance Literature

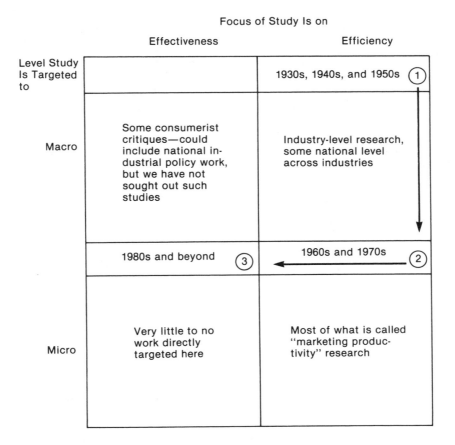

Note: Numbers in small boxes indicate the historical flow of research into marketing productivity, and hence give a sense of the evolution of the discipline from macroeconomic to microeconomic work and from efficiency toward effectiveness concerns.

In modeling "doing things right" (efficiency), we examine the skills that managers of a given marketing program must exercise and the support structures a firm provides to the program. By assessing both, we approximate the overall effort an organization has had to expend to obtain the level of satisfaction derived above. Obviously, the less effort or resources a program uses to produce a given level of satisfaction, the more efficient the program is. By maximizing satisfaction (effectiveness) relative to effort, we ensure that a given program is becoming efficient at producing effective outcomes.

Finally, the MPA model incorporates explicit measures of the factors beyond a firm's control that affect a given program's performance, including competitive actions, distribution channel actions, and changes in the legal, economic, and demographic variables of the overall market environment. These variables attempt to sort among programs that succeeded or failed because of luck rather than effort.

We will explore the components of the model in detail, but we note here that the three main lessons researchers and managers should take from this model parallel these three components. Any comprehensive measure of marketing performance must measure (1) the degree to which a program satisfies strategic objectives and management concerns, (2) the effort the program expends to produce that satisfaction, and (3) the effect of uncontrollable forces on the program. The first lesson, although well known to managers, is treated lightly in the research literature. While the other two lessons are more straightforward, combining them with the first and measuring them in the fashion we propose is a radical departure from previous practice.

Organization of the Book

This book explores both the specifics of the MPA model and the more general issues in marketing performance assessment raised by our research and that of others. The book is divided into ten chapters, and supported with three appendices.

The rest of this chapter outlines the approach we took in reviewing the voluminous research literature in marketing performance and productivity. The literature review examines both the research underlying our work and alternative approaches that we considered provocative. By understanding the strengths and weak-

nesses of past approaches, readers will obtain maximal guidance toward evaluating our efforts. We also note a number of related marketing and general management works not specifically aimed at marketing productivity per se, but which have important insights to offer those who wish to think carefully about assessing marketing performance.

Chapter 2 describes a series of landmark macroeconomic studies of marketing productivity; although our model is aimed at the microeconomic concerns of specific firms and programs, the measures these scholars applied to the U.S. economy established a significant tradition and approach that later authors have built upon. Chapters 3 and 4 review more recent microeconomic approaches to assessing marketing performance.

The remaining chapters offer and develop the MPA model. Chapter 5 draws lessons from the literature, and introduces concepts critical to the definition and specification of marketing performance assessment. Especially salient to our model is an overview of previous work in marketing implementation which serves as a base for the present work. The chapter also sketches the basic MPA model. Chapter 6 analyzes the model in detail, and fully develops the derivation. Chapter 7 examines the methodological concerns in operationalizing and validating the model. Chapter 8 provides initial qualitative data on the model's validity, based on interviews, preliminary questionnaire data, and three case studies. Chapter 9 outlines a set of implications and testable propositions that arise from MPA, while Chapter 10 concludes the book and describes in some detail the appended materials. Three research appendices offer a preliminary questionnaire to measure marketing performance, the full texts of the clinical case studies undertaken to derive and develop the model, and an annotated bibliography of sources on marketing performance.

Literature Dynamics and Plan of Review

The literature classification scheme presented here distributes studies along the two cleavage points discussed above, the effectiveness versus efficiency and the macroeconomic versus microeconomic focuses of inquiry. As Figure 1 shows, virtually all relevant work has been targeted at efficiency measures. Given marketing's historical lack of investigatory depth into output measures generally, this is surprising, for it might be thought that the nature of which output variables are useful for measurement would have preceded the attempt to improve the ones at hand (e.g., sales, profit). This has not been the case; whether "everybody knows" that sales and profit are the key measures of marketing performance, or whether the matter has not been investigated, it is hard to say.

Scope of the Literature Review

The scope of the literature survey sometimes goes beyond marketing's boundaries, especially when particularly seminal or provocative pieces exist that have informed or should inform new thinking on MPA. Existing work on productivity across disciplines is broad and far-flung, concerning everything from productivity of production plants (Garvin, 1984) to software systems design (Boehm, 1978). Existing work on marketing productivity is equally divergent. Therefore, the literature review takes a somewhat broader perspective than is often encountered, attempting to categorize and overview both general productivity work as it has addressed marketing or is useful to marketers in a perspective-setting way, and specific work directed at marketing productivity under some common headings. Work on the marketing audit is reviewed separately because of its importance as a line of thought, its unique status as a part effectiveness, part efficiency tool, and its direct focus on performance. Finally, we examine marketing performance works that are not explicitly productivity-oriented.

As a basis for the review, we conducted both a computerized and manual literature search for articles addressing both "marketing" and "productivity." We then carried out successive searches through the bibliographies of the core articles, and through the bibliographies of secondary articles. We continued this "snowball" search until the citations referred to each other rather than to new articles. A search of the *Business Periodicals Index* was also done under the heading "performance." By these methods, we reviewed over 130 books and articles that examine some aspect of marketing productivity and performance. In addition, we drew on works from other disciplines as appropriate, especially psychology and organizational behavior. These 150-plus articles form the core of the literature we discuss in the next three chapters.

We have made a conscious effort in the literature summaries presented below to strive for depth rather than breadth. That is, if five or ten studies discuss the same concept, we elected to report at length on the classic, illustrative, or best sample of the subspecies, rather than bore the reader with redundancy-by-citation. Our approach was to illustrate the most important concepts and methodologies in the literature, not to conduct a detailed critical review of individual studies. The annotated bibliography, therefore, contains many more sources than we elected to reference in the text, and should serve as a good as well as comprehensive reference listing for those inclined to read further than our primary sources discussed in the text proper.

Chapter 2

Macroeconomic Studies of Marketing Performance

Marketing Efficiency

As long as there has been commerce, there has been criticism of commerce. In the twentieth century, analysts have focused much of their scrutiny upon the marketing function in particular in modern businesses. Indeed, antibusiness sentiments could be considered a prime motivation for the original interest in marketing productivity.[1] In the first half of this century, U.S. researchers, practitioners, and policymakers were concerned with the cost of marketing activities, especially in the area of distribution (see the Twentieth Century Fund, 1939, reviewed below). Was the consumer paying too much for goods because of marketing? And what was the productivity of marketing compared to that of manufacturing?

Some of the difficulties authors have had in dealing with these questions implicates definitional issues for marketing input and output. In many ways, the macroeconomic literature on marketing productivity is mired in confessed compromises between need for quantification and the reality of available data. Most scholars agree that the true output of marketing includes a series of services performed for the customer, such as delivery, credit, warranties, and so on. However, the measurement of such services on a national or even industry level is virtually impossible. Researchers have therefore relied on the more gross data that are available, such as sales, value added, and units shipped.

Barger's Work on Distributive Efficiency. Given the mass of data the U.S. government now regularly publishes, it is hard to imagine a time when we did not have it. The early macroeconomic productivity researchers studied in such a time. With only fragmentary data at best, Harold Barger (1955) at the National Bureau of Economic

---

1. For some interesting discussions of the place of marketing in society, see Cox et al. (1965), Schudson (1984), Fisk (1964, Chapter 23), and Homans and Enis (1973).

Research compiled a seminal list of sources on U.S. distribution costs in the period 1869 to 1949.

Barger wanted to study productivity in retailing and wholesaling in the United States longitudinally, as he previously had for agriculture (Barger and Landsberg, 1942), mining (Barger and Schurr, 1944), and transportation (Barger, 1951). Unfortunately, the first national surveys of distribution costs were not performed until after World War I, and both the Bureau of the Census and the Bureau of Labor Statistics did not examine distributive costs until after 1929. Therefore, Barger and his associates returned to primary source materials of the nineteenth and early twentieth centuries, including news accounts, trade journals, accountants' files, and interviews with executives. The result was a forty-five-page compilation of individual and serial data sources dating back to 1865.

In examining his data, Barger was concerned with three areas: (1) the amount of the labor force involved in distributive activities, (2) the output of the distribution industry in physical volume of goods distributed, and (3) the cost of these activities. The first two factors, Barger thought, would give him a labor productivity figure (output per man-hour) which he could then compare with that of other industries. The third factor, adding a pecuniary dimension to his previous economic calculations, would answer the cost question that interested the critics of marketing expenditures.

For output, Barger used the unit volume of goods shipped by the distributive industries; for input, the number of persons engaged in the distributive trade and the number of hours they worked. Combining these two measures, he discovered that productivity in retailing and wholesaling rose much more slowly over the period from 1870 to 1950 than did the productivity of "commodity-producing" industries such as agriculture, forestry, fishing, mining, and manufacturing. Virtually all of the difference in growth rates seemed to be accounted for by a dramatic increase in the number of people employed in distribution relative to production, while output in both sectors grew at roughly the same rate. However, by analyzing gross margins, Barger concluded that the cost of distribution as opposed to the total retail value of an item had changed little, if at all, in eighty years, remaining constant at about 37¢ on each dollar of goods purchased.

Though others emphasize the numerical results of his analysis, Barger thoughtfully attempted to explain his puzzling data (i.e., constant cost despite low productivity gains) by turning to qualitative evidence. Defining distributive productivity as the services provided by retailers and wholesalers, Barger described a variety of changes that occurred over the period of his study that seemed to argue distributive productivity had actually risen substantially over the period, though his method of measuring distributive productivity could not detect these changes. He cited much anecdotal evidence of the expansion of distributive services in areas such as store facilities, service at the point of sale, packaging, free home trial of merchandise, return privileges, credit, and delivery.

In more quantitative terms, Barger also described the changing channels of distribution over the eighty-year period surveyed by his study. Over the period from 1869 to 1929, the percentage of producers' goods distributed through wholesalers dropped from a peak of 70 percent in 1889 to 60 percent in 1929, while the percentage distributed through retailers rose from 71 percent to 81 percent. Traditional wholesaling functions, Barger observed, were being absorbed by the growing retail sector on the one hand, and by manufacturers on the other. The middleman, in effect, was being squeezed out of the distribution system.

Barger's study serves as an important milestone and interesting template for understanding the macroeconomic, industrywide type of efficiency research that has characterized much of marketing productivity's history. It is instructive to enumerate some of these characteristics.

First, note that Barger's measures assume that higher output per employee or lower distributive costs, for example, represent higher productivity. As we noted above, the efficiency literature presumes knowledge of what is effective. Clearly, Barger's results do not and cannot demonstrate this linkage. Indeed, his main finding of greater numbers of employees entering distribution while efficiency stayed constant might well be used as an argument that distributive efficiency decreased in this industry over time.

Second, although Barger's conclusions are very useful in an overall descriptive sense, they say little about what an individual firm, or even industry segment, could or should do to improve its productivity. Macroeconomic work is often implicitly normative when it comes to presumed effectiveness measures, but it is weak when it comes to applicable findings for specific firms (cf., e.g., Beckman, 1961).

Third, as Barger himself pointed out, a too narrow or just too quantitative definition of productivity in marketing is likely to give misleading or illusory results, as with Barger's own main finding of slow to no growth in distributive productivity. There is a real danger in the quantification process of losing sight of the nature of the phenomenon of interest. To his credit, Barger quickly turned to qualitative supporting evidence when his main quantitative ratios did not seem sensible.

Finally, follow-up studies to Barger's work suggest the elusiveness of quantitative "truth" altogether. In the course of his major studies of productivity in the American economy, John Kendrick (1961, 1973) revised and extended Barger's work. Improved data from the U.S. government and inclusion of a wider variety of wholesaling firms led Kendrick to argue that retail and wholesale productivity increased twice as fast as Barger had reported in the period from 1929 to 1949 (Kendrick, 1961). Doubly confounding is that Kendrick's later revision of his own figures for the period from 1948 to 1953 indicate that he himself underestimated retail and wholesale productivity in his first study (Kendrick, 1973; see also Bucklin, 1978, pp. 49–52 for a more detailed discussion of Kendrick's extension of Barger).

Beckman's Inquiries into Wholesaling and Retailing. A second distinguished student of the macroeconomic marketing productivity problem was Theodore N. Beckman (1957, 1961). In a paper delivered in 1960 to the Business and Economic Section of the American Statistical Association, Beckman (1961) described his attempts to measure marketing productivity.

Like Barger, Beckman suffered from limited data on marketing productivity relative to his needs. Beckman nicely stated the traditional distinction, for example, between the utility that manufacturing provides relative to that supplied from marketing. Manufacturing, he said, concentrates on providing mostly "form utility," meaning the function of the product itself. Marketing, on the other hand, concentrates on providing place, time, and possession utility to the consumer—that is to say, on providing the product to the consumer where, when, and in a form suitable for ownership. In this sense,

Beckman argues, "marketing permeates in some degree every phase of our economy" (p. 308). However, such ubiquity is difficult to tease out for measurement and analysis. Beckman therefore chose to examine marketing "structurally" by studying the same industries that Barger did: retail and wholesale trade.

Unlike Barger, Beckman restricted himself to the most reliable data available, the *U.S. Census of Manufactures*, and therefore limited the time period that he could study to the years between 1935 and 1958. To represent wholesale productivity, he selected data on merchant wholesalers (slightly more than 40 percent of wholesale industry revenues) and manufacturers' sales branches (about 15 percent of industry revenues). For retailers, he was able to use all census data except those on restaurants and bars, therefore covering about 90 percent of total retail sales.

If his sample was only a portion of distributive enterprise, his measures were yet more restrictive. Beckman's preferred output measure was value added, which may be defined as the difference between the price commanded for a product and the cost of raw materials, energy, supplies, containers, and contract work required to produce the product. This difference represents the work a company performs plus the profit it receives and, therefore, the value added by its labors. Unfortunately, the government had just begun to collect value-added data at the end of the 1950s, so Beckman instead used constant (1958) dollar sales as a proxy for value added.

For input measures, Beckman initially chose man-hours, but he had to use all employees as his base, again largely because of the constraints on the available data. His data reveal that between 1935 and 1958, wholesale output per man-hour increased more slowly than the comparable statistic for manufacturing, but that retail output per man-hour (especially in food stores) increased more rapidly than did manufacturing productivity.

Of special interest is Beckman's extension of Barger's pure man-hour data by the inclusion of capital intensity measures. Most economists agree that a more accurate measure of productivity is obtained when not only labor is included in the assessment (single-factor productivity), but when measures of land, capital, and management costs are considered as well (total-factor productivity). This, of course, is a much more difficult estimate to make, but it can yield results far different from labor calculations alone (see Beckman and Buzzell, 1958, for a good discussion). Beckman used total assets as his capital measurement (the only data available), and found that capital productivity between 1939 and 1958 actually peaked in the late 1940s. Furthermore, using a weighted combinatorial model of capital and labor productivity, Beckman found that merchant wholesaling increased only 15 percent in productivity from 1939 to 1958, or less than 1 percent per year.

Looking at Beckman's work in a different, broader way than he intended, it might be said that for any marketing endeavor like retailing or even product management, there are available at any given time the skills (labor and management input) of the workers as well as the overall facilities available to a company, an industry, or the economy as a whole (capital and land). Relative to facilities, which tend to give up their value over a long period of time, skills are a more variable input, because of both employee turnover and development of the skills of those who stay.

Clearly, Beckman's total-factor productivity approach contains many of the assumed elements of effectiveness found in Barger's work, but the addition of more than just man-hours as determining productive marketing output seems to make for a more coherent account. Beyond their obvious overall descriptive value, however, it is difficult to know just what to make of the findings. As Beckman himself noted late in his career, industry-level analyses are of limited value in helping managers improve, or even understand, the productivity in their companies: "What is needed, above all, is fundamental research of productivity in marketing on an individual enterprise basis" (Beckman, 1965, p. 71).

Also, some low-level assumptions in the macroeconomic work about marketing as an enterprise do not sit so well when they are exposed: whether "marketing is essentially a process like farming, manufacturing, mining, or construction" (Beckman, 1961, p. 308) clearly is both highly debatable and vaguely unsettling.

Value Added: Cox et al.

Cox, Goodman, and Fichandler (1965) ultimately made the value-added study that Beckman desired. Taking as their primary source of data the U.S. Bureau of Labor Statistics' comprehensive *1947 Interindustry Relations Study*, the authors constructed the flow of products among 190 industries. Using worksheets and unpublished papers from the massive report, they constructed charts analogous to double-entry bookkeeping ledgers to avoid double counting of purchased goods. By this means they were able to identify purchased inputs and vended outputs to and from each industry studied. Aiming to examine the societal worth of distribution, Cox et al. chose value added as the measure of marketing performance.[2] Their study, which is in the tradition of the Twentieth Century Fund (1939, reviewed below), devotes a substantial portion to describing the history and functions of distribution, and rebutting earlier arguments against its worth to the economy and the consumer.

As with the simpler measures discussed above, however, powerful presumptions about effectiveness are implicit in the choice of value added as an efficiency measure. Is the goal of a value-added measurement to add more value or less? The complaint that inspired much of the macroeconomic line of research was that marketing provided too much value added to consumers because it made products too costly (Twentieth Century Fund, 1939). Although concentrating on providing less value to the customer from distribution may lower the cost, it may also lower the customer satisfaction gained from purchases. It is simply not clear what efficient adding of value means regarding marketing effectiveness.

Cox et al. develop a novel view of the outputs of distribution, conceiving distribution as a series of flows: one through space, a second through time, and a third "intangible." The first two flows are the physical tasks of distribution; the third relates more closely to the extended marketing services that Barger describes, such as credit and packaging. Included in intangible flows are flows of ownership, negotiation, information, payment, risk, and capital. Within a distribution channel, Cox et al. maintain, different channel members affect different parts of these intangible flows. For example, merchant wholesalers take ownership of the goods they sell, thereby assuming the market risk that the

---

2. Value added, Cox et al. note, is an absolute, and therefore not a traditional, measure of productivity. They define productivity as a relative measure of outputs and inputs.

goods might not sell. Similarly, retailers might offer extended payment plans and training on sophisticated products such as personal computers.

Cox et al. outline three approaches to studying marketing productivity. The first is the Institutional approach, which examines marketing from the standpoint of the activities of various enterprises. The second is the Commodity approach, which analyzes marketing according to the type of goods involved. The third is the Functional approach, which divides marketing into its component activities, such as advertising, selling, and distribution. To get a broader view of the spectrum of marketing productivity statistics, Cox et al. included the transportation, storage, and advertising businesses in addition to the retailing and wholesaling industries. Approximately 21 percent ($34 billion) of the output delivered to household purchasers ($161 billion) was value added by these five industries in 1947.

The Institutional approach encompasses the type of analysis that Barger and Beckman performed. In each case, they looked at the output of a type of enterprise, whether retailing or wholesaling. As Cox et al. point out, this type of data is easiest to gather because so much of the work is done by the U.S. government. They consider the Commodity approach much more informative.

On a Commodity basis, a more detailed analysis of the Bureau of Labor Statistics information reveals that over 18 percent of the 21 percent value added contributed by distribution was applied to products (59 percent of total household purchases), while the remaining 3 percent was applied to services (41 percent of total household purchases). Examining the products category further reveals that depending on the product, the contribution of distribution to the total value the consumer purchases varies widely, from 22 percent to 40 percent of the final purchase value. (See Table 8-5, p. 135 of Cox et al., 1965, for a detailed array of products and the contribution each received from distribution.) The wide variation in contribution, Cox et al. explain, arises from characteristics of both the products and the industry structure. For example, fish are expensive to store and transport because they require refrigeration, but distribution also contributes more to seafood products because the fishing industry is composed of many small operators who simply do not have the financial ability to conduct distribution activities.

The Commodity approach findings made by Cox et al. strongly imply that any measure of sales to marketing expense will vary widely by product. Therefore, if we use sales/marketing expense as a productivity measure, some industries will have inherently higher marketing productivity than others simply because of the characteristics of their products, industry structure, and marketing practices. Comparing marketing productivity among companies would then require a careful weighing of the companies' product mix in addition to the actual efforts of the marketing department.

The data on the Functional approach are more fragmentary. Cox et al. note that the government does not collect information on a number of marketing activities. A second data-gathering problem is that businesses themselves rarely collect information in convenient functional categories, such as advertising. Instead, business accounting tends to use "natural" categories, keeping an account for each organization or individual to whom payments are made rather than according to the type of work performed. (This accounting practice also confounds numerous profitability analysts, whose work is reviewed in Chapter 3.) Cox et al. attempt to get around this problem by reorganizing the institutional data, assuming that all value added by distributive industries consists of distributive activities. This obviously overstates the case, but the authors argue that the practice is justified because there is no discernible "personal selling" or "marketing research" industry from which they can draw data.

Clearly, the Cox et al. study represents a valuable extension of earlier macroeconomic work on marketing efficiency in several ways. First, value added was employed as a dependent measure, a much more sophisticated approach than had been used before. Second, Cox and associates began the move away from the easy convenience of distribution, studied so frequently in the history of marketing productivity, toward an admittedly imprecise, but nonetheless ambitiously broadened, definition of marketing. And third, these authors were among the first to display sensitivity to product-by-product, and even product life cycle, differences in marketing productivity *just because* of each product's varying requirements for marketing inputs and outputs.

Bucklin's Total Factor Productivity Approach. The most recent major investigation into marketing productivity on a macroscopic level is that of Bucklin (1978). Reviewing the work of Barger, Beckman, Kendrick, and a number of other scholars, Bucklin takes a hard stand against using pecuniary measures of marketing efficiency.

The problem with measures such as sales per employee or profit divided by expense, he notes, is that they obscure the difference between *real* changes in input and output and *price* changes in input and output. He argues forcefully that the true output of a marketing department is the service level provided to the customer, and that the true input is the labor, capital, land, and management that the organization has available. Sales or profit, whether deflated or not, is at best a rough proxy for this service level, since these variables represent the monetary reward the organization can command for its services. Number of employees or marketing expense is at best an incomplete measure of input; to achieve a total-factor marketing productivity measure, one must account for capital and land as well, the value of which appears imperfectly on the income statement, if at all.[3]

Bucklin begins his work with an algebraic demonstration of what productivity in marketing is—and is not. Using S for sales in dollars, C for cost in dollars, O for unit output, I for unit input, P(o) for cost per unit of output, and P(i) for cost per unit of input, marketing productivity in Bucklin's terms is based on the following identities:

$$S = O \times P(o) \quad and \quad C = I \times P(i),$$

which is to say, sales result from total number of units sold times price per unit, while cost equals number of units input times unit cost. Rearranging these identities, Bucklin defines marketing productivity (real output per real input) in the following equation:

$$\frac{O}{I} = \frac{S/P(o)}{C/P(i)}.$$

Because price is represented both in the numerator and denominator (i.e., as components and supplies) of the equation, unit output and input in Bucklin's terms are separated from price effects.

However, it is anathema to Bucklin that some scholars have used productivity and profitability interchangeably (see Sevin, 1965, reviewed below). Because of the confounding of price changes with the ratio of outputs to inputs (productivity), Bucklin sees these two terms as distinctly different. One way to think about profitability, he suggests, is to look at the ratio of sales to costs. To the extent that sales exceed costs, the organization has a profit. Shuffling his equations, Bucklin thus produces the following:

$$\frac{S}{C} = \frac{O}{I} \times \frac{P(o)}{P(i)}.$$

From this viewpoint, profitability is the result of the firm's productivity, O/I, and the relative price ratio of inputs and outputs. The latter equation component Bucklin calls the "terms of trade" (p. 3).

It is on the measurement front that much of Bucklin's theoretical elegance breaks down, though he spends much space on constructing plausible if hard-to-obtain measures that might satisfy his needs. He argues that outputs from the firm's activities are measured both by the transactions the firm has with its customers and the more traditional measures of product units others cite. In measuring inputs, he wishes to include material, marketing effort, labor, and capital, all depreciating over time and all subject to the opportunity costs of other possible uses of that capital. The potential confusion between the seemingly identical effects of product quality improvements and sheer price inflation is also discussed at some length. Assuming all these data were collected, or even collectible, Bucklin finally illustrates what he calls a "synthetic index" approach to measuring the productivity of marketing in the economy (pp. 62–64). This index tries to weight each industry's marketing intensity with its productivity in order to get a weighted contribution to the sum total of marketing work done in the economy.

In defining output and input, discussing types of services and their quality, and analyzing the cost (or value) of marketing, Bucklin expands greatly on the previous works we have examined, but the area in which he makes his

---

3. Of course, the "services output" measure is no less vulnerable to challenges about its assumed effectiveness goals than are sales or value-added measures. More services are not necessarily better, as the rapid growth of off-price retailing clearly shows. The trouble, as we suggest above in our discussion of value added, is that adding services for the customer also often requires adding costs that will force a price level some customers are unwilling or unable to pay.

strongest contribution to our understanding of marketing productivity in a national economy is his discussion of the external forces that affect the productivity of a given economy's efforts in marketing.

Terms of trade, for example, represent a gross quantification of the market conditions that an organization faces. If the organization faces strong competition, its price per unit of output is likely to be lower than if it faces no competition, and terms of trade will also be less favorable. Similarly, if the organization can get a critical material from only one supplier, its price per unit of input is likely to be higher than if the supplier industry is very competitive. Again, terms of trade will be less favorable. The more unfavorable terms of trade are, the less profitable the company will be. This is a valuable notion.

In relating productivity to overall economic growth, Bucklin raises the intriguing notion that an expanding economy can contribute to increased productivity as well as result from it. As an economy expands, higher demand provides opportunities for companies to expand their scale, invest in new facilities, and so on. From a marketing standpoint, expanding demand might mean that an organization could achieve scale economies in distribution and selling efforts, or that add-on products would become economically feasible.

Bucklin reviews several other empirical works that address the impact of market conditions on productivity. Two studies of particular note are Denison (1967) and George (1966).

Edward Denison, then a senior staff member of the Brookings Institution, studied national income growth[4] between 1950 and 1962 in nine Western countries (the United States, West Germany, Belgium, the Netherlands, Denmark, France, Norway, Italy, and the United Kingdom). He used data from governments, international organizations, books, and periodicals to analyze why national income growth rates differed across countries in the twelve-year period. The result was an extremely comprehensive measure of total-factor productivity. Although many of the factors Denison uncovered were similar to those we have discussed—for example, land, labor, and capital inputs—he also identified two new influences that contrib-

uted to productivity growth: advances in knowledge and improved allocation of national resources.

Advances in knowledge, Denison argues, contribute to national income growth by introducing technological and managerial changes that improve productivity. Unfortunately, Denison's derivation of this component is strictly theoretical; he offers no way of measuring advances in knowledge. Instead, he develops his assessment of this factor by subtracting the other growth factors that he has identified, and assigning the residual growth to advances in knowledge.[5]

Denison found improved allocation of national resources in three areas: a decline in the agricultural sector, a decline in self-employment, and lower trade barriers. All three of these changes, he claims, improve overall economic efficiency, thereby generating more output (in the form of national income) for the same input.

George (1966) analyzed retail productivity in 160 British towns with populations of 30,000 or more and retail sales of £10 million or more, using sales per person engaged as his productivity measure. Drawing on government publications, he discovered three economic and demographic characteristics that influenced the productivity of different towns: income per capita, population, and tightness of the overall labor market. The first two characteristics reflect simple scale opportunities: larger towns and larger incomes lead to larger total spending, which provides opportunities for expanding scale. Labor tightness is slightly more complex. George hypothesized that the labor effect is strong because retail wages tend to be lower than manufacturing wages. When demand for workers is high (the labor market is tight), retailers therefore have a more difficult task in finding workers, forcing shops to get by with a lean staff.

George also discovered that industry characteristics such as size of retail stores and market share of multiples (department stores) and cooperatives increased labor productivity. Large shops and branches of multiples, George explains, allow their owners to fine-tune labor usage and take advantage of scale and specialization opportunities. The more a town is dom-

---

4. Net national product rather than gross national product. NNP is "the amount of its output a nation could consume without changing its stock of capital" (p. 14).

5. He does recognize this measure thus includes the net error of his other measurements (see p. 281).

inated by these outlets, the greater its productivity. Finally, like Cox et al., George notes that different types of businesses (groceries, confectioners, clothing stores, etc.) have different productivity levels, and the mix in a given town will thus change that town's productivity.

Marketing Effectiveness

As noted above, if we are to categorize a work as effectiveness-related, it must explicitly discuss the "right things" to do, as opposed to "doing things right." Although Cox et al. come close to this standard in their attempt to answer criticisms of marketing, they are much more descriptive than prescriptive. We found only one piece that we would categorize as effectiveness-oriented in the macroeconomic literature on marketing performance: that of the Twentieth Century Fund (1939).

The Twentieth Century Fund was founded in 1919 by merchandising magnate Edward A. Filene. A private research organization, the fund appoints and finances research committees to investigate and report upon major social and economic issues of the day. In many ways, the Twentieth Century Fund's distribution study was the first great cost study of distribution. Drawing heavily upon U.S. census data, especially the 1929 census, the fund study examines a wide variety of distributive and marketing activities, including labor productivity, price spreads, distributive costs and profits, and government regulation. The study is divided into two parts: "the factual findings," similar to those of Cox et al. (1965) and Barger (1955), and "the program," offering numerous government and business policy recommendations.

The facts, reported by Paul Stewart, J. Frederick Dewhurst, and Louise Field, cover much of the ground that Barger and Cox et al. expand upon in their later studies. Like Barger, the fund study examines goods distributed per production worker and employment patterns in the distribution industries. Like Cox et al., it draws a chart of the flow of goods in the U.S. economy.

The fund study, as its authors note, involves "a considerable amount of estimating on the basis of inadequate statistical data" (p. 334). They restate census data to estimate certain figures (pp. 11–12). Despite this limited data, the fund study manages to glean some general trends in distributive costs. Like Barger, the

fund study concludes that labor productivity in distribution grew far more slowly than in manufacturing over the period 1870–1930. Internal Revenue Service figures in the study reveal that distribution companies were not exceedingly profitable relative to manufacturing companies (pp. 120ff). The study also finds that cost of the majority of finished goods in 1929 was the product of distribution rather than manufacturing.[6]

What makes this an effectiveness rather than an efficiency study is that it compares the performance of marketing in the U.S. economy to a set of explicit goals. In this case, the authors proclaim their goal to be determining how minimum cost is to be obtained, within three assumption sets:

a. free choice for the consumer, with the inevitable costs necessitated by the consumer's demands for variety, immediacy, and convenience;

b. freedom of opportunity for the distributor, which means the opportunity to develop new methods and techniques that will yield him a profit, but which also means . . . the opportunity to fail and in doing so to injure his own and others' interests; and

c. a system of competition, which should be regulated with two ends in view: (1) the promotion of the long-run interests of consumers and (2) the protection of the public interest; not merely to preserve the status quo or defend the position of particular groups of distributors (pp. 347–348).

Comparison of results and objectives create in this case a qualitative but explicit evaluation of the effectiveness of marketing in the U.S. economy:

we can say with confidence that there is waste in distribution, but we cannot reduce it to a percentage figure—as a whole, or in any of its parts. Nor can we say that distribution is more or less wasteful than production. We can, however—even with limited statistics that we have—point out specifically many ways in which the costs of distribution can be reduced or its efficiency increased. . . . (pp. 348–349)

In examining the causes of waste, the fund authors condemn many features of marketing,

---

6. The fund claims that distribution costs in 1929 accounted for 59 percent of finished goods cost, compared to 37 percent in Barger and 45 percent (for 1947) in Cox et al. See Chapters 9 and 10 of Cox et al. for a thoughtful discussion of the differences among Barger, Twentieth Century Fund, and Cox and co-workers.

including duplication of sales efforts, multitudes of brands, unnecessary advertising, unreasonable or misinformed consumers, and the management practices of distributors themselves (p. 348). The authors go on to make over a dozen specific recommendations to help U.S. marketing realize its goal of minimum cost while retaining free choice. They divide these recommendations into three categories: improving consumer knowledge, improving management practices and information available to distributors, and making regulatory reforms of laws affecting the distribution industry (Chapter 11).

By clearly stating its goals and comparing marketing results to them, the fund study avoids making the assumptions of later studies such as those of Barger, Beckman, and Bucklin (e.g., "more productivity is better"). It is this factor that makes the fund study an effectiveness one. "Doing the right thing" is very explicit here, leading to a much more prescriptive slant in the fund study.

The Twentieth Century Fund takes a more avowedly "consumerist" stance in its approach than the efficiency studies we have reviewed. It is possible that other consumerist critiques could be considered effectiveness studies. In this sense, some of the societal role of marketing pieces we cited in footnote 2 (Fisk, 1964; Homans and Enis, 1973; and Schudson, 1984) could be on the periphery of the matrix. Schudson (1984), for example, critiques the effect of advertising on American society. To the extent that we as a society have certain interests in the way advertising is conducted, a macroeconomic effectiveness study might examine how well advertising addresses these interests. If, for example, the number of legal actions brought for deceptive advertising is rising, we might say

this is societally ineffective advertising, since the societal goal for deceptive advertising is presumably zero.

Summary: Macroeconomic Marketing Research

One way to construe the macroeconomic efficiency inquiries follows psychologists who speak of "S-O-R" models in human behavior. In these models, a Stimulus acts on an Organism to provoke a Response. The stimulus may be seen as the inputs of a marketing productivity equation, either for a particular industry, like the distributive or retailing ones, or for all industries. The response side of the equation, obviously, is analogous to the output measures used to study marketing productivity. The unobservable "black box" that constitutes the organism is fair game for theorists' attempts to specify any number of mediating variables or constructs that seem to help in explaining how inputs (stimuli) are translated into outputs (responses). Tables 2, 3, and 4 offer a summary view of such inputs, outputs, and mediating constructs in the macroeconomic forays into marketing productivity analysis.

Table 2 shows the various input measures used by macroeconomic scholars interested in marketing productivity. The basic distinction in the table is between the first two rows and the remaining rows—that is, between simple use of labor as a measure of marketing productivity inputs and assorted total-factor approaches that variously incorporate capital, land, management skills, R&D intensity, and other measures to get a more complete picture of marketing's inputs. The former has generally been regarded as an incomplete and unsatisfactory way of

Table 2 Summary of Input Measures in the Macroeconomic Literature Concerned with Marketing Efficiency

Measure	*Author*
Man-hours	Beckman (1961), Barger (1955), Bucklin (1978), Kendrick (1961, 1973)
Number of persons employed	Barger (1955), George (1966)
Capital	Beckman (1961), Bucklin (1978), Kendrick (1961, 1973)
Land	Beckman (1961), Bucklin (1978)
Management	Bucklin (1978)
R&D intensity	Bucklin (1978)
Advertising expenses	Bucklin (1978)
Knowledge and technology	Denison (1967)

measuring marketing inputs; the latter have been a measurement nightmare.

Table 3 gives a summary of the output measures focused on by macroeconomic efficiency studies. Clearly, the most popular measure has been a straight sales one, either in dollars or units, with services, the provision of channel or customer "extras" that enhance the product, a close second. Again, each of the simple and the complex efficiency measures brings with it strong assumptions about what is effective. These can often be challenged: for example, it is easy to imagine a situation in which enhanced service lowers sales, at least under the right competitive conditions. The simpler measures have traditionally had a good measure of dissatisfaction associated with them as adequate measures of what is meant by productivity in marketing, while the complex ones have been difficult or impossible to calculate.

Finally, Table 4 lists a host of organismic "mediating factors," which we might think of as items that help explain variations among more standard productivity measures. These are some of the external, uncontrollable factors we discussed in our preview of the MPA model. Macroeconomic mediating factors may be divided into three overall categories: demographics, economic environment, and industry-specific modifiers. The particular ones chosen by each analyst, of course, sometimes have more to do with theoretical leanings than with anything necessarily observable from the data. This should not be surprising, as it is in the mediating factors that each writer has most fully imposed his or her understanding on marketing productivity.

Note the similarities and differences between the input-output formulation of the efficiency studies and the results-goals comparison of our lone effectiveness study (Twentieth Century Fund, 1939). There is an "output" of distribu-

Table 3 Summary of Output Measures in the Macroeconomic Literature Concerned with Marketing Efficiency

Measure	Author
Dollar sales	Beckman (1961), Bucklin (1978), George (1966)
Units shipped	Barger (1955), Kendrick (1961, 1973)
Value added	Beckman (1957), Cox, Goodman, and Fichandler (1965)
Services	Bucklin (1978), Barger (1955), Beckman (1961), Cox, Goodman, and Fichandler (1965)

Table 4 Summary of Mediating Factors in the Macroeconomic Literature Concerned with Marketing Efficiency

Measure	Author
Demographics	
Population density	Bucklin (1978)
Population growth rate	Bucklin (1978)
Age of settlement	Bucklin (1978)
Economic	
Terms of trade	Bucklin (1978)
Resource shifting	Denison (1967)
Market expansion	Denison (1967), Bucklin (1978)
Per capita income	Bucklin (1978), George (1966)
Tightness of labor market	George (1966)
Trade wages	Bucklin (1978)
Industry-specific	
Industry structure	Cox, Goodman, and Fichandler (1965)
Product characteristics	Cox, Goodman, and Fichandler (1965), Bucklin (1978)
Channel structure	Barger (1955)
Marketing practices	Cox, Goodman, and Fichandler (1965)
Quality of inputs and outputs	Bucklin (1978), Barger (1955), Beckman (1961)
Sales size of stores	George (1966)
Percentage of chain stores present	George (1966)
Number of retail stores per capita	Bucklin (1978)

tion that the fund measures, distribution's costs, but there is no input. Instead, the comparison standard is the goal of minimal cost. Both formulations, however, include mediating factors, the fund's most notable one being government regulation. In addition, many of the underlying calculations in the fund study, such as labor productivity figures, are similar or identical to those in the efficiency studies; it is the use to which these calculations are put that makes the difference between effectiveness and efficiency clear.

Several general points can be made about the macroeconomic researches overviewed here. First, remember that most of the major studies reported have been on some aspect of distributive industry, often concerning wholesaling or retailing. The reasons for this are manifold, but among them are the early historical evolution of these functions compared, say, to other service businesses, the availability of public data on these sorts of enterprises but not on many others, and the difficulty of separating marketing expenses within manufacturing businesses compared to the ease of measuring such expenses in businesses dedicated to distribution. All these things have led researchers to single out distributive industries for frequent study, and these industry studies form the bedrock for what is known macroeconomically about marketing efficiency. But it is not terribly clear how far, or indeed whether, what has been learned is generalizable to other kinds of businesses, or to the marketing function per se.

Second, efficiency measures have dominated macroeconomic productivity researches, while measures of effectiveness have been nearly absent, except as implicit presumptions underlying the efficiency work. One reason for this, which can be overlooked because it is so prominent, is that many authors who have written on this topic consider the question of effectiveness in marketing to be quite obvious—effectiveness *is* sales, profits, value added, or whatever. Clearly, on reflection, that simple logic cannot be correct, because it is easy to generate questions about whether any of these simple goals is to be preferred all the time; about whether satisfying one goal does not conflict with attaining another; and about the limits of a firm's capabilities, even if all possible goals could be harmonized. Our one effectiveness study (Twentieth Century Fund, 1939) alone discusses trade-offs among goals at all.

We started this chapter by noting that many of the original marketing productivity studies were conducted because of wide-ranging criticisms that marketing costs too much. Clearly, such criticisms themselves presume the effectiveness of what is being criticized; otherwise, the critic cannot justifiably complain about the expense. Just as department stores in the early 1900s were widely criticized by clerics as "works of the devil which made people spend too much and forget their morals along with their children" (Schudson, 1984), so marketing's effectiveness was not so much questioned as presumed.

The predominance of efficiency work in the macroeconomic literature on marketing productivity is also owing, we speculate, to the foundations of productivity study itself in the measuring of "work" in physics. In its physical definition it is clear that work is effective, by definition—in marketing, the same may not always be true.

Clearly, the macroeconomic analysts provide much insight into the satisfaction, effort, and external factors components of any performance measure. It is apparent that each of these global variables can be measured in a variety of ways. In terms of satisfaction as a comparison of results to expectations, we find a desire to discover what marketing does for the consumer, especially in the tangible services formulations. We will see in the next chapter that microeconomic analysts judge marketing in terms of what marketing does for the rest of a given organization. This is one of the strongest distinctions between the macroeconomic and microeconomic literatures, perhaps reflecting the differing interests of users of macroeconomic and microeconomic data.

In terms of measuring effort, the lesson we draw is the distinction between single-factor productivity (Twentieth Century Fund, 1939; Barger, 1955) and total-factor productivity (Beckman, 1961; Denison, 1967; Bucklin, 1978; and to some extent, Cox et al., 1965). Total-factor assessment is preferable on both practical and theoretical grounds, but it is complicated to measure. The decision one makes is where to draw the line on methodological complexity in the pursuit of theoretical accuracy.

Concerning external factors that mediate between marketing effort and results, the question is simply which of many to choose. While we elucidate our preferences in developing the model below, the breadth of possible choices is worth pondering.

Despite this diversity, approaches of macroeconomic analysts appear homogeneous compared to the widely varying methodologies advocated by microeconomic researchers. At least with the former, a relatively clear semblance of progression from simple measures of sales to the complex ones of value added and "total productivity" can be constructed. With the latter, no such simplicity offers itself to allow easy classification. It is to the microeconomic, level-of-the-firm researches, we now turn.

Chapter 3

Microeconomic Studies of Marketing Efficiency

Introduction

If the macroeconomic literature asked, "What role does marketing play in the economy, and how efficient is it?" the microeconomic literature asks, "How can managers do a better marketing job within a given organization?" These are very different questions, and it is not surprising that scholars in the two areas differ concerning definition, methodology, and prescription. They agree on only one point—the presumption that effective (i.e., properly goal-directed) work is being accomplished, which wants only an addition of increased efficiency for success. The microeconomic schemes may be loosely grouped in two categories: pecuniary and nonpecuniary measures.

Pecuniary Attacks on Efficiency: Profit, Sales, and ROI

Profitability Analysis

One strong strand of microeconomic marketing productivity research examines the relative profitability of different portions of a company's business. Although Bucklin and other economists tilt against this interpretation of the word "productivity," the subject still draws considerable attention from numerous scholars in the marketing field (see Feder, 1965; Goodman, 1967, 1970, 1972; Beik and Buzby, 1973; Mossman, Fischer, and Crissy, 1974; Corr, 1976; Dunne and Wolk, 1977; Hill, 1978; and Takeuchi and Salmon, 1985, for a representative sampling of researchers who have measured marketing productivity with a profit-based approach). The father of much profitability work in marketing productivity is Charles Sevin, whose *Marketing Productivity Analysis* (1965) is a small masterpiece in the marketing literature.

Sevin's Marketing Productivity Analysis. Sevin defines marketing productivity as "the sales or profit output per unit of marketing effort" (p. viii). He deals with the assumed goals problem at the outset of his work:

> expositions of business practice and microeconomic analysis both usually proceed from the assumption that the objective of the individual business firm is to maximize its net profits. Twenty years of management-consulting practice, however, make it clear to the author that this assumption about objectives is naive and unrealistic. . . . But no matter what the objectives of the firm, all managements are (or should be) interested in increasing the productivity of their marketing operations, thus favorably affecting such factors as "growth," sales volume, market share, and net profits. (p. viii)

While this seems innocuous enough, Sevin in no way escapes the problem of working on efficiency while remaining uncertain about what constitutes effectiveness. Certainly growth, sales volume, market share, and profits are common measures, but they do not necessarily operate in concert. Nor are the causal connections among these measures clear. Strict profitability measures also avoid the "quality of services rendered" questions raised by the macroeconomic analysts whose work we reviewed in Chapter 2, although Sevin is explicit in his dismissal of qualitative measures for his purposes. Sevin's summary of his aims could, with few changes, serve as a statement of purpose for many microeconomic investigations of marketing productivity: his work is intended to show

> [h]ow any business firm can increase its sales volume or its net profits very substantially, and more than once, by obtaining and using (1) marketing-cost and profitability information and (2) marketing-experimentation information to do a better job of allocating its marketing efforts to the various segments of its business. (p. vii)

It is these two areas, profitability analysis and experimentation, that Sevin explores in detail. The key virtue of both approaches, Sevin explains, is that they provide information not generally available to marketing management.

Insufficient information, Sevin continues, results in any of a number of problems, including a budget that is too large or too small for a given product or customer segment, an inefficient marketing mix, or a gross misallocation among segments (pp. 6–7). Without the right information, the marketing manager has no way of knowing whether these problems exist; with this information, the marketing manager can uncover those areas in which results and allocated efforts are out of sync.

For his profitability analysis, Sevin first identifies the costs against which revenues will be matched. He does this by classifying costs into "functional" cost groups that reflect marketing activities rather than the "natural" accounts that businesses tend to use, as we discussed in the last chapter. Sevin groups costs into seven categories: (1) direct selling costs, (2) indirect selling costs, (3) advertising, (4) sales promotion, (5) transportation, (6) storage and shipping, and (7) order processing. He then allocates these costs to product groups, account-size classes (small, medium, and large accounts), and geographic areas by the volume of activity performed in each area (not the dollar expense of the activity). The logic is similar to a sales per man-hour equation, where man-hours are assumed to represent a standard of activity. When all costs have been allocated, their sum in each segment is compared to the revenue or profit that that segment produces, giving a measurement of productivity.[7]

Once the analyst has grappled with the very real and difficult problems intrinsic in the cost allocations Sevin recommends, and after he or she has calculated the relevant productivity ratios, Sevin recommends a variety of tactics for improving ratios in underperforming areas. Most of these tactics involve reallocating efforts either to reduce costs or to increase revenues for a given segment. However, the very notion that a change in allocations will produce a corresponding change in sales or profits ignores both market factors and quality of execution—Sevin's way of thinking, like that of many of the authors on macroeconomic productivity, defines the marketing activities of the firm as a "black box" that can be tweaked simply by

---

7. Although Sevin uses somewhat different allocation bases for manufacturers, wholesalers, and retailers, the underlying principle is the same: allocate on the basis of activity, then compare segment costs to segment revenues or profit (see Sevin, Chapters 2 and 3 for the exact allocation rules).

changing its inputs toward more efficient responses.

To get an empirical understanding of whether changing effort will indeed improve results, Sevin advocates a program of vigorous and sometimes ad hoc experimentation, especially with products, customers, and advertising. Sometimes the results of experiments do suggest dramatic possibilities for profit improvement.[8] However, experiments are themselves prone to error, and experimental results to misreading, as Sevin readily admits. Strict experimental control of markets is usually impossible. Because of expense and internal practicality, experiments often measure short-term outcomes when long-term results may be more relevant. Uncontrolled variation across units may overwhelm differences generated by the independent variable. The proliferation of national channels of distribution and media can make it difficult to isolate control units. Competitors may sabotage experiments by changing their efforts within the test markets. Sevin argues that exact accuracy is not the issue, but merely a "better-worse" distinction (see Sevin, Chapter 8). By this criterion, he claims, experimentation provides valuable answers to crucial information needs.

Sevin's ultimate argument for his analytic approach, including information gathering on profit ratios plus experimentation to assess sensitivities, is essentially that it works. In Sevin's experience reallocation of effort has always worked, "even in large and efficiently managed businesses" (p. vii). This may, however, be "hitting the broad side of a barn." The average manager will probably improve his or her sales/effort ratio by applying Sevin's scheme. Looking at mismatches between revenues and costs will often reveal areas that will benefit from almost any attention, much as changing the lighting levels in a factory can cause increased output more because of management attention than the specific action (Roethlisberger and Dickson, 1934). Thus virtually any nondestructive management action can improve sales or

profit in some fashion. Hitting optimal targets, though, may require considering market factors and execution issues that Sevin excludes.

Profitability is no less controversial than productivity when it comes to definition. Just as we found for effort in productivity equations, the question of what costs are appropriate to subtract from revenue does not admit of an easy or univocal answer. One consistent debate in this area is whether the fixed costs of an organization should be allocated to individual marketing programs. Sevin says they should. Others argue that only variable costs should apply (see, for example, Christopher, in Shapiro and Kirpalani, 1984; for other views on this debate, see Rayburn, 1973; Beik and Buzby, 1973; Dunne and Wolk, 1977; and Band, 1983).

Goodman's "Marketing Accounting" Scheme. Another profitability analyst, Goodman (1967, 1970, 1972), describes what he calls relevant costs as the key to accurate profitability measurement. Costs are relevant, he asserts, if they produce a negative answer to the following question: "If we did not do this—make this product, serve this customer, use this channel, and so on—would we still have this cost?" One advantage of this approach is that it is decision-oriented, and therefore immediately relevant to a manager evaluating his or her programs. A second advantage is that the definition cuts across the fixed cost–variable cost debate; the question is one of relevance, not of cost behavior as a function of volume.

To understand relevant costs, Goodman recasts the traditional income statement, grouping variable marketing and manufacturing costs to reveal a variable profit, then fixed product costs to show a direct product profit, then direct division costs and fixed overheads to calculate division and corporate profits. Table 5 shows one example of Goodman's scheme.

Goodman's adaptation of the traditional income statement leads to his important notion of direct product profits, or the profit remaining after manufacturing, storage, distribution, advertising, and promotion of the good, but before its sale through the channel (sales management and promotion). The critical problem with this way of thinking, however, has always been the inability of managers to decompose their costs in the manner recommended by Goodman (see also Kotler, 1984, for a similar analysis based on market segments rather than on products). Usually, it just is not known how much

---

8. Others have, of course, used experiments to assess the potential for sales improvement through marketing efforts. See, for example, Ackoff and Emshoff's classic study (in Enis and Cox, 1985) of advertising at Anheuser-Busch, Dhalla (1977), and other studies cited by Sevin. In addition to sales versus expense measures, Dhalla advocates using experiments to judge the quality of decisions in areas such as pricing, advertising, promotion, and the mix of marketing tactics employed.

advertising or promotion, for example, to allocate to $\frac{3}{16}$-in. drill bits in a thirteen-thousand-item industrial equipment line.

Beyond this distinction, Goodman raises some more readily executed modifications of traditional profitability. In *Techniques of Profitability Analysis* (1970) he illustrates his approach to profitability measurement. First, he distinguishes between profitability and profit. Profit, he argues, is concerned with the past. It is a static, residual number based on subtracting costs from revenues in a given period. Profitability, on the other hand, is future-oriented. It represents the organization's potential to create wealth over time. A company that is profitable, therefore, is one that has built a sustainable momentum.

Table 5 Specimen of Goodman's Adaptation of the Income Statement for Marketing Profitability Analysis

Proceeds from sales		100.0
Variable cost of goods sold		
Raw materials	10.0	
Packing	10.0	
Direct labor	5.0	
Variable gross profits (manufacturing contribution margin)		75.0
Other variable expenses		
Freight	3.0	
Warehousing	2.0	
Spoilage	1.0	
Commissions	5.0	
Discounts	3.0	
Variable profit (distribution contribution margin)		61.0
Direct product costs		
Advertising	9.0	
Promotion	3.0	
Direct product profits		49.0
Direct division costs		
Sales management	12.0	
Product management	3.0	
Sales force	2.8	
Sales incentives	1.0	
Market research	.2	
Division profit contribution (net contribution margin)		30.0
Allocated period expense		
Factory overhead	21.0	
Supervision	4.0	
Other overhead	19.0	
Corporate administration	5.0	
Net division profit before taxes		(19.0)

Source: Adapted from Goodman (1970, p. 38).

The sustainability of this momentum is what Goodman approaches with his second methodological innovation. Goodman argues that the "quality of profits" differs depending on the position of a given product in the product life cycle. Profits from development and growth products are more valuable than those from saturation or decline products because the former class of profits indicates greater potential for the future. He illustrates a "life-cycle worksheet" that reveals the proportion of profits provided by products in the different stages. (See Goodman, 1970, pp. 90–91 and Chapter 5 for a detailed discussion of this worksheet.) Presumably this life-cycle argument would hold no matter the performance measure.

Goodman also explains that different profit measurements are useful at different levels of an organization. Using the income statement described above, he produces operating statements for different organizational levels. At a product-manager level, the most important figure is the direct product profit. The direct profit and variable profit are the best quantitative measures of product management performance because they separate the division and period expenses over which the manager has no influence from the variable product-related expenses, which product management does influence.

The division operating statement adds direct divisional expenses, such as general management and the division sales force, and allocated period expenses, such as factory overhead and plant depreciation, to furnish a net division profit. The net division profit represents profit that would disappear if the division disappeared, following the relevant cost discussion above. Finally, the corporate operating statement subtracts corporate period expenses from divisional profits.

From a marketing performance standpoint, the concept of different productivity ratios at different organizational levels is not surprising, especially given the widespread use of manufacturing productivity measures at line, plant, firm, and economy levels. However, manufacturing activities are more discrete than is marketing. Once one has the materials for an assembly operation, a worker can perform his or her task with little concern about the activities of other assembly lines. Marketing programs, on the other hand, may be intimately linked with the activities of other programs or the division and corporate levels, particularly in regard to the overall image the organization attempts to project. This can be beneficial to a given program (see "free-riding" in Anderson and Weitz, 1986, discussed below) or detrimental, depending on circumstances. One may assume that the marketing productivity of a breakfast cereal program at General Foods would be very different from the marketing productivity of the same program if it were launched by a small regional cereal maker.

Goodman connects all these threads in return on investment (ROI) calculations. ROI, he comments, measures "the efficiency of profits rather than [absolute] profit dollars" (p. 110). It is calculated by dividing the appropriate profit by the investment in the segment. The investment in the segment consists of the total assets employed in that segment less the current liabilities due against those assets. Goodman calls this the "tangible net worth" of the segment. He goes on to apply ROI analyses to problems ranging from corporate acquisitions to sales staffing decisions (Goodman, Chapters 6–10; see also Hayes, White, and Williams, 1984; and Takeuchi and Salmon, 1985, for applications of ROI in retailing).

Although Goodman does not label it this way, ROI is very similar to some of the productivity measures we examined in the macroeconomic citations. Bucklin or Beckman might call it a measure of capital productivity, since the ratio reveals the amount of output (profit) generated by each dollar of capital (investment). ROI is in turn very different from Sevin's conception of sales or profits divided by expenses. To the extent that many marketing expenses represent some form of labor performed (e.g., selling compensation, staff payroll), Sevin's measure more closely resembles a labor productivity measure than it does one that accounts for invested capital.

Feder's Marginal Revenues/Marginal Costs Approach. Feder (1965) adds another twist to the traditional profitability concept. He defines good marketing performance (he calls it the "marketing objective") as an investment "in each market area up to the point where an additional dollar would produce greater immediate profits if spent elsewhere"; spending beyond this level depends on "the future potential which justifies the sacrifice of immediate profits" (p. 134). The goal of marketing profitability analysis, then, is to "identify areas in which the company over-

spent or underspent relative to the immediate profit potential" (p. 136). This goal is quite similar to Sevin's, and is also reminiscent of treatments of the 80/20 rule, which postulates that approximately 80 percent of an organization's business derives from 20 percent of the organization's customers (see, for example, Dubinsky and Hansen, 1982). Feder's approach represents, of course, a marketing application of the traditional marginal revenues over marginal costs argument so familiar from economics.

To accomplish this marginal cost analysis for marketing, Feder recasts the income statement in a fashion similar to that of Goodman (see Feder, p. 135 for a detailed example), but he adds a timing factor. Feder points out that marketing expenses such as advertising and sales promotion are often directed at the consumer, and thus are most likely to affect retail sales in the immediate future. Factory sales will change later, as retailers restock their shelves. Feder suggests using market research to determine the length of this time lag so that the company can account for it in financial information provided to marketing management. Researchers can do this by expanding the time period examined until market share, gross profit, and market size move together consistently.

Feder adds outside factors to examine the efficiency of marketing spending. In addition to measuring market share, market research should calculate the size and trend of the retail market, retail distribution characteristics (what percentage of the total retail market do the stores carrying a company's product control?), and media efficiencies (cost per thousand). These factors influence the impact of the company's spending, and thus suggest why profits may differ from area to area.

Once he has compiled the data, Feder compares results for different market areas across time periods to identify over- and underspending. He does this by calculating "opportunity rates" for a given area. We might say these rates represent the potential sales inherent in a product or area. Feder develops average opportunity rates for an area by dividing "gross marketing earnings," a profit measure, by the sum of advertising and sales promotion expenses. In this sense, his opportunity rates are similar to the profit divided by cost measure Sevin uses. From this level, Feder proceeds to calculate incremental opportunity rates. These rates demonstrate the effect of a change in marketing expense relative to a change in profit. If reducing spending by $100,000 increases profit $50,000, the incremental opportunity rate is $.50 (fifty cents of profit for every dollar of reduction in spending; see Corr, 1976, for another treatment of opportunity rates).

Opportunity rates are another future-oriented performance measure, similar to Goodman's quality-of-profit concept. The rates become more useful as the market research department assembles historical information over time. Combined with adjusted profit figures, opportunity rates (profit/marketing expense) and incremental opportunity rates (change in profit/ change in marketing expense) give measures of past profit, current profit/expense ratios, and potential profit/expense ratios.

Anderson and Weitz's Vertical Integration Measures. Anderson and Weitz (1986) use a profitability perspective to examine marketing productivity in the much narrower context of vertical integration decisions for marketing. Common "make-or-buy" decisions in marketing, they explain, include such issues as whether to develop an in-house sales force or use manufacturers' representatives, or whether to create an in-house advertising agency. They define marketing productivity in terms of what they call "long-term efficiency," which in turn rests on "net effectiveness" and administrative overhead, as follows:

Net effectiveness = Revenue − Direct cost;

$$\text{Efficiency} = \frac{\text{Net effectiveness}}{\text{Administrative overhead}}$$

Administrative overhead consists of costs incurred to monitor and control activities within a firm. (Etgar, 1976, discusses the operational efficiency of some of these integrated activities in distributing insurance.) When an activity is brought within the firm, such as personal selling, any increase in effectiveness is partially offset by the increase in the cost of management due to the increase in the complexity of the tasks managed. Vertical integration, Anderson and Weitz argue, increases marketing productivity when integration's advantages (increased revenues and/or reduced costs) outweigh its disadvantages (increased administrative overhead to manage the new task internally).

Anderson and Weitz's use of efficiency and effectiveness is contrary to our use of these terms, but even stripped of the labels, the scheme they propose differs from other profitability measures. Goodman might call Anderson and Weitz's net effectiveness a measure of variable profit. Administrative overhead, on the other hand, resembles a fixed cost in that it is added periodically, and does not vary directly with the amount of the new activity performed. Therefore, we can redefine their productivity measure here as a measure of incremental variable profit divided by incremental fixed cost. This is similar to Feder's treatment of opportunity rates, except that the denominator there was a period program cost, advertising and sales promotion expense, while for Anderson and Weitz the denominator is a period administrative cost.

Given the framework they propose and the problems with which the framework grapples, Anderson and Weitz pose an interesting set of factors that increase or decrease what they call marketing productivity (efficiency, in our usage). They review several marketing studies of vertical integration and conclude that the key issues in the marketing literature center on a trade-off between scale economies and control. Using an external agent can lower unit costs because the agent performs the same activity for a number of companies, thereby building scale economies and developing expertise. However, an individual firm has less control over the activities of the external agent; companies sometimes complain, for example, that independent distributors resist providing information in a format the company finds useful. Internal agents increase the control, but diminish the productivity improvement opportunities inherent from increased scale.

Anderson and Weitz then turn to economics, where they conclude that the key issues in vertical integration are cost reduction and environmental control. Vertical integration reduces costs when the efficiency of the total process requires the close coordination of several tasks. They cite the example of the steel industry, where integrating blast furnaces, converters, and primary reduction mills reduces overall handling costs of the metal by eliminating reheating between stages.

Firms vertically integrate for environmental control when they need to secure access to supplies or markets. This argument differs slightly from the control argument above. The interest here is not so much controlling how an activity is performed but whether the firm has access to critical resources and constituencies.

Both these reasons, Anderson and Weitz submit, are ultimately grounded in market imperfections within the supplier and buyer industries. If a supplier market is perfectly competitive, they claim, the suppliers will compete with one another to provide the maximum cost reduction to the firm (someone will locate a blast furnace near the firm's converter and mills). Similarly, competing suppliers will strive with each other to provide the firm access to critical resources.

Anderson and Weitz carry the steel example one step further to demonstrate another concept. Once a supplier has located a blast furnace near a firm's processing plant, that supplier has a tremendous competitive advantage relative to other suppliers—operating blast furnaces on site. The supplier is able to monopolize blast furnace services to the firm's processing plant, giving rise to "opportunism," or monopolistic behavior (high prices, inadequate service, etc.).

This blend of scale economies, control issues, and market imperfections falls under a discipline called transaction cost analysis (Williamson, 1975), which Anderson and Weitz use to develop their framework. In applying this set of ideas to marketing, they demonstrate a variety of factors that change the productivity with which a firm executes its marketing activities.

A number of factors, for example, reduce efficiency by reducing variable profit. Lack of competition in supplier (or, by implication, buyer) industries reduces net effectiveness by increasing costs to the organization. Noncompetitive industries for marketing arise principally from two sources: company- or person-specific capabilities and scale economies within the supplier industry. Obviously, if only one external agent has the capability to service a firm properly, that agent can be opportunistic. If the supplier industry lends itself to scale economies, certain agents may develop sufficient scale to preclude entry by new competitors. These types of competitive factors are ones that we can imagine influencing Bucklin's (1978) terms of trade. Prices of inputs and outputs will be affected by the competitiveness of supplier and buyer markets.

Other factors reducing net effectiveness include environmental uncertainty, the difficulty of assessing performance, and "free-riding" potential. If a firm operates in a rapidly changing environment, it is less able to specify the tasks external or internal agents need to perform. If it is difficult to assess good performance of a task, the firm cannot evaluate external or internal agents. If an agent may derive benefits from other agents without paying for them (for example, a franchisee who runs his or her own business poorly, but benefits from the reputation built by the operations of other franchisees), the agent may underperform. All of these factors, Anderson and Weitz note, increase opportunism on the part of agents.

To control opportunism, companies traditionally resort to two tactics: administrative control and organizational culture. Administrative control consists of traditional management control: increased analysis of information leading to a more sophisticated range of incentives and punishments. Organizational culture attempts to socialize agents into behaving in the organization's interest. One could compare this to the contrast between the "hard" and "soft" controls of the McKinsey 7-S model of organization (see Waterman, Peters, and Julien, 1980). Administrative controls are, we believe, usually structural: information flows, incentive systems, and so on. Organizational culture depends more on the attitudes and skills of the individuals who run the structures.

Finally, Anderson and Weitz contend that the nature of the task itself often dictates the productivity with which a company may perform it. If the task is performed infrequently, the company will develop few skills or structures because they have too little experience upon which to base rules to improve efficiency. If the task involves a small amount of dollars, the company will not be justified in devoting administrative costs to managing the activity in-house. A highly differentiated product may dictate a unique marketing approach, limiting competition in supplier and buyer industries. The place of the product in its life cycle will also affect the productivity potential: in the introductory phase, for example, environmental uncertainty, the ability to monitor performance, and company-specific capabilities will all be high because management is unable to forecast ultimate market acceptance and the speed with which that will occur, reducing net effectiveness. This is similar to Goodman's (1970) life-cycle notion.

Some form of profitability analysis is by far the most popular choice among microeconomic analysts of marketing performance. In addition to the studies we reviewed above, one may examine Beik and Buzby (1973—profitability by customer segment), Dubinsky and Hansen

(1982—on the 80/20 rule), Dunne and Wolk (1977—using a database and diagrammatic income breakdowns), Hill (1978—profitability by customer), Jackson and Ostrom (1980—methods of grouping costs), Mossman, Fischer, and Crissy (1974—a residual income approach), Takeuchi and Salmon (1985—departmental ROI for retailers), Hayes, White, and Williams (1984—gross margin ROI for retailers), and Rayburn (1973—a management accounting perspective). The point is the same: maximum profits at minimum costs are said to equal maximal performance.

Sales Analyses

Conceptually related to profitability analysis is sales analysis, which compares sales versus expense rather than profit versus expense. Although the results of a sales analysis will often differ from those of a profitability analysis, the two methods share the scheme of measuring a monetary output versus a monetary input. Thus, sales analyses also share most of the virtues and vices of profitability analyses.

Sales measures appear particularly common in examining the subfunctions of marketing, such as advertising (McNiven, 1980; Ackoff and Emshoff, in Enis and Cox, 1985) and personal selling (Hall, 1975; Bilon, 1979). Because of their closeness to profitability analysis, and because this line of research is significantly narrower in its implications for performance analysis, it is not reviewed further here. See Gross's work, however (discussed below), for one scheme that relies on unit sales as a core measure.

Nonpecuniary Measures of Performance

Other researchers have not been convinced that dollar measures are the sole arbiter of superior performance. Peter Drucker (1986) addresses this question by comparing business performance feedback to the various dials on an automobile dashboard.

Drucker's Multiple-Criterion Measure

The first dial Drucker suggests is market standing, measured by market share. Drucker emphasizes that an organization should use multiple measures of market share in determining the organization's "true" share, because single or aggregate share figures can be as mis-

leading as quarterly earnings figures. Aside from overall market share, Drucker maintains that top management of a company needs to know share by key customer segments, key geographic areas, and key product categories. On a macroscopic level, the organization needs to know its market standing versus substitute product markets: steel versus pre-stressed concrete, for example.

Drucker's second dial is "innovative performance." He thinks of this primarily in the development of new products and services, but there is no particular reason why it would not apply to marketing tactics, promotional schemes, or advertising creatives. Drucker divides innovation into two submeasures: how well does the company innovate relative to its competitors (a kind of "share of innovation" measure), and how quickly does it innovate? He again categorizes innovation by segments and product categories, as for market share. Deciding where to innovate in the product mix, he suggests, can be as important as how much a company innovates. By concentrating innovation on a specific market segment, a company may develop a powerful advantage there that can be used to approach other segments. Drucker cites Digital Equipment Corporation's work in the minicomputer segment of the data-processing equipment industry as a successful example of this approach.

Dial three rates productivity performance. Drucker defines a company's productivity as the real value added of a company's output divided by the amount of capital, materials, and labor the company uses. While the total factor measure is important, Drucker also argues strongly that the individual single-factor measures should be evaluated as well in order to reveal whether productivity gains for one factor are being produced by degrading the productivity of other factors. He accuses American industry of doing this quite often, frequently boosting labor productivity at the expense of capital productivity. Within labor productivity, he further champions analyzing output versus the number of employees in labor categories. In another essay (Drucker, 1985), he explains that much of the U.S. auto industry's problem versus Japanese manufacturers is owing to the much larger white-collar staff, particularly clerical workers, relative to the number of cars manufactured in the United States. A simple marketing application of this analysis would involve examining unit output of an organization versus the size of its marketing management group.

The final two dials are cash flow and profitability. For cash flow, Drucker advocates examining standard financial projections. One good example is a cash-based sources-and-uses statement, usually found in an organization's annual report. For profitability, which Drucker defines (in a fashion similar to that of Goodman) as the ability of a company to produce a profit, he uses a thirty-six-month moving average of operating profit.

Drucker's article raises the question of how many measures we need in an aggregate assessment of marketing performance. While most of the authors we review do advocate a single measure, Drucker is not alone in championing several. Thomas (1984) and Bucklin (1978) propose a multitude of measures to judge marketing performance.

BCG and PIMS Market Share Studies

Drucker's first dial, market standing as measured by market share, is almost as popular as profit as a yardstick of marketing performance. Part of this popularity undoubtedly arises from market share's prominence in a number of strategic planning treatments that were widely discussed in the 1970s.

The first of these is the growth-share matrix developed by the Boston Consulting Group (BCG) for portfolio planning (Henderson, 1973; see also Abell and Hammond, 1979; and Mahajan, Varadarajan, and Kerin, 1987, for critical appraisals of this model). The object of this planning approach is to develop a balanced portfolio of businesses regarding cash generation and cash use. A portfolio with too many cash-using businesses will require constant external financing, while a portfolio with too many cash-generating businesses is accumulating cash rather than investing it in future business.

The growth-share matrix argues that the cash-generating potential of a business may be approximated by examining the growth of that business's market, and the relative market share of the business in that market.[9] High-growth,

high-share businesses produce fairly neutral cash flows, because while high-share businesses should throw off cash, high-growth businesses require increasing amounts of working capital to finance growth. Low-growth, low-share businesses are similarly neutral: low working capital needs offset low cash flow potential. High-growth, low-share businesses are heavy cash users, since they are not yet large enough to provide internal funding for their working capital needs. Low-growth, high-share businesses have large positive cash flows because they require little financing for growth relative to the strong cash positions their competitive strength provides.

Mahajan, Varadarajan, and Kerin (1987) note three assumptions underlying the growth-share matrix:

1. Cash generated is a function of relative market share due to scale economies and experience effects.
2. Cash required is a function of market growth rate and market share strategy.
3. Net cash flow is a function of relative market share, market growth rate, and market share strategy. (p. 5)

Given the plausibility of these assumptions (they are by no means uncontroversial; Mahajan et al. term them questionable at best) it is obvious that market share is extremely important to a business unit's prosperity. Thus, companies that use the BCG matrix are likely to judge a business unit's performance, and particularly its marketing, by the unit's market share.

A second strategic marketing analysis that leans heavily on market share is the propositions generated by the Profit Impact of Market Strategies (PIMS) model. The PIMS model is based on a database of almost 3,000 business units from some 450 corporations. Comprehensive information has been collected on these units, with some data going as far back as 1972. Using this financial, market, and operational information, researchers have constructed a model of the relation between profit and marketing strategy. The heart of this model is a thirty-seven-variable regression equation that predicts pretax return on investment (ROI).[10] (See Abell and Hammond, 1979, for a detailed description of the PIMS project.)

---

9. Relative market share is computed as a business unit's sales divided by the sales of the unit's largest competitor.

10. ROI equals pretax profit divided by the sum of equity and long-term debt.

One of the most important independent variables in this equation is market share. Buzzell, Gale, and Sultan (1975) first publicized this finding in an article in the *Harvard Business Review*. A 10-percentage-point increase in share of the market the business unit served accounted for a 5-point increase in ROI.[11] Like BCG, the authors suggest that economies of scale could be one reason this relationship holds true. They also suggest that greater market share means greater market power—large companies should be able to bargain more effectively with buyers and suppliers, and to administer prices to their advantage. (Again, this recalls Bucklin's terms of trade; see Bucklin, 1978.) Finally, Buzzell, Gale, and Sultan propose that quality of management may have a great deal to do with both high share and high ROI. In their review of the "PIMS principles," Buzzell and Gale (1987) conclude that the share-profitability relationship is based on the following sequence of events: (1) a business unit develops superior relative quality in its products or services; (2) this superiority attracts customers, building market share; (3) by gaining share, the business attains scale or experience-based cost advantages in production; and (4) these cost advantages combine with the premium prices that superior products may command to produce high profitability.

This relationship is not as straightforward as the 10:3.5 ratio might suggest. First, there is substantial variation depending on mediating factors that influence the business unit's position. For example, Buzzell, Gale, and Sultan note that market share is more important (i.e., influences ROI more) for infrequently purchased products and for business units with weak, fragmented buying groups. Second, as is often the case with complex regression analyses, there have been substantial methodological criticisms leveled at PIMS (see Abell and Hammond, 1979, p. 376; and Mahajan et al., 1987, Table 3 for more on this topic).

Still, there is no denying the prominence market share retains in the minds of many executives. Mahajan et al. remark that (1) scarcity of capital and slower market growth has refocused management attention on pruning low-share businesses in the hope that higher return on capital will result; (2) many institutional inves-

tors "often rely on market share positions when making stock recommendations"; (3) the recent wave of mergers and acquisitions has often been driven by market share concerns; and (4) the work of market share advocates and new concerns about global competitiveness have put increasing emphasis on being "big" to compete (pp. 25–26). We make some arguments on the inadequacy of share measures for marketing-performance measurement below.

Mehrotra's Brand Franchise

Some authors deny the validity of profit and share measures altogether. One outspoken advocate of this position is Mehrotra (1984), who claims that measures such as profit and market share miss the true purpose of marketing: "identifying and meeting the needs and wants of the end-users" (p. 10). Instead, he claims that most marketing managers are evaluated on their "ability to produce the 'numbers'" (share and/or income) without exceeding the budget (p. 10).

Instead of share and profit, Mehrotra argues that the best measure of a consumer marketer's productivity is the "consumer franchise" or "goodwill" the organization builds over time. Borrowing a consumer model from an internal report at General Electric, Mehrotra claims that consumers can be arrayed on a continuum based on their probability of buying a given brand. Consistently high-probability buyers are the brand's core consumer franchise. Consistently low-probability buyers are uncommitted or committed to another brand. Mathematically, therefore, a brand's sales can be represented as

Sales = P (buy if committed)
    × Number of committed buyers
    + P (buy if uncommitted)
    × Number of uncommitted buyers.

Given this view, Mehrotra continues, there are two ways one can increase sales. First, one can increase the immediate probability that a consumer will purchase the brand. Second, one can increase the number of consistent, high-probability buyers, the brand franchise. Mehrotra associates the former approach with sales promotions such as coupons, and the latter with advertising and product improvements. Although both methods work, Mehrotra cites research that suggests that continual promotions tend to erode profitability.

11. In more recent work, Buzzell and Gale downgrade this effect to about 3.5 points of ROI increase for every 10 points of share increase. See Chapters 1 and 5 of Buzzell and Gale, 1987.

In a study to test the model, the correlation between franchise and market share was high (.87), and between franchise and relative price low (.08). The highest correlation, however, was between franchise and the product of share and relative price (.95). Mehrotra outlines the implications of this finding:

> the size of a brand's consumer franchise predetermines what a brand's value is in the market place, but the marketer has the option to "realize" this value through many share/price combinations, because infinitely many combinations of share and relative price will result in the *one* product of share and relative price that is governed by the consumer franchise. (p. 13)

The conclusion that follows is that in the short term, market share can be made to increase by price reductions through promotions, but that for a fixed relative price, the brand's market share is determined by the size of its consumer franchise. The implication Mehrotra draws from this is that market shares in the short term can be manipulated up or down through pricing actions without the consumer franchise changing (p. 13).

The problem with using market share measures of performance, therefore, is that they give no indication whether share is high because buyers are committed to the product, or because buyers are committed to getting a low price. Given the pressure on marketing managers to produce numbers, Mehrotra suggests that managers have strong personal incentives to use price promotions in hopes of boosting share even though this may erode the franchise in the long run. The straightforward conclusion is that some marketing tactics are protective of the brand franchise, and hence productive, while others destroy the franchise even as they produce high profits, share, or sales in an efficient (but ineffective) manner.

This is a very different conception of performance than those we reviewed that used profit. Although he does mention profit in the context of franchise, Mehrotra relies more heavily on such traditional statements of marketing's purpose as the "marketing concept."

Bucklin's Markets, Services, and Technology

Bucklin (reviewed in Chapter 2) has some powerful ideas on what the true productivity of marketing is at a microeconomic level. Although *Productivity in Marketing* (1978) focuses on macroeconomic productivity, he also develops a conceptual framework for marketing productivity within firms (see Bucklin, Chapters 5 and 6).

As outlined above, Bucklin believes that marketing productivity at the macro level is based on the real output marketing produces divided by the real inputs it uses. Inputs include hours of labor, investment of capital, and so on; output consists of services. At the micro level, Bucklin looks at three factors that affect output/input: market forces, market services, and marketing technology.

Market forces are factors external to the organization that affect its marketing productivity. Bucklin focuses on four. First, he examines competition within the organization's industry. Organizations within highly competitive industries, he hypothesizes, will have higher productivity; if they do not, they will swiftly lose ground to competitors. Bucklin believes his "terms of trade" (price of outputs/price of inputs) is a conceptually valid approach to quantifying levels of competition. Greater competition should reduce the ratio, because the organization would be forced to price its units of output as low as possible to attract purchasers.

Bucklin's second market factor is growth. Whether in the economy, the industry, or the individual firm, he argues, growth increases demand, leading to better capacity utilization. He also believes high-growth industries and companies are more attractive to managers, and thus tend to attract a higher caliber of management skills.

Timing of a firm's entry into the market, which Bucklin calls "age of market," can also affect productivity. Early entrants can have a significant advantage over late entrants, both in terms of reputation among buyers and learning curve effects. The degree of power this factor holds is not as clear as for the first two. Bucklin remarks, for example, that if an entire industry has long been established, the relative entry points of the industry members will be less important. Also, riding down the learning curve in terms of marketing is by no means inevitable. Bucklin's argument on this factor produces results similar to Goodman's logic about product life cycle stage—early-stage products are "better" than late-stage ones.

Finally, the transaction size of the firm affects marketing productivity. Many marketing services are the same whether the buyer purchases a small or a large amount of goods. An example is a one-year warranty covering a wide variety of products. Bucklin claims that most determinants of transaction size are beyond the control of the firm; thus he classifies it as a market force.

Concerning market services, Bucklin reiterates his argument that changes in quality of service must be incorporated in output measures of marketing, or marketing productivity measures will understate real service rendered. He divides market services into three parts: logistical, informational, and product functional.

Logistical services cluster around the convenience with which the buyer may purchase an organization's product. These include delivery time, availability, order size limitations, and product quality (freshness of baked goods and snack foods is directly related to speed of delivery, for example). Informational services provide guidance to the consumer in choosing the product the consumer needs or wants. Information services, Bucklin contends, are the most complex of the three marketing services. Dimensions on which information service can vary include waiting time for information, quantity and quality of information, product return policies (which allow the buyer to learn about the product in his or her home at no risk), breadth of product assortment, clustering of different items in a product category to allow easier comparison, and product standardization. Product functional services enhance the value of the product to the consumer. Organizations may provide assembly or installation services in relation to a product, product adjustments (tailoring of suits in a retail store, for example), warranties, protective packaging, and credit.

Marketing technology may be the most interesting aspect of productivity that Bucklin analyzes at the microeconomic level. He observes that the notion of technology in marketing management is often overlooked, or at best appears only in certain aspects of marketing research (Bucklin, p. 94). He asserts that technology is by no means a static factor on which marketing management overlays itself. He argues that, over time, marketing departments have steadily substituted capital for labor, not only in the form of structural changes in distribution and retailing, but also in the shift away from personal

sales to advertising and promotion. Further changes reflecting the revolution in microelectronics, he predicts (in 1978), will only speed this capital substitution. Recent innovations such as planogram models for analyzing retail shelf space allocations, the use of self-service information terminals in stores, and "direct product profit" schemes all support this contention (Takeuchi and Salmon, 1985).

Bucklin borrows concepts from manufacturing productivity to discuss the effects of different dimensions of marketing technology on productivity. Scale of operation, he hypothesizes, should have a positive impact on marketing productivity. Larger scale should provide the opportunity to routinize more tasks, possibly by automating them. Most growing small companies, for example, reach a point where they process a sufficient number of transactions to justify automated order processing. Similarly, degree of fixed capacity utilization, such as warehouse space utilization, should be positively related to marketing productivity. Capital intensity (in the form of advertising "investments," R&D investments, and physical plant) will definitely improve labor productivity, and may improve total productivity as well. Organization of human resources influences productivity to the extent that it puts an adequate quantity of marketing staff in place to support an adequate amount of market research, R&D, and other technological investments. Bucklin also notes that the quality of the personnel has a profound impact as well. Finally, he hypothesizes that the degree and mode of coordination within distribution channels will affect productivity. Controlled channels will, he claims, be more productive than uncontrolled ones, on average, because vertical integration eliminates duplication of effort.

Though Bucklin cites empirical research on a few of these forces, services, and technologies, the results are surprisingly mixed and not always confirmatory (see Bucklin, pp. 97–105 for details of this work). He attributes part of this to the absence of any framework within which to research marketing productivity. But although he stresses the need for a net measurement of total marketing services provided, he suggests no means of aggregating these individual measures.

Bucklin's framework is comprehensive, but its very complexity makes it difficult to develop comprehensible measures, much less useful ones. His framework is designed as a spur to future research rather than as a useful yardstick. Most of what he discusses on a micro level are the ways to account for services in a real output measure, although his technology considerations must affect input as well.

Still, as we suggested above, it is not clear whether more services are better. Rather, we suspect, certain mixes of services appeal to certain target markets. Thus, unit output of a marketing system plus an accounting for services will not provide a clear measure of productivity because, although it will reveal the effort for a given level of outputs and services, it will not indicate whether the given level is optimal. Although Bucklin's framework examines different components of marketing's black box at quite a low level, once again we encounter an assumed goals problem.

Gross's Ratio Approach

Gross (1984) proposes a much less comprehensive but more parsimonious framework for calculating marketing productivity. Taking as a theoretical starting point the question of how one might isolate the contribution of marketing to a business, Gross uses the general output/input equation of manufacturing productivity.

He contends that the overall productivity of a business is largely financial. Its outputs include such items as the value of its assets, its cash flows and profits, and its competitive position. Its inputs include investments, technology, expenses, reputation, and people, among others. Financial analysts do not have any single means of measuring this productivity, but rather produce a variety of measures such as return on assets, value added per employee, and others that, viewed together, "reflect reasonably how well the business' management has utilized its resources" (p. 5).

Below this level of analysis, continues Gross, lie the individual functions that comprise business activity, such as manufacturing, marketing, and R&D:

> Each functional unit is expected to contribute to the business' overall performance by producing certain results. . . . The "productivity" of the function ought to be a measure of how well the resources are used to produce those results. (p. 5)

For manufacturing, claims Gross, the contribution is obvious. The output is the quantity and quality of product produced, and inputs are the same as those we noted in a variety of studies above: labor, plant investment, raw materials, and so on. For marketing, Gross suggests that unit sales volume is a good starting measure. Since selling and servicing the product line are two of the key tasks of marketing,[12] sales volume is an appropriate measure. Other advantages of sales volume include the ease with which it can be related to financial performance, the ease with which sales can be attributed to individual organizational units or tactics, and the fact that sales volume information is readily available. Gross does note disadvantages of this measure as well, including what we call the assumed goals problem, the timing differences between marketing expenditures and results, and the impact of market forces, but he still thinks sales is the best measure for isolating marketing's ultimate influence.

Gross separates various intermediate steps in marketing productivity analysis, beginning with marketing resources, such as expenses and personnel, which an organization converts into marketing activities, such as sales calls. Gross calls the quantity of activities an organization produces relative to the quantity of its resources that organization's "functional efficiency." If Company B's one-hundred-person sales force makes twice as many calls per month as Company A's one-hundred-person sales force, Company B has greater functional efficiency. Such measures are not uncommon in the business world, particularly in sales work. See, for example, the evaluation by Burstiner (1974) of a telemarketing sales force.

Of course, Company A's sales calls may produce better immediate results than Company B's. Gross calls this the company's "functional effectiveness."[13] If two hundred Company A sales calls produce twice as many bid requests as two hundred Company B sales calls, Company A has greater functional effectiveness.

---

12. This is, of course, a challengeable assertion.
13. We would not be inclined to label Gross's indices in this manner. His work seems to us directed squarely at marketing efficiency, not effectiveness. That is, neither making nor closing sales calls indicates to us that personal selling is the most *effective* medium by which to market the hypothetical product in question; it only says that personal selling, whatever its effectiveness, certainly is efficient.

The product of an organization's functional efficiency and functional effectiveness is its functional productivity:

$$\text{Functional efficiency}$$
$$\times \text{ Functional effectiveness}$$
$$= \text{Functional productivity},$$

which is to say,

$$\frac{\text{Marketing activity}}{\text{Marketing resources}} \times \frac{\text{Functional results}}{\text{Marketing activity}}$$
$$= \frac{\text{Functional results}}{\text{Marketing resources}}.$$

Functional productivity measures the immediate results of a marketing operation relative to the resources available to that operation. The remaining measurement is the fate that befalls this immediate result in the marketplace. Gross calls this "market effectiveness." It measures market results (sales, for example) divided by functional results (sales leads, for example). If one hundred Company B sales proposals produce twice as many orders as one hundred Company A sales proposals, Company B's efforts have greater market effectiveness.

The aggregate measure, marketing productivity, is the product of market effectiveness, functional effectiveness, and functional efficiency:

$$\text{Market effectiveness}$$
$$\times \text{ Functional effectiveness}$$
$$\times \text{ Functional efficiency}$$
$$= \text{Marketing productivity},$$

which is to say, substituting terms,

$$\frac{\text{Marketing results}}{\text{Functional results}} \times \frac{\text{Functional results}}{\text{Marketing activity}}$$
$$\times \frac{\text{Marketing activity}}{\text{Marketing resources}}$$
$$= \frac{\text{Marketing results}}{\text{Marketing resources}}$$
$$= \text{Marketing productivity}$$

Gross writes:

Hence, Marketing Productivity is conceptualized as the product of three kinds of performance, Marketing Functional Efficiency, Marketing Functional Effectiveness and Market Effectiveness. The first is a measure of a unit's ability to organize and control its resources in order to produce di-

rected, potentially productive, activities. The second is a measure of the immediate tactical results of a unit's activities per quantity of those activities. The third reflects the strategic potency of the choice of tactical objectives. (pp. 9–10)

The reason Gross breaks up his measure of marketing productivity in this manner is precisely the same reason Bucklin breaks out price changes from his marketing productivity conceptualization. Both argue that marketing productivity is the product of efforts internal to a marketing organization (services provided per unit input, functional productivity) and effects beyond a marketing organization's control (industry price changes, the functional efforts of other departments, and marketplace variables). Like Bucklin, Gross is not bold concerning the exact measures of productivity a manager should use; he explains his model as laying a theoretical framework within which others may work.

Obviously, Gross's equation is much more easily calculable than the myriad individual measures Bucklin uses to assess levels of service. His choice of sales volume as an output measure, however, leaves his work open to the question of whether higher sales is a universal goal. He admits it is not always appropriate. Beyond this, his use of the terms efficiency and effectiveness seems imprecise and indeed, inaccurate, given that what results are produced is posed as a matter already determined.

Worse, the simplicity attained by Gross's model comes at a price. Even if one is content to settle on a complete efficiency focus as the appropriate universe for marketing productivity inquiries, it is still questionable whether Gross's conceptualization correctly identifies the outputs and inputs in the traditional output/input equation. While his measures seem suitable for the sales function, it is unclear just how they might be applied to *marketing*.

Summary: Microeconomic Efficiency Approaches

In looking at the firm-level literature on marketing productivity, a myriad of efficiency measures have been proposed by many authors wishing to improve management performance in marketing. Despite the diversity offered, however, the preponderance of what has been written endorses, follows, or extends the profit-to-expense ratio measures of Sevin. Tables 6, 7, and 8 summarize the input, output, and mediating variables the microeconomic authors suggest for improving marketing efficiency.

Input measures (see Table 6) are quite varied, although some form of marketing expense quantification represents the popular choice. Researchers argue over what is a marketing expense, and there is great disagreement over what are "relevant," "complete," or just "direct" marketing expenses, much as there is for the outputs to be discussed below. Investment measures have been the clear second choice of measuring marketing inputs. In most cases, authors use investment as the denominator of an ROI calculation.

It is interesting to ask the somewhat obvious question as to why marketing inputs have traditionally been quantified either as expense dollars or as investment of capital, since not only do other effort surrogates (head count, man-hours) exist, but also the quantity of any of these measures in no way reflects the quality with which marketing moves are made. We believe the focus on marketing expense is driven by corporate budgeting processes. The company knows it is spending a certain amount of money on programs labeled "marketing." Does the company get its money's worth? This relates to the questions with which we began our chapter. While the macroeconomic authors are more interested in the role that marketing plays in the economy, microeconomic scholars—and the managers they serve—want answers about how they can do the marketing job better. On a global level, the first marketing consideration a company must answer in a budget is how much money it wants to spend on its marketing.

Examining output (Table 7), we see that profit measurements are by far the most frequent choice among the firm-level analysts, followed by sales and then a host of yardsticks advocated by one or two individuals. This is especially interesting when Table 7 is compared to Table 3 in the macroeconomic efficiency summary, where profit is not mentioned once. We attribute this to two differences. First, individual profit figures are virtually impossible to calculate for the distribution industries as a whole (upon which the macro analysts focus), while this information is readily available for an individual firm. Second, individual firms are much more likely to be judged on their profitability by the capital markets; profit is less relevant in most policy evaluations of the distribution industry.

Of course, like the macroeconomic discussion of "real services," there is no consensus on exactly what "profit" is. Some authors use full-costing profit (e.g., Sevin, 1965); others use only "relevant" costs (Goodman, 1967, 1970, 1972), gross margin (Hayes, White, and Williams, 1984), or contribution (Anderson and Weitz, 1986).

Table 6   Summary of Input Measures in the Microeconomic Literature Concerned with Marketing Efficiency

Measure	*Author*
Marketing expense	Sevin (1965), Feder (1965), Corr (1976), Band (1983), Dhalla (1977), Ackoff and Emshoff (1985), Donath (1982), McNiven (1980), Thomas (1984), Hall (1975), Beik and Buzby (1973), Dubinsky and Hansen (1982), Gross (1984)
Investment	Goodman (1970), Hayes, White, and Williams (1984), Takeuchi and Salmon (1985), Drucker (1986), Thomas (1984), Bucklin (1978)
Number of employees	Drucker (1985), Hall (1975), Bilon (1979), Gross (1984)
Man-hours	Gross (1984)
Quality of employees	Bucklin (1978)
Quality of decisions	Dhalla (1977)
Number of transactions	Bucklin (1978), Bilon (1979)
Square feet (retailing)	Hayes, White, and Williams (1984), Bucklin (1978)
Technology	Bucklin (1978)
Administrative overhead	Anderson and Weitz (1986)
Effort	Bucklin (1978)

Table 7 Summary of Output Measures in the Microeconomic Literature Concerned with Marketing Efficiency

Measure	Author
Profit	Sevin (1965), Feder (1965), Goodman (1967, 1970, 1972), Anderson and Weitz (1986), Corr (1976), Drucker (1986), Dhalla (1977), Beik and Buzby (1973), Dubinsky and Hansen (1982), Dunne and Wolk (1977), Hill (1978), Jackson and Ostrom (1980), Rayburn (1973), Mossman, Fischer, and Crissy (1974), Band (1983), Hayes, White, and Williams (1984), Takeuchi and Salmon (1985)
Sales (dollars)	Gross (1984), Bucklin (1978), Drucker (1985)
Sales units	Sevin (1965), McNiven (1980), Ackoff and Emshoff (in Enis and Cox, 1985), Dhalla (1977), Hall (1975), Bilon (1979), Thomas (1984), Hayes, White, and Williams (1984), Gross (1984)
Market share	Drucker (1986), Donath (1982), Feder (1965)
Cash flow	Drucker (1986)
Intermediate activities	Gross (1984), Burstiner (1974)
Stock turnover (retailing)	Hayes, White, and Williams (1984)
Innovation	Drucker (1985, 1986)
Services	Bucklin (1978)
Quality of services	Bucklin (1978)
Value added	Drucker (1986)
Consumer franchise	Mehrotra (1984)

In general, the microeconomic authors use many more monetary measures than the macroeconomic analysts. This may again reflect the capital market interest in financial performance. However, we also find unusual measures such as innovation, "consumer franchise," and stock turnover (for retailers).

Microeconomic analysts also list a broader range of mediating factors than their macroeconomic counterparts. We divide these factors into four categories: market characteristics, product characteristics, customer characteristics, and marketing task characteristics (see Table 8). Most of the factors we list in the macroeconomic section were market characteristics, such as per capita income growth, which are usually external to marketing as a function or distribution as an industry. Industry-specific characteristics, such as channel structure, are usually internal to the industries studied.

For the microeconomic unit of analysis, the firm, virtually all of the industry-specific characteristics are market (external) characteristics, and the microeconomic analysts then add a new set of company-specific (internal) characteristics, which we classify under product, customer, and task characteristics.

Stepping back to examine the measures as a whole, the microeconomic equations epitomize the black box phenomenon of "money in, sales out." Note, for example, how few authors discuss quality of effort in any form. And although they cite myriad mediating factors, most researchers provide no means of incorporating them into a productivity measure. Finally, we find that advocating a single measure inevitably elevates the output of that measure to assumed desirability.

Concerning the three components of the MPA model, satisfaction, effort, and external factors, effort is usually measured in dollar terms. External factors overlap heavily with the macroeconomic analysts' choices, but also include many task-, product-, and customer-specific variables, suggesting the difficulty of comparing performance across industries and firms. Concerning satisfaction, the micro efficiency literature adds a dazzling array of possible measures we could use in comparing results and expectations. Not only can we choose between financial and nonfinancial measures, but within each we see a wide variety.

We do not mean to suggest that efficiency researchers ever make this comparison. Indeed, that they never do defines the limitation of their contributions. What efficiency measures fundamentally omit is a clear sense of what measure is appropriate for the company in question, what will be effective in meeting those goals. One measure is not as good as any other for a

Table 8 Summary of Mediating Factors in the Microeconomic Literature Concerned with Marketing Efficiency

Factor	*Author*
Market Characteristics	
Supplier industry structure	Anderson and Weitz (1986)
Channel structure	Beik and Buzby (1973), Hall (1975), Dunne and Wolk (1977), Feder (1965)
Competition	Donath (1982), Bucklin (1978), McNiven (1980), Drucker (1985, 1986)
Market volatility	Anderson and Weitz (1986), Bucklin (1978)
Market size changes	Bucklin (1978), Hall (1975), Feder (1965)
Timing of market entry	Bucklin (1978)
Per capita consumption of product category	McNiven (1980)
Inflation	Bucklin (1978), Hall (1975)
Product proliferation	Hall (1975)
Marketing practices	Bucklin (1978)
Technological change	Bucklin (1978), Donath (1982)
Product Characteristics	
Life-cycle position	Sevin (1965), Goodman (1967, 1970, 1972), Anderson and Weitz (1986)
Product differentiation	Anderson and Weitz (1986)
Product cost structure	Feder (1965), Dunne and Wolk (1977), Sevin (1965)
Product mix	Dubinsky and Hansen (1982), Sevin (1965)
Customer Characteristics	
Cost of servicing	Sevin (1965), Hill (1978)
Customer growth	Donath (1982)
Customer mix	Sevin (1965), Dubinsky and Hansen (1982), Mehrotra (1984)
Brand loyalty	Mehrotra (1984)
Task Characteristics	
Magnitude and frequency of activities	Anderson and Weitz (1986)
Ability to monitor task performance	Anderson and Weitz (1986)
Transaction size	Bucklin (1978), Dunne and Wolk (1977), Donath (1982)
Transaction frequency	Donath (1982)
Company or employee capabilities	Anderson and Weitz (1986)
Economies of scale	Anderson and Weitz (1986), Bucklin (1978)
Vertical integration	Anderson and Weitz (1986), Bucklin (1978)

given company. Hitting the broad side of the barn with "adequate" assessments is not sufficient. What marketing performance assessment requires is an equation that encompasses both a sense of specific appropriateness for a given company (effectiveness), and a sense of optimal resource utilization (efficiency) toward meeting the appropriate goals. For the next piece of the puzzle, we move first to the marketing audit, which straddles efficiency and effectiveness concerns, and finally to the effectiveness literature.

Chapter 4

Microeconomic Studies of Marketing Effectiveness

Introduction

Before treating the microeconomic effectiveness literature proper, we pause briefly at a recent development in the marketing performance literature that occupies a cusp between efficiency and effectiveness. This is the growing body of work dealing with "marketing audits."

Straddling Efficiency and Effectiveness: The Marketing Audit

The need for a means of evaluating marketing performance has provoked some scholars to borrow the idea of a financial audit from accounting. A marketing audit is a formal inquiry into the effectiveness of the marketing function, both on a strategic and a tactical level. Philip Kotler (1984), one of the first proponents of auditing in marketing, defines it as

> a comprehensive, systematic, independent, and periodic examination of a company's—or business unit's—marketing environment, objectives, strategies, and activities with a view to determining problem areas and opportunities and recommending a plan of action to improve the company's marketing performance. (p. 765)

Kotler sees auditing as the ultimate control measure, one that checks on all marketing management tasks as they are performed within an organization. In contradistinction to this view, we see marketing audits as a hybrid of the efficiency and effectiveness literature in marketing performance. Rather than describing an efficient or effective measure of marketing performance, audits describe an efficient process for developing effective measures and actions. Audits evaluate the performance of the marketing organization and the underlying assumptions of its marketing strategy. In this manner, an audit examines not only the efficiency with which the organization executes its marketing ("doing things right"), but also the effectiveness of the execution relative to strategy and the organization's overall health ("doing the right things").

On its face, auditing seems to be a good idea, perhaps even more from an effectiveness standpoint than from an efficiency one. The very comprehensiveness that Kotler emphasizes, however, albeit with a lack of definition, makes auditing very expensive and time-consuming—not attributes we would ordinarily associate with efficiency. Still, there is a growing literature that shows companies can benefit from stepping back and examining the assumptions and execution underlying their business. Roseman (1979), for example, relates a story of gaps between management assumptions and performance facts that are so vast as to seem a caricature. Efficiency here arises more from a dramatic boost in results than a reduction in effort.

Exactly what an audit should examine, and how one should be conducted, has been debated extensively. One question is whether the entire marketing function is the logical unit of analysis, or if individual marketing subfunctions such as sales or advertising may be fruitfully explored. Kotler is a firm advocate of doing an overall audit, which he calls a horizontal audit because it crosses subfunctions (Kotler, Gregor, and Rodgers, 1977; Kotler, 1984). Other authors claim that subfunctions can be examined alone (cf., Browne and Reiten, 1978; Cook, 1985). Kotler calls this a vertical audit. To some extent this is a semantic distinction. Kotler has no problem with companies that conduct vertical audits; he merely wants them to call the audit by the subfunction being examined (a "sales audit" rather than a "marketing audit") to avoid confusion (Kotler et al., 1977). We agree with Kotler's contention that the most appropriate level at which to examine marketing is above the subfunction level. We believe it is impossible to evaluate the effectiveness of a subfunction such as sales or advertising outside the context of the rest of the marketing program. (See Bonoma, 1985a, or below for a detailed exposition of this argument.)

Looking at horizontal audits, what might one include? Kotler, Gregor, and Rodgers (1977) suggest six areas for analysis: (1) marketing environment, which the authors divide into the "macro-environment" surrounding the industry (legal and demographic trends, for example) and the task environment (customers, competitors, and suppliers, for example); (2) marketing strategy; (3) marketing organization; (4) marketing systems (sales forecasting, inventory control, and order processing, for example); (5) marketing productivity, which the authors examine using a Sevin-style profitability analysis; and (6) marketing functions, specific vertical audits of subfunctions which the auditors conduct if the previous five segments seem to suggest them.

Other authors usually cover much of the same ground, but with different emphases and some intriguing additions to the list put forth by Kotler et al. Tye (1983) conceives of a marketing department as consisting of a set of information flows, the adequacy of which the auditor must evaluate.[14] Cook (1985) includes the organization's image in the eyes of customers, competitors, employees, and the public as an area for exploration. Corey (personal communication) adds to traditional strategic analysis an assessment of "management attitudes and orientation." Roseman (1979) examines "intracompany activities" such as the relationship between marketing and other departments, and the length of time it takes for actions to be approved.

A second question often asked is who should perform the audit. Kling (1985), in his excellent review of the audit literature, discusses six possibilities: (1) a "self-audit" by the marketing department; (2) an audit from across conducted by members of another department at the same management level; (3) an audit from above, by the executive to whom the department manager reports; (4) an audit by a company auditing office; (5) an audit by a special company task force; and (6) an audit from outside. Most authors agree that an outside audit is usually the best approach because the auditor then has greater independence and objectivity; different methods, however, have their strengths as well as weaknesses. In their survey of firms that had undergone marketing audits, Capella and Sekely (1978) discovered that at one extreme, self-audits tended to have great problems find-

---

14. Tye's work covers the motor carrier industry. One would speculate that other service industries that depend heavily on information (e.g., airlines, hotels) would also benefit from an information flow treatment.

ing the best data, while at the other extreme, outside audits were more expensive and generated higher levels of friction between auditors and company personnel.

Many different kinds of firms can and do benefit from audits. The literature contains examples of audits done in banking (Campbell, 1973), hospitals (Sherlock, 1983), and trucking (Tye, 1983) in addition to more traditional marketing-oriented manufacturers. Kotler et al. (1977) suggest five types of organizations likely to benefit from audits: production and technically oriented companies, troubled divisions, high-performing divisions, young companies, and nonprofit organizations.

The process of the audit itself consists of a three-step procedure (Kotler et al., 1977; Kling, 1985). First, management and the auditors define the scope, objectives, and methodology of the audit. Second, the auditors collect the relevant data and analyze it. Third, the auditors present their findings and recommendations to management; sometimes auditors will also aid in implementation.

Problems can arise at each step of this process. Kotler et al. describe vague or inappropriate objectives as a very common problem because it is often difficult to determine in advance what the best objectives might be. Capella and Sekely (1978) found that by far the most frequent problem in the audit was that needed data were unavailable. Half of their thirty-eight respondents cited this problem. Friction between auditors and company personnel can create difficulties, as noted above. Overly optimistic expectations can dash the most accurate audit. Finally, the link between analysis and implementation can be poor (Kotler et al., 1977). The depth of some of these potential problems may be estimated in advance. (See Cook, 1985, p. 471 for a good list of nine warning signs that say "don't use an audit.")

Conducted periodically (Kling suggests yearly), audits can provide the capstone to a marketing control system by providing an independent perspective on the system. Note, though, that the audit literature is very brief on the type of performance measurements we discussed in the microeconomic efficiency section of the literature classification. The audit outlines we have reviewed concentrate more on illuminating the context within which marketing implementation occurs, such as strategy, environment, and information systems capability. This,

we believe, is the beginning of effectiveness evaluation. The context provides meaning that simple profit/expense ratios cannot capture. What a marketing performance measure provides in turn is an assessment of implementation results within this context. Evaluating effectiveness thus requires an understanding both of performance and the context of performance. It is this understanding that efficiency measures sadly lack.

Microeconomic Effectiveness Work

In our issues tutorial above, we distinguished effectiveness from efficiency by observing that efficiency measures assume overall goals will be met by maximizing some ratio of outputs over inputs ("doing things right," in Drucker's words), while effectiveness examined results against these goals ("doing the right things"). We called the former means-related measures and the latter ends-related.

While measuring the efficiency of marketing performance is a worthwhile endeavor, we believe that efficiency measures in the absence of effectiveness measures give an incomplete picture of marketing performance at best, and an inaccurate one at worst. Organizations must assess marketing's results against specific goals to complete the picture. Not only does Organization X produce a large amount of sales relative to expense, but it must also produce a level of sales the organization can service adequately.

The notion of relating results to goals as a performance measure is fairly common outside marketing. We find it in the general management literature (Andrews, 1980; Bower, 1983), the nonprofit/public management literature (Gleason and Barnum, 1982; Kanter and Summers, 1987), and the accounting and control literature (Stephens, 1976; Anthony and Dearden, 1980). The table below gives some representative quotations from leading authors in each of these disciplines.

There is also a substantial literature in the organizational behavior area concerning organizational effectiveness (for detailed reviews and bibliographies in this area, see Spray, 1976; Goodman and Pennings, 1977; Lewin and Minton, 1986; Kanter and Summers, 1987). Two viewpoints dominate this literature (see overviews in Campbell, 1976; Kahn, 1977). One group of researchers argues that the "goal-centered" or "goal-attainment" model best

Area	Author	Quotation
General management	Bower (1983)	"The only way to measure whether an organization is effective is relative to the common purpose around which it is organized." (p. 16)
Nonprofit/public administration	Gleason and Barnum (1982)	"An effectiveness indicator should measure the extent to which an objective has been achieved." (p. 380)
Accounting	Anthony and Dearden (1980)	"By effectiveness, we mean how well an organization unit does its job: that is, the extent to which it produces the intended or expected results." (p. 8)

evaluates effectiveness. This model closely follows the reasoning of the authors cited in the previous paragraph. A second group, however, criticizes the goal-attainment model and proposes what is called the "natural systems" view. These scholars

> make the assumption that if an organization is of any size at all, the demands placed upon it are so dynamic and so complex that it is not possible to define a small number of organizational goals in any way that is meaningful. Rather, the organization adopts the overall goal of maintaining its viability or existence without depleting its resources. (Campbell, 1976, p. 31)

We maintain the goal-attainment viewpoint. Although it is probably unreasonable to expect a small number of goals to apply to all institutions, it is reasonable that an organization may specify (or have specified for it) a small number of goals that apply to itself. For example, Buzzell, Nourse, Matthews, and Levitt (1972), using a conception of performance not dissimilar to our own in some regards, propose a hierarchy of objectives for marketing (see Chapter 26).

In addition, survival is too overarching a goal to provide any meaningful feedback to those managing the organization. If the organization is surviving, this does not give managers any information on how it might be improved, while if the organization has not survived, none of the managers remain to improve. There are also numerous temporary organizations, such as task forces, which attain their goals but are then dissolved.[15]

Marketing goals arise from the strategy of the organization. Note that this does not mean that effectiveness measures evaluate marketing

strategy; they evaluate execution *relative* to strategy. The difference may be conceived as one between long- and short-term goals, and overall versus subgoals. There is a substantial literature on marketing strategy that addresses the long-term positioning and mix of the business (see, for example, Abell and Hammond, 1979; Mahajan et al., 1987). Effectiveness measures, as we envision them, measure what current operations of the marketing department contribute to achieving the goals of strategy.

Goals, then, arise from the strategy of the organization. The organization may decide that it wishes one product to dominate a product category. A specific goal for that product's management might thus be a market share goal. An effectiveness measure would compare the product's actual market share to this goal, while an efficiency measure might compare how much incremental effort it required for management to gain incremental share. In the long term, the company's overall performance—probably, as Gross suggests, financial performance (Gross, 1984)—will rise or fall based on the soundness of the strategy.

Within the microeconomic literature, the importance of meeting objectives is examined at two levels. At the program level, articles discuss the effectiveness of focused marketing mix efforts around a brand, a product, or a customer group. At the subfunction level, there is a large literature in the area of what is called selling and advertising effectiveness. We concentrate on program-level effectiveness, in line with our research goals, and then conclude with some remarks on selling and advertising effectiveness.

Program Effectiveness

Hulbert and Toy's Marketing Budget Variances. Within a firm, an effectiveness measure should compare some aspect of the firm's marketing results

---

15. Indeed, Bonoma (1986) believes that one of the skills good managers have is the ability to orchestrate these temporary "subversive organizations" across the formal organizational structure.

to its marketing goals, as generated by the marketing strategy. One obvious way to attempt this is by comparing actual results to budgeted results for a given program.

This is precisely what Hulbert and Toy (1977) do in developing a strategic framework for marketing control. Working from the strategic parameters described by the Boston Consulting Group and the Profit Impact of Marketing Strategies (PIMS) studies, Hulbert and Toy apply variance analyses usually employed in managing production processes to marketing performance. They focus on market share, market size, and market growth as especially important marketing variables.

The easiest way to explain their scheme is by example. Table 9 represents planned, actual, and variance figures for the operating results of an imaginary product, "alpha."

The $100,000 unfavorable variance in total contribution reported in the table may arise from two sources: differences between actual and planned quantities (volumes), and differences between actual and planned contribution per unit (price/cost). The volume variance may further be disaggregated into quantity differences based on market size changes and market share changes.

The price/cost variance may be represented as follows:

$$(C_a - C_p) \times Q_a,$$

where C = contribution per unit, Q = quantity, and the subscripts "a" and "p" represent actual and planned values, respectively. Using the example in the table, the price/cost variance equals $(.1773 - .20) \times 22,000$, which equals ($500) in contribution.

The volume variance, in turn, is calculated as follows:

$$(Q_a - Q_p) \times C_p.$$

Here, product alpha's figures total $(22,000 - 20,000) \times .20$, or a contribution of $400. Note that the price/cost variance of ($500) and the volume variance of $400 add up to the total contribution variance of ($100).

Hulbert and Toy further decompose the volume variance into market size and market share variances. For market size,

$$(M_a - M_p) \times S_p \times C_p = (50,000 - 40,000)$$
$$\times .5 \times .2$$
$$= \$1,000,$$

where M = market size and S = market share. Market share variance is

$$(S_a - S_p) \times M_a \times C_p = (.44 - .50)$$
$$\times 50,000 \times .2$$
$$= (\$600).$$

Note that the sum of the last two equations equals the total volume variance of $400.

As shown in Table 9, these four equations disaggregate the actual market performance of a product or service relative to expected performance. Each equation attempts to isolate the impact of one factor on total variance in contribution—that is, all other things being equal, factor X accounted for so much variance.

Table 9 Operating Results for Product Alpha

Item	Planned	Actual	Variance
Revenues			
Sales (000 lbs.)	20,000	22,000	2,000
Price per pound ($)	.50	.4773	(.0227)
Revenues (000 $)	10,000	10,500	500
Total market (000 lbs.)	40,000	50,000	10,000
Market share (%)	50	44	(6)
Costs			
Variable cost per pound ($)	.30	.30	—
Contribution			
Per pound ($)	.20	.1773	(.0227)
Total (000 $)	4,000	3,900	(100)

Source: Adapted from Hulbert and Toy (1977), Exhibit 1, p. 13.

Using this scheme, the total variance indicates the overall effectiveness of the product's marketing, while the subvariances indicate possible reasons for differing performances. In the product alpha example, Hulbert and Toy note that the favorable volume variance was caused by a positive market size variance and a negative market share variance. Even the market size variance is not so "positive," they say, since it indicates alpha's managers underestimated the market size by a whopping 25 percent. Similarly, the price/cost variance indicates that alpha did not realize its planned price per unit, which although it may have increased volume, also lowered contribution per unit.

Hulbert and Toy's methodology to this point varies little from standard management accounting practice. However, they use this base to develop an ingenious "ex-post-performance evaluation." At the end of the period in question, say a year, managers look back and see how market events differed from expectations. The object is to separate the proportion of the total variance caused by planning deficiencies from that caused by performance deficiencies. From this exercise, Hulbert and Toy develop a schedule of performance and planning variances in the price/cost and volume variance. The authors argue that marketing plans are by nature based on ex-ante information, so it is desirable to evaluate performance by comparison with ex-post conditions. Hulbert and Toy call this the "what should have happened under the circumstances" scenario (p. 16).

This process involves retrospectively revising the plan forecasts. The difference between revised and plan estimates is the planning variance, under the assumption that more perfect planning would have anticipated all events during the plan period. The difference between actual and revised outcomes is the performance variance; even if the company had had perfect foresight, the performance variance demonstrates where its results fell short of or exceeded expectations.

The calculation of actual market forces' impact on planning assumptions is not a trivial one. Continuing with the product alpha example, the authors provide ex-post information that an expected new entrant to the industry debuted with an unexpectedly aggressive low-price promotion. This dragged down the mean industry price per pound, and increased market size. Also, a fire in a European competitor's plant led to unforeseeable demand of one million pounds of alpha's product category. The authors assign the remaining nine million pounds of the market size variance to planning. Thus, while $M_a = 50,000$ and $M_p = 40,000$, $M_r = 49,000$ because alpha's planners should have foreseen this market expansion, while they could not have foreseen the fire. By similar adjustments, Hulbert and Toy compute a value of 49 percent for S_r, \$0.18 per unit for C_r, and 24,010 pounds for Q_r.

Hulbert and Toy plug these revised figures into planning and performance variance equations. Concerning market share,[16] for example, the planning variance equals

$$(S_r - S_p) \times M_r \times C_p = (.49 - .50)$$
$$\times 49,000 \times .2 = (\$98),$$

while the performance variance equals

$$(S_a - S_r) \times M_a \times C_r = (.44 - .49)$$
$$\times 50,000 \times .18 = (\$450).$$

Other equations produce planning and performance variances for market size and price/cost. Overall, these equations provide feedback to managers on marketing's performance, highlighting planning issues in particular. Although it is geared to contribution analysis, there is no conceptual reason why budget variance analysis cannot be applied to virtually any measure. The object met here is an explicit comparison of results to goals, factoring out planning shortfalls.

Buzzell and Chussil's Cash Flow Potentials. While Hulbert and Toy analyze performance relative to an organization's plan, Buzzell and Chussil (1985) examine performance relative to a potential defined outside the organization. They borrow from financial methodology to measure the long-term cash flow and capital market value of companies against operating potential.

Buzzell and Chussil use return on investment (ROI) as their starting point. They argue that there are two ways of improving a company's ROI: the first is to adopt a more profitable strategy; the second is to improve its operations for a given strategy. Using the PIMS database (see p. 29 for a more complete account), Buzzell and Chussil find that, although strategic position

---

16. The total share variance here does not equal the total share variance we calculated previously because of derivational differences. See Hulbert and Toy's appendix for an algebraic derivation of these and other equations.

made a great difference in ROI, some 30 percent of the companies in the database reported ROIs at least 15 points above or below the average ("par" ROI) for a given strategic position. This suggests that given the same strategic situations, some companies execute their activities better than others—hardly an extraordinary finding, but an effective foundation for Buzzell and Chussil's elegant model of business potential.

For each of 178 businesses in their sample, Buzzell and Chussil identify "strategic lookalikes" in the PIMS database, companies with identical strategic positions on dimensions such as market share, vertical integration, and relative product quality. Buzzell and Chussil divide the lookalike companies into those that perform above and those below the par ROI of the group as a whole, and they define the potential of a given strategic position as the average of the ROIs for the above-par group. Using these ROIs, they project potential cash flows over a period of five years, then compare them to actual flows of the businesses in their sample.

Buzzell and Chussil calculate cash flows using the discounted cash flow method borrowed from finance. This method allows them to determine the value of future cash flows given the investment return available from other investment options. Second, the researchers calculate the capital market valuation of each firm at the end of five years using a price-to-book-value model, and adjust this "terminal" value with the discounted cash flow procedure. The final performance measure expresses performance as a percentage of potential:

$$\frac{\text{Actual cash flows} + \text{Actual market value}}{\text{Potential cash flows} + \text{Potential market value}} .$$

Buzzell and Chussil find that only 12 percent of all companies exceeded their potential. The hallmarks of success on this measure appear to be aggressive marketing expenditures supported by higher than normal investments in plant and equipment (although the authors admit that these could be effects of success rather than its cause).

Rather than the results-over-efforts measures we saw in much of the efficiency literature (cf., Sevin, 1965; Feder, 1965), Buzzell and Chussil outline a results-over-results scheme. Their rationale is similar to the use of market share measures, as we discussed above, where results

are compared to the rest of an industry under the assumption that performance should at least match the growth of the overall market (that is, that market share should be stable), although cash flow potential lacks some of the methodological weaknesses of market share measurements (see Oxenfeldt, 1959; Mehrotra, 1984). By setting an external standard that companies should meet, Buzzell and Chussil also part company with simple accounting variance analysts (although it is possible that the variance methodology could be used on a "potential" scenario). While one may argue that the finding that few businesses exceeded potential may be unsurprising given how potential was defined, the notion of comparing a business's cash flow to a strategic twin is an ingenious one.

Ruekert et al.: Marketing Organization and Performance. Ruekert, Walker, and Roering (1985) examine marketing effectiveness in the context of the same question that Anderson and Weitz (1986) investigated: when should a company perform an activity internally versus externally? To this question Ruekert et al. add the query, "Whether a firm performs an activity internally or externally, how should the organization of the workers performing the activity be structured?"

Like Anderson and Weitz, Ruekert and co-workers specify that these decisions should be based on performance outcomes; but unlike Anderson and Weitz, they argue that there are three different types of relevant performance outcomes: efficiency, effectiveness, and adaptiveness. Ruekert et al. define efficiency and effectiveness as we do (outputs/inputs and meeting objectives, respectively); they relate adaptiveness to the external environment.

The authors begin by critiquing the traditional organizational work relating to functional, product management, market-focused, and matrix organizations, contending that such structural work masks interfirm and interindustry differences, ignores the vertical integration question, does a poor job of linking structure to performance, ignores environmental contingencies, and is too macroscopic in that it tends to focus on corporate structure rather than smaller, activity-based units.

Rather than use this standard structural framework, Ruekert et al. build a "contingency theory" of structure and performance based on two alternative formulations: the system-structural perspective and the transaction cost economics perspective.

The systems-structural perspective relates certain structural variables to outcomes. Ruekert and associates explain:

> Within this perspective, the structural dimensions of centralization, formalization, and specialization/differentiation are considered to be of central importance in understanding the functioning of social systems. . . . *Centralization* reflects the extent to which decisions are shared within the social system. *Formalization* represents the degree to which activities and relationships are governed by rules, procedures, and contracts. *Specialization/differentiation* examines the degree to which tasks are divided into unique elements. (p. 15)

Reukert et al. link the three structural variables to the three outcome variables we mentioned above, leading, in turn, to three suppositions: (1) *centralization leads to greater effectiveness* due to the ability of the decision maker to plan, coordinate, and control activities; (2) *formalization leads to greater efficiency* because such rules serve to routinize repetitive activities and transactions; and (3) *greater specialization/differentiation leads to greater adaptiveness,* in that specialists understand problems more clearly, adapt more readily to changing conditions, and discover new ways of doing things (p. 15).

Transaction cost economics, as we outlined in our discussion of Anderson and Weitz (1986) in Chapter 3, argues that under competitive market conditions, tasks should always be performed externally because the internal organization cannot improve on the market. It goes on to depict scenarios under which imperfect market conditions hold, such as a small number of suppliers, which make internal organization more attractive.

Ruekert et al. combine these two perspectives in their contingency framework. The contingency model suggests that "the kind of performance that results from marketing activities is dependent upon the nature of the task, the way in which the task is organized, and the nature of [the task] environment" (p. 17).

Based on these influences, Ruekert et al. suggest four propositions:

Proposition 1. External (or market) organization of a given task leads to more efficient performance than internal organization when (a) no, or very few, idiosyncratic assets, either physical or human, are required; and (b) many competitive suppliers are available.

Proposition 2. The greater the formalization of a given task, whether organized internally or externally, the greater the efficiency of its performance, when (a) the task is of short duration; (b) the task is repetitive; (c) performance outcomes can be easily and accurately assessed; and (d) the task environment is stable and not complex.

Proposition 3. The greater the centralization of a given task, whether organized internally or externally, the greater the effectiveness of its performance when (a) the task is routine and repetitive; (b) performance outcomes can be easily and accurately measured; and (c) the task environment is stable and not complex.

Proposition 4. The greater the specialization/differentiation of a task, whether organized internally or externally, the greater the adaptability of its performance when (a) the task is nonroutine; (b) performance outcomes are difficult to assess; (c) the task environment is rapidly changing and uncertain; and (d) the task environment is complex (pp. 17–19).

Ruekert et al. argue that these propositions, if valid, have a number of managerial implications. First, no single organization structure is appropriate for all task or environment types. Second, no single structure will perform well on all performance dimensions. In particular, they discern a trade-off between short-run efficiency and effectiveness on the one hand, and adaptability and long-run effectiveness on the other. They would argue that the tempting call to maximize efficiency and profits in the short term can become the cause of long-term inflexibility and thus eventually be ineffective. Third, Ruekert et al. believe that corporate and other high-level structures are too centralized and formalized, suppressing innovation, while low-level task or work units are not specialized enough relative to their work.

Reukert and co-workers use the dimensions of their model to build a matrix of four "archetypal organizational forms" that are determined by two dimensions, locus of activity and structure. The three structural variables are included in one dimension because the authors claim that centralization and formalization tend to be positively related to each other and negatively related to specialization. (Figure 2 is a simplified version of their matrix.)

Figure 2 Archetypal Organizational Forms

Locus of Activity

Structure	Internal Organization	External Organization
	Bureaucratic form	**Transactional form**
Centralized Formal Unspecialized	Appropriate usage -noncompetitive supplier markets -low environmental uncertainty -repetitive, assessable tasks -requires specialized assets Performance -high efficiency -high effectiveness -low adaptability	Appropriate usage -competitive supplier markets -low environmental uncertainty -repetitive, assessable tasks -no specialized investment Performance -very high efficiency -high effectiveness for appropriate tasks -low adaptability
	Organic form	**Relational form**
Decentralized Informal Specialized	Appropriate usage -noncompetitive supplier markets -high environmental uncertainty -infrequent tasks, difficult to assess -requires specialized assets Performance -low efficiency -high effectiveness for specialized task -high adaptability	Appropriate usage -competitive supplier markets -high environmental uncertainty -infrequent tasks, difficult to assess -no specialized investments Performance -low efficiency -high effectiveness for specialized task -high adaptability

Source: Adapted from Ruekert, Walker, and Roering, 1985, Table 2, p. 20.

Ruekert et al. add two further general considerations. First, they contend that the type of task and environmental uncertainty differ across the product life cycle. Therefore, new products are often better served by decentralized internal organizations that can develop assets necessary for the new product, and that can adapt to new situations. Mature products, on the other hand, face a more stable environment, a more competitive supplier market, and higher needs for efficiency, arguing for a more centralized, external organization. Second, they note the competitive strategy work of Porter (1980), remarking that a cost leadership strategy should stress efficiency, leading to centralization, while a differentiation strategy stresses specialization, suggesting decentralization.

They do not provide an explicit measure of effectiveness beyond their definition that it involves meeting objectives, but nevertheless Ruekert et al. add greatly to our consideration of effectiveness by relating it and other performance measures to the organization of activities. Addressing the efficiency/effectiveness distinction in itself makes this a rare piece in the marketing literature; the addition of the adaptiveness dimension makes the theory more intriguing.

Stefflre: Organizational Behavior and Marketing Effectiveness.

Given our definition that effectiveness is performance that meets management objectives, Volney Stefflre has a great deal to say about the negative impact management interests can have on marketing performance. His 1985 book discusses developing and implementing marketing strategies, focusing on problems within the organization.

Stefflre tends to take the natural systems view of marketing effectiveness, which we discussed above. He argues that the critical problem facing organizations is to remain adaptable and flexible enough to survive in a changing environment (p. 209). One of the key aspects of this adaptability, in his view, is an organization's ability to introduce new products, an ability that is reduced as the organization grows larger.

Stefflre claims that one of the reasons for the spectacularly high failure rate of new products is that the objectives different groups of managers have are often based on the internal political environment rather than the external market environment. Therefore, rather than choosing the right option, the organization chooses the option that is minimally dissatisfy-

ing to the largest number of people. Stefflre calls this the "line of least resistance" (p. 68).

From this concept, Stefflre draws two hypotheses:

> [1] The larger the organization making the decision, the higher the probability that the internal aspects of the decision will dominate the external implications. . . .
> [2] The larger the organization, the higher the probability that its collective decision processes will focus upon short-run internal problems (like succession) and select minimally dissatisfying solutions to them, rather than focus on long-run opportunities or the aspect of alternatives relating to those consequences. (p. 69)

In general, Stefflre associates size with more bureaucratic behavior driven by short-term objectives, leading to an efficiency and profitability focus that is antithetical to long-term investments in innovations.

This bureaucratic style, Stefflre argues, is aggravated by information filtering:

> the fact that bad news is often selectively filtered out and recognition of the problem delayed until the resources for the implementation of the necessary solutions are badly depleted. . . . we have found that if the bad news had arrived, the type of decision rules typical of major bureaucratic institutions seems to effectively preclude innovations that would alter the internal balances of power. (pp. 71–72)

Stefflre calls this the "social information-processing" aspect of an organization. A variety of factors, he contends, increase the probability of information filtering, including the number of links in the reporting system, the time-horizon of the problem (longer is worse), the novelty of the problem relative to senior management's operating experience, faster personnel turnover, and the proportion of organizational rewards assigned on the basis of short-term efficiency and compliance measures.

Politics, Stefflre argues, can be so crippling that no decisions are made at all. He finds this particularly likely in cases in which each of several factions has the ability to blackball solutions, the factions differ radically in their views of the situation, and the issue is central to the distribution of power within the organization.

Stefflre's depiction of irrational objectives is a marketing version of the criticisms that the natural systems theorists in organizational behavior level at the goal-attainment theorists. Bad goals make bad performance. Certainly this is true, but we believe it is equally true that a good planning process should minimize bad goals, and that a good board of directors (or, in these takeover times, another company) will eventually impose order on egregiously irrational management. Still, Stefflre serves as a warning that blind adherence to meeting objectives is as culpable as blind adherence to efficiency measures.

Bonoma: Performance and Peace of Mind. In the last chapter of *The Marketing Edge*, Bonoma (1985a) makes a first attempt to conceptualize a measure of good marketing practice, or "marketing quality." In his admittedly exploratory attempt to make sense of twenty-eight clinical case investigations illustrating both good and poor marketing practices, Bonoma synthesizes the work of two nonmarketing writers on quality: Robert Pirsig, author of the 1974 best-seller *Zen and the Art of Motorcycle Maintenance*, and Thomas Gilbert, who presented his conception of "competence engineering" in his book *Human Competence* (1978).

Pirsig aims to define "quality" in human life, both on the ivory-tower level of the philosopher and the earthbound one of the craftsman. In his observations of both everyday life and philosophical discourse, Pirsig notes a profound cleavage in the ways people approach the idea of goodness. On one side of the cleavage stand those who are highly analytic and rational in their thought processes, persons who revel in the intricate chain of causes and effects that make up a motorcycle engine or a logical argument. They advocate scientific method, and grapple with "objective" reality. On the other side of the cleavage are those who are completely uninterested in the technical aspects of life. Rather than spending their time in analyzing and manipulating facets of their environment, such persons immerse themselves in the romantic, subjective side of reality, thirsting for sight, sound, and experiences.

Pirsig concludes that these two viewpoints are not mutually exclusive, but rather are opposite sides of a quality coin. Quality, he argues, occurs when the scientific/technical and the romantic/subjective views meet in such a way that observer is at one, and at peace with that which is being observed. Quality is, quite simply, the peace of mind that occurs when the observer is no longer distinguishable from the observed—when reality breeds no dissonance in the actor.

This concept, that "[q]uality is no more and no less than the perception that what we're doing to manipulate, change, observe, interact with . . . or otherwise relate to the world makes us peaceful about the interaction between us and events" (Bonoma, 1985a, p. 186), struck Bonoma as powerful though over-general. From his observations of managers executing programs in the field, he noted that successful managers "felt good" about their efforts to cope with the repetitive execution fires that threatened program success.

There was something missing, however. As his students pointed out, sometimes one is at peace because of achievement, and sometimes one is at peace because one is asleep. How does a manager know if marketing actions that make him or her feel peaceful are good? Here Bonoma turned to Gilbert (1978). Bonoma writes:

> Stripped to the bone, Gilbert's thesis is that (1) we spend too much time looking for quality *behavior* when what we want is quality *performance*, and (2) we often mistake effort for performance. Gilbert claims that even complicated performances, like those of the marketing manager, can be measured, if only by looking at the best existing performance of the exemplar in question. (p. 186)

Trained as an engineer, Gilbert consults widely to industry, particularly in human productivity areas. His basic method is to find the best example of performance for a particular job, such as welding, and measure all other performance of this job against this exemplar. By breaking down the work of the exemplar, Gilbert learns what to teach other workers to improve their performance. This is similar to the idea of Kotler et al. (1977) of auditing top marketing programs to find out what they are doing right and disseminate it through the rest of the organization. It is also a more radical formulation of traditional management-by-objective (MBO) work. (For a good review of MBO in marketing, see Etzel and Ivancevich, 1974.)

Gilbert's emphasis on performance is critical to his model. He does not care how a worker does a job if the output of that work is superior. He cites the example of a subcontractor who was "mining" an old rifle range for lead bullets, and who hired a crew of college students to aid his regular crew. The students were undisciplined, disorganized, and ignored the complex work system the subcontractor had developed for the job. He fired them at the end of the day, but was chagrined to discover that they had mined three times as much lead as the regular crew.

Bonoma concludes that these two standards, performance and peace of mind, must be part of any measure of good marketing. He folds these in with his earlier work (1985a) on individual managers' implementation skills, arguing that the mark of marketing quality is the quality of coping with execution crises, substituting managerial skills for shortcomings in the corporate marketing structure, and therefore "subverting" the organization toward quality. Although Bonoma holds that good marketing is a set of managerial behaviors that produce good results in the marketplace, he differs with Gilbert in maintaining that these behaviors are the evidence of good marketing, not the results. The best marketing practice, he argues, could produce indifferent results due to factors external to the company, such as competitive activity.[17]

Performance and peace of mind are both marketing effectiveness measures because both focus on congruence between outcomes and goals. Pirsig's notion of peace of mind implies satisfaction with the relation between a worker and his or her work. Presumably, this satisfaction arises not only from the "oneness" of effort and the object of effort, but also from the oneness of result and expectation. Poor outcomes relative to expectations must reduce peace of mind.

Gilbert is more explicit. He is not concerned about the effort side of the equation, but merely with results. Measuring output against a standard, the exemplar's performance, his focus is on what we call effectiveness.

Unfortunately, Bonoma's work does not quantify, measure, or indeed offer any empirical evidence beyond his case clinical data for this conception of good marketing. It was this shortcoming that led us to our current work on analyzing marketing performance.

Advertising and Selling Effectiveness

There are substantial bodies of work in the marketing literature on the topics of "advertis-

ing effectiveness" and "selling effectiveness," but these do not fit our definition of effectiveness measures for two reasons.

First, examining effectiveness at the subfunction level is neither conceptually nor methodologically valid because it is impossible to separate one part of the marketing mix from the influences of the other parts. The selling task, for example, is always influenced by the character of the product; the product is a joint determination of its own characteristics along with those of the distribution channel and the price. Parts of the channel will in turn be receptive to high-priced goods sold with powerful service support, while other channel members will reject such a price/sales approach, and the communications mix both determines and is determined by these other variables. In our view, it is inappropriate to raise questions of effectiveness (but very appropriate to ask ones about efficiency) until and unless the goals of the marketing program dictating the employment of any one subfunctional marketing element, like selling, has been specified. The lowest level at which these goals are encountered in any form *is* the program level, at which marketers try to select segments and adjust marketing mixes to maximize some sought goal, like sales or profit.

Second, many of the alleged subfunctional effectiveness measures, particularly in advertising, are by our definition efficiency measures, in that they aim to maximize some output for a given input. The assumption made in many of these researches is the same as is encountered in so much of the literature—that what works well is the right thing to be doing. This is tantamount to suggesting that a neutron bomb is a useful tool because it can more efficiently dispatch humans while leaving structures intact. That a neutron bomb is an efficient tool is not in dispute—but commenting on its effectiveness requires moving a step up on the ladder to ask about the goals of the conflict. It is no different with marketing "tools." But because of the size of these two research areas, we will discuss them briefly here.

Kotler (1984) divides advertising effectiveness research into two sets: communication effects and sales effects. The former measure how well an ad communicates a message. This involves both pre-testing, as in a test in which consumers are asked to look through a portfolio of prospective ads, and post-testing, typically for recall or recognition. Lavidge and Steiner (1961), for example, advocate testing for the effect ads

---

17. We take up this interaction between marketing structures and management skills below, when we formulate our MPA model.

have on particular attitudes about a product, viewing sales as too simplistic a measure. Gallup (1966) uses the idea of "playback" to examine consumers' recall of advertising.

Sales-effects tests study the actual sales response to advertising. Sevin (1965) advocates experimentation to illuminate this response curve. Ackoff and Emshoff (in Enis and Cox, 1985) studied sales responses for Anheuser-Busch advertising over a five-year period; Ginter and Starling (1979) examine both sales and communication effects in comparative advertising.

These studies are classic output/input works, emphasizing maximum "bang for the buck"; in our terminology, this makes them clear efficiency evaluations. The one cry for something like an effectiveness evaluation of ads comes from Paul Harper (1981), chairman of the Needham, Harper & Steers agency in New York. In a special *Advertising Age* section on advertising productivity, Harper followed three other authors who all advocated efficiency measures. Harper expressed his belief that productive advertising may be defined as "the consistency with which an agency is able to produce acceptable advertising efficiently" (p. S-1). In terms reminiscent of Bonoma's peace of mind formulation discussed above, Harper defines acceptable advertising as "advertising an agency feels good about selling a client, and that the client feels good about buying" (p. S-1). As the studies indicate, however, this is not a usual point of view. It also agrees with our position that one cannot evaluate the effectiveness of a marketing subfunction like advertising per se, since presumably advertising the client feels good about buying is advertising that meets the strategic goals of the marketing program.

The sales effectiveness literature is again very much shaped by the output/input model, essentially proposing a string of measures by which to evaluate selling efficiency. As in the advertising work, little attention has been given to *whether* selling (versus direct mail or telephone selling, for example) is the most appropriate tool for a given marketing program. Also as with advertising, there is both communications- and sales-effect work, although the latter dominates.

Weitz (1981) identifies three streams of research in this area. One examines the effect of sales behaviors and behavioral dispositions on performance, a second looks at the capability and resources of salespeople versus perfor-

mance, and a third takes a dyadic view, studying the consequences of the interaction between customer and salesperson. All these studies approach effectiveness from an output maximization standpoint (i.e., efficiency) rather than a performance versus goals standpoint (effectiveness). We cited some of these types of studies in Chapter 3 (see, for example, Hall, 1975; Bilon, 1979; LaForge, Cravens, and Young, 1985).

One selling piece that begins to examine what we call effectiveness is that of Zabriskie and Browning (1979), who examine the industrial selling activities of five firms in each of three industries. Through interviews with sales executives, the authors determine that industrial selling activities can be divided into four parts: sales seeking, marketing intelligence, channel assistance, and goodwill. Only sales seeking encompasses explicitly trying to get an order, and sales-seeking behaviors occupy anywhere from 45 percent to 75 percent of a salesperson's time.

Zabriskie and Browning note that virtually all sales performance measures focus on some aspect of sales as the output variable. Wondering how sales executives evaluated salespeople on behaviors in the other three areas, where there is no explicit causal link with sales, they discovered that managers turned to a "logic based on managerial objectives" (p. 170). If the manager assigned a certain activity to a salesperson, the manager would later ask "Did he do it?" and "How well did he do it?" (p. 170). For Zabriskie and Browning, this is a "pragmatic productivity rule," one that compares results to goals; the goals for selling tasks are presumably driven by the broader goals of the marketing program under consideration.

One area in which we often see this kind of pragmatic productivity rule is in sales quotas. Sales quotas are perhaps the most explicit example of the use by management of an effectiveness measure in marketing, although they are often mistaken for efficiency tools. Shapiro (1977, p. 308) notes over a dozen types of quotas that companies use.

Salespeople are evaluated, and often compensated, on how closely they meet a set of expectations negotiated at the beginning of the quota period. These sales expectations are in turn most often negotiated between sales and marketing executives on the basis of what the target market requires in terms of call frequency and what the distribution geography requires in terms of coverage. Thus, in the best cases they are driven directly by the marketing strategy for the program in question, tempered by the sales force's responsibility to sell the company's other programs as well. Quotas are usually based on an overall sales forecast, which in turn is based on the adjudged potential of an area (Kotler, 1984, pp. 694–696). The overall forecast is then broken down into goals by territory for individual salespeople.

Kotler (1984) notes three schools of thought concerning setting sales quotas. The *high-quota school* sets quotas higher than most sales representatives will achieve but that are nevertheless attainable. Its adherents believe that high quotas spur extra effort. The *modest-quota school* sets quotas that a majority of the sales force can achieve. Its adherents feel that the sales force will accept the quotas as fair, attain them, and gain confidence. The *variable-quota school* thinks that individual differences among sales representatives warrant high quotas for some, modest quotas for others (p. 695).

As Kotler explains it, the quota-setting logic can be applied to setting expectations in general in some of the other works we have cited. Gil-

bert (1978) and Buzzell and Chussil (1985), for example, both use a "high-quota" method. They admit that many if not most individuals and companies will fail to match the best performer, but also maintain that striving to match the best—Gilbert's "exemplar," or Buzzell and Chussil's above-par performer—is the optimum goal against which to compare performance. Looking at budget variances as Hulbert and Toy (1977) do, on the other hand, uses a modest-quota assumption; it is assumed that a company should meet its planned performance, and that variances from planned performance are unusual and must be explained.

Summary: Microeconomic Effectiveness Approaches

Unlike the efficiency literature, the effectiveness literature does not lend itself easily to a simple tabular treatment listing inputs and outputs. The theme in this chapter has been one of context and contingencies. Table 10, which summarizes some of the studies and viewpoints

Table 10 Summary of Work on Marketing Effectiveness

Author	*Concepts and Variables*
1. The marketing audit	Straddles efficiency/effectiveness issue by addressing an efficient process for developing effective actions
Kotler (1984)	Control of marketing activities
Roseman (1979)	Uncovering errors in management's marketing assumptions
Kotler, Gregor, and Rodgers (1977)	Horizontal cross-subfunctional audit
	Marketing environment, strategy, organizations, systems, productivity, and subfunction audits
Campbell (1973)	Specific industry audits
Sherlock (1983)	Specific industry audits
Tye (1983)	Specific industry audits
2. Marketing effectiveness	
a. Program effectiveness	
Hulbert and Toy (1977)	Variance analysis; planned vs. performance variances
Buzzell and Chussil (1985)	Cash flows and market value: actual vs. potential
Ruekert, Walter, and Roering (1985)	Organization, integration, and short- vs. long-term effectiveness
Stefflre (1985)	Organizational politics and marketing effectiveness
Bonoma (1985)	Peace of mind and performance of best existing exemplar
b. Advertising/selling effectiveness	Such work is not really concerned with effectiveness in our view—marketing effectiveness is measurable only at the level of the program, not the subfunction.

discussed, reinforces the view that effectiveness work has been both less frequent and more complicated than the numerous marketing efficiency studies. In any organization, "doing the right things" must take into account the situation in which the organization finds itself and the goals it sets itself. It is only by measuring marketing results against marketing goals, given the situation, that an organization's marketing effectiveness can be measured. This says nothing, of course, about effort expended; effective actions can always be carried out more efficiently. Our objection to the efficiency literature is simply that it usually does not question whether the actions at which a firm becomes more efficient are effective.

The closest we have to efficiency ratio measures in the effectiveness literature is the cash flow potential developed by Buzzell and Chussil (1985). As we noted, though, this measure calculates results relative to a standard deemed reasonable for the strategic position of a given organization, thus meeting our definition of effectiveness. Similarly, the variance analysis made by Hulbert and Toy (1977) compares results to a plan, which presumably bears some

relationship (although not necessarily a direct one) to organization goals. Gilbert (1978) and Zabriskie and Browning (1979) also measure results versus goals, though in a less formulaic manner.

Organizations differ, say the effectiveness researchers, so one should measure organization results against specific goals. And as there were systematic external modifiers to efficiency measures, there are systematic external modifiers to effectiveness measures. Ruekert et al. (1985) propose that centralization should increase overall effectiveness because the organization will be better able to monitor goal achievement. They also contend that certain task and market characteristics will mediate for or against effectiveness. Stefflre (1985) argues that organization size limits communication and politicizes debate, constraining effectiveness. The sharpest acknowledgment of contingencies comes from the "peace of mind" formulations in Bonoma (1985) and Harper (1981); what could be more situation-specific than "feeling good" about a marketing program?

It is from this base that we attempt our own conceptualization of MPA.

Chapter 5

A Model for Measuring Marketing Performance

Introduction: Lessons from the Literature and a Practice Road Map

Taking the literature as a whole, a number of observations can be made about assessing marketing performance.

1. There has been an enormous preoccupation with efficiency measures in the macroeconomic as well as microeconomic literature, with little attention given to what makes for effective marketing practices. This should not be surprising for a number of reasons, as we have pointed out above. First, salespeople call on accounts they think are likely to buy, and marketing researchers measure phenomena that appear measurable. Marketing efficiency is eminently measurable, as the literature review shows. Quality of marketing practices, whether marketing policies are pointed in a useful direction, and other indicators of marketing effectiveness are notoriously difficult to measure (cf., Bonoma, 1985a). Indeed, those who have tried to do so have been driven to case study and other clinical methods; a clean and quantifiable method to capture effectiveness has proved elusive.

2. Physical, manufacturing, and other productivity analogues have a dominant "share of mind" in traditional marketing productivity and performance researches, leading to ratio methods and financial measures. There are two parts to this lesson: the analogues employed and the measures used. As to analogues, we have noted before that it is highly questionable to us whether either physics or manufacturing productivity is close enough in process to marketing's lagged and multivocal character to be useful as a theoretical template. There is a great deal of difference between measuring the number of non-operating air conditioning units coming from an assembly line (also an efficiency measure, since it is presumed the air conditioners are technically well designed) and measuring marketing performance. The latter is much more complex and intimately involved with the skills of the managers doing the job. Although of course we recognize the parsimony of the physical "effort/expenses in, results/profits out" hydraulic, we are not convinced that the assessment of marketing performance, which includes an assessment of its effectiveness as well as efficiency, is best captured by such a simple mechanism.

As to the measures, we find financial ratio approaches dangerously incomplete and often misleading, and the various nonpecuniary measures even more so. Profit (or sales, or value added), for instance, is implicated with more of a firm's functions than just marketing; this makes it difficult to determine an a priori correlation between good marketing and profits. We are familiar with one firm, for instance, that makes most of its profit through an exceptionally able chief financial officer who invests the firm's cash in a manner that can only be called astoundingly fruitful. While this might be a good index of the firm's treasury productivity, it is not one of its marketing productivity.

Similarly, market share and other customer franchise measures (a) are determined by many factors, only some of which (and not the bulk) are under marketing's control; (b) are time-lagged measures that do a poor job of reflecting current marketing performance but a better job at reflecting past marketing performance; and (c) are affected by the competitive environment and distribution channel's efficiency in ways that no previous account has handled.

3. *Curiously, the previous work on marketing performance appears to be "management-free."* There is little mention in past models of management's capabilities at executing marketing plans, programs, and policies, either in an *efficiency sense or an effectiveness one*. We find this difficult to comprehend, and more difficult to accept. Marketing (or sales, production, or finance) gestalts are, by definition, a joint function of, on the one hand, the structures put in place to execute the functional plans and, on the other, the people doing the job. That all behavior is a joint function of the person in an environment (structures) has been an accepted precept since Kurt Lewin (1951) first wrote on psychological field theory. We find the previous literature, with only a few passing exceptions (Bucklin, 1978; Bonoma,

1985a; Anderson and Weitz, 1986), to be completely focused on the structures and completely unfocused on the people. If and when management becomes fully automated, this may be the correct approach. For now, however, it seems unwise and unthoughtful to neglect the key aspect of how marketing gets done either efficiently or effectively—the managers.

4. *Not only have managers' actions been defined out of the literature in previous approaches, but so has managerial judgment.* As the measures proposed are scrutinized, it can only be said that the literature has made more room for experts' and academicians' proposals about relevant input and output decisions than it has for managerial judgments about the behavior of other managers. One way of summarizing the literature on marketing performance might be to see it as a relatively single-minded attempt to define out of the various equations and ratios proposed the only two variables that in our opinion seem directly related to both marketing and productivity—the marketers' behaviors, and the judgments of the managers who supervise them about whether these behaviors are productive. Some of our confusion here no doubt stems from our personal psychological backgrounds, which tends to validate behavior and even verbal behavior more than some other disciplines. But some of the confusion is just that—wondering why both macro- and microeconomic theorists have so persistently worked with distal, results-proxy measures, without even trying to include the more proximal behaviors supposedly generating the results.

5. *Finally, and despite what we believe are some serious shortcomings in the literature to date, it can be said that much of value has been learned through both the general consensuses that exist in the literature and the specific findings of numerous studies.* Despite our negative comments, we recognize in the literature the building blocks of a good performance measure; we synthesize as well as invent in producing the MPA model. First, the efficiency literature demonstrates a consistent sense among scholars that performance assessment must incorporate some measure of output relative to input. Whatever the specific measure, both practitioners and academicians feel that there must be some assessment of the return generated by the resources used in any given program.

Second, the effectiveness literature illustrates

a similar consensus, less powerful only because it is the product of fewer studies, that the output or return that any program generates must be measured against some relevant organizational standard or goal.

Third, both the efficiency and the effectiveness literatures reveal the need to consider the effect of events external to the firm. In the macroeconomic literature, these external, or mediating, factors consist of grand trends in the economy and society as a whole, and smaller structures that characterize specific industries (see Table 4). In the microeconomic literature, researchers add factors within an organization which are yet beyond the immediate control of a marketing manager. Of the product, task, and customer characteristics we list in Table 8, many can be ultimately influenced by marketing acts, but in the short run most are uncontrollable.

These consensus building blocks helped drive us toward a model incorporating all three. What we found in reviewing the literature was a curious sense of incompleteness. When efficiency was measured, effectiveness was assumed. When effectiveness was evaluated, effort was often incompletely modeled. And when external factors were considered at all, they often were modeled in unoperationalizable construals or were treated with equally unoperational vagueness. Certainly some scholars have made good efforts along these lines (e.g., Bucklin, 1978; Ruekert et al., 1985; Cox et al., 1985), but the current state of the art falls short of integrating these concepts.

Despite a lack of integration, however, specific concepts and methods cast great light on the assessment problem. Picking at random from some of the work reviewed above, we find Goodman's life-cycle notion regarding profits and the marketing behaviors that should be used to engage maximum profits at various life-cycle stages quite intriguing. Bucklin's various and important contributions to the marketing productivity literature, whether his notion of "terms of trade" or his good typology of the "ancillary factors" that must be considered when evaluating marketing, can only be called marvelously important lines of thinking as well. Gross's important reconceptualization of work in this area as a simpler, and therefore powerful set of cross-canceling identities is a third important contribution. It is useful as well to cite the marketing auditing work of Kotler and oth-

ers, with its unique blend of efficiency measurement of effectiveness-seeking, as a useful tool not only to scholars but a directly applicable one for managers.

What follows is a first attempt to integrate effectiveness questions—psychological as opposed to physical science analogues and measures—and most important, the management doing the marketing job into marketing performance assessment, or MPA. As important background, we begin with an overview of some work done in the recent area of marketing implementation, and move from there toward model specification. The marketing implementation work is reviewed because it represents the cornerstone of our thinking and the base of our model. In addition, we incorporate a number of the notions that we find valuable from the literature, but in many ways have attempted to "zero-base" our work from a marketing practice perspective.

First Looks at Marketing Performance: Marketing Implementation

The primary impetus for a new look at MPA comes from the progress made in marketing implementation by Bonoma (1985a, b, c; Bonoma and Crittenden, 1988; Bonoma, Crittenden, and Dolan, forthcoming; also Kotler, 1984; Stefflre, 1985). Bonoma felt strongly that, while marketing strategy formulation was becoming more and more sophisticated, little attention was being paid to the principles that underlie the execution of those strategies. He set out on a multiyear research project in order to determine if there might be a set of principles that explained "quality marketing practice," or as he put it, "the doing of marketing as opposed to the conceiving, planning or strategizing of it" (1985a, p. xiii). While Bonoma can be said to have succeeded in identifying factors critical to marketing execution, and in partially explaining the operation of those factors in "getting the marketing job done," he can also be criticized for having neglected to specify the nature of "quality marketing practices" or the principles that produce it. It is that failure (see above, p. 50) that spurs the present work.

Bonoma claims that two characteristics of much strategy work in marketing make any useful commentary on marketing practices, as distinct from plans, difficult. First, he notes, the strategic literature offers disturbingly universal, management-free "rules," presumptively as applicable to managers in a $10 million regional soap company as to those at Procter & Gamble (Bonoma and Crittenden, 1988). Omitting factors like firm size, industry, company organization, managers' backgrounds and skills, and corporate culture, he thought, made such recommendations suspect and possibly useless.

Second, he points out (1985a) that much of what has been done to improve marketing strategy reflects a unidirectional strategy-causes-practice causal presumption that does not account for a powerful and active reverse causal linkage, practice-causes-strategy. The practice of marketing, as strategies are translated into acts, can have far-reaching effects on what strategies management finds congenial or even possible to use. In particular, Bonoma contends that in many marketing situations firms find habitual, comfortable, or just possible modes of execution that come to shape the formulation of future strategies. Hence, he ascribed prime importance to learning about execution, for it was strategy-as-practiced that he saw as the engine for the corporation's marketing efforts.

After reviewing work from social psychology, organizational behavior, and marketing (1984), Bonoma describes a field research project (1985b) to identify the determinants of marketing execution. Essentially, this project consisted of a preliminary interview phase with top managers, coupled by a several-year case clinical investigation of an evolving taxonomy and model of marketing implementation. Bonoma investigated some thirty situations in the field, situations in which marketing practice was problematical to managers and firms. From this research and from the literature, he "evolved" (1985a) his major theoretical notions on marketing execution.

Essentially, Bonoma sees marketing practice as the attempt to attain targeted results by managers possessing certain execution skills. These managers in turn practice their craft in an organization guided by established marketing execution structures. The structure-by-skills interaction, which is at the heart of quality practices in marketing, occurs in a double field flooded by marketing strategy at the local or proximal level, and environmental conditions more re-

motely, or distally.[18] Figure 3 illustrates this model of marketing practice. As Bonoma puts it,

> Marketing practice
> = f (Environment, Structure, Skills),

where it is understood that part of the firm's environment is its marketing strategy.

Marketing Structures: Habits of the Corporation

Bonoma (1981, 1986) considers the structures for executing marketing plans and strategies akin to habits in the corporation's marketing operations, much like habits of individuals. These habits act to routinize, systematize, and organize a myriad of recurrent decisions made by marketing in such a way that they become repetitively executable by the organization, but also, like most "ruts of behavior," invisible or preconscious under ordinary circumstances.[19] The purpose of these habits is to routinize repetitive action so that it need not be thought about, and serve as an "automatic pilot," which allows the organism (individual or corporate) to get about more important business. (This routinization is also an aspect of Bucklin's, 1978, and Ruekert et al.'s, 1985, conception of performance.)

Bonoma describes four habitual or structural levels in firms as regards marketing: actions, programs, systems, and policies. The first level, marketing actions, describes the execution of low-level subfunctions in marketing like selling, sales management, pricing, and the like. Bonoma claims that these subfunctions are characterized by many implicit rules of thumb, so that in a particular firm "everybody knows" advertising is not supposed to exceed 5 percent of

---

18. The terms *proximal* and *distal* here are used in the specific senses that Egon Brunswik originally wrote about them in his essays on "probabilistic functionalism." See Kenneth Hammond's (1966) edited version of these lectures for a powerful psychological model of interactive behavior which has much to offer marketing.

19. The *preconscious* is a less familiar term than the *unconscious*, which has entered the popular lexicon, though both are from Freud's *The Interpretation of Dreams* (1950). Basically, a preconscious concept is not ordinarily conscious (e.g., "What was the address of the house in which you grew up?"), but can be recalled to consciousness with effort. It is the same with most habits in individuals; we are not often aware of our own accents in speech, for example. The phrase "ruts of behavior," of course, is that of William James in his famous description of the functions of habits.

Figure 3   A Rudimentary Model of Marketing Implementation

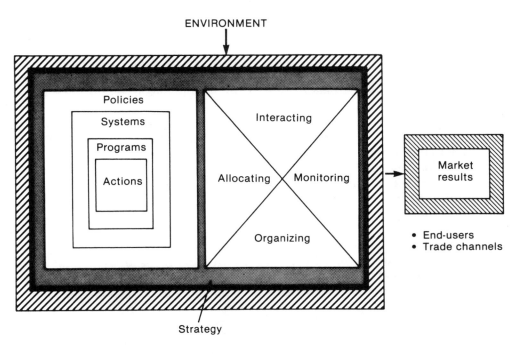

Quality practice = f (Marketplace results) = f (Environment, Strategy, Structure, and Skills)

Implementation

Source: Adapted from Bonoma and Crittenden (1988).

sales, for instance, or that price to distributors is 50 percent of the price to the end-user. Such habits, Bonoma contends, can be helpful or hurtful to the organization, but often are the latter.

The second structural level is marketing programs, which are combinations of subfunctions intended to perform synergistically to market a brand or serve a customer segment. Bonoma cites brand management, in which a particular brand may get specialized pricing, advertising, promotion, and selling effort, as an example of programs targeted at brands, and national account management as an example of a program serving a special customer segment.

The third structural level is marketing systems, by which Bonoma means everything from the telecommunications and electronic data processing support for marketing activities to the marketing organization chart and budgeting system. Singled out for special attention, however, are two systems: those directed at marketing allocation (i.e., the apportioning of money, time, and people across marketing activities), and those directed at marketing control (i.e., knowing the firm's performance as a result of its efforts).

The final level of marketing structure Bonoma calls marketing policies; he defines these as all those things that top management says and does which affect how the rest of the organization executes the marketing job (1985a, p. 99). Bonoma breaks marketing policies into what he calls "policies of direction" and "policies of identity." The first concept refers to marketing strategy (in Bonoma's view, execution dominates strategy, and therefore he incorporates strategy as part of the policies directing execution) and the quality of marketing leadership in the firm. The second concept refers to the firm's sense of "who it is and what it does vis-à-vis the customer," and includes notions such as marketing theme and culture.

Marketing Skills: The Abilities of Management

Cross-cutting these four structural levels are management's behavioral skills at four central implementation processes: interacting, allocating, monitoring, and organizing. These skills inhere in the individual marketers doing the job, and are distinct from corporate ritualizations of similar activities. Thus, while there is a

formal organization system, the behavior of managers organizing efforts for a marketing task may be very different, informal, and indeed, at variance with the formal structure's guidance.

Interaction skills include managers' own behavior styles and their attempts to influence or manage the behavior of others (Tedeschi et al., 1973). The marketing job is by nature one of influencing others within and outside the company, often under conditions of no formal power. For example, a product manager wishing to convince the sales force to devote more attention to his or her line occupies a near-perfect persuasion setting. Such central variables as negotiation (Druckman, 1977), conflict management (Tedeschi et al., 1973), and persuasion (Hovland, Janis, and Kelley, 1953) are captured by this managerial implementation skill.

Allocation skills involve parceling time, money, and people across different marketing tasks. Regardless of a marketer's scope of responsibilities, he or she needs to make these allocation decisions so that tasks will be well executed. Allocating behaviors, Bonoma (1985a) claims, have generally been neglected in marketing.

Monitoring skills involve the construction and maintenance of feedback mechanisms used to measure and, sometimes, to control marketing activities. Finally, organizing skills are managers' informal "networking" abilities, which help managers supplant, replace, or even defeat the formal organization structure in an attempt to better execute marketing tasks. While a good deal is known about formal organization structures in marketing (e.g., Corey and Star, 1971), very little is known about this critical behavioral skill.

Structures and Skills: The Critical Tension

Bonoma's clinical research seems to confirm the plausibility of these dimensions across a number of situations in interpreting, if not explaining, marketing practices. The model allows him to offer a set of propositions (Bonoma and Crittenden, 1988) about both structures and skills that seem to provide disconfirmatory specificity about marketing execution. The most interesting dynamic in the Bonoma model, however, is the contention that structures and skills coexist in almost constant tension.

According to Bonoma, structures, like habits, are put in place by the corporation at a given point in time in order to routinize activity usefully, and indeed, they serve this function admirably for a period. Over time, however, the world "slips away" from the conditions the structures were designed to help cope with, and the firm's structural habits for marketing routinization act almost as does a boat's frozen autopilot long after the occupants have changed their preferred destination—the structures may take the ship toward the shoals rather than the harbor.[20] It is only by top management's permitting, encouraging, and allowing marketing management to subvert the organization toward quality (Bonoma, 1986) by exercising their personal execution skills to overcome shortcomings in the marketing structures that Bonoma believes good marketing practices come about.

Thus, for Bonoma, "quality marketing practices" (1985a, Chapter 11) can come from one of two sources: (a) an unchanging or stable environment, which preserves structural appropriateness over time, or (b) the exercise of management skills to subvert structural inappropriateness. The question, however, of just what "quality marketing practices" might be is not specifically answered in Bonoma's work.

Quality Marketing Practice

At various points in *The Marketing Edge*, Bonoma (1985a) defines quality of marketing execution as (a) the "quality of coping" with the various diversions, problems, and "fires" that come up every day, and (b) a combination of "performance" and "peace of mind." While these are not terribly specific definitions, it is useful to inquire further into what he means by these notions, and also into his much clearer explanation of what marketing quality is not.

Bonoma dismisses much of the work on marketing performance (his term then was "quality") as "equivocal." For example, he considers share of market at best correlative with, not an effect of, quality marketing practice. Regarding profit versus expense ratios, he says they measure only whether what is done is efficient, not whether it is effective. None of these measures, furthermore, give any attention to the very important practice side of marketing that forms the basis of marketing execution work. Bonoma cites both the work of Gilbert (1978; see above, pp. 49–50) on human competence, with its notion of "worthy behavior," and the philosophical work of Robert Pirsig (1974; above, p. 49) to get at his conception of quality.

Bonoma was unable to quantify, measure, or indeed offer any empirical evidence beyond his case clinical data that certain of his combinations of structures and skills produced demonstrably better performance than others. However, the admittedly psychological, behavioral, and executional way of looking at performance which he advocates avoids many of the deficiencies of the "traditional" marketing performance work we have discussed. First, a definition of marketing performance which is based on management's behaviors as well as the structures of the firm for marketing certainly builds management's skills back into performance equations, which is as it ought to be. Second, this quality construct does not constrain marketing performance indices to either physical analogies or manufacturing ones; if done well, it can incorporate financial ratios in marketing performance analysis without relying on them alone as a standard for evaluation. Finally, and most important, starting from this admittedly managerial and executional understanding of marketing allows the question of what effective marketing behavior is to serve not only as a building block for marketing performance analysis, but as its foundation. It is this foundation from which we have developed our notions for a new view of MPA.

A Model of Marketing Performance Assessment (MPA)

Our interest lies in developing a measure of effective efforts and results of marketing behavior within firms. We call this measure "marketing performance," by which we mean the "adjudged goodness" of a marketing program. In measuring the performance of marketing programs, we add to the literature of microeconomic articles, but what we measure is as much implementation oriented as anything else. Consequently, we are as much concerned with effectiveness as with efficiency.

Also, we are not willing to leave management out of the equation. Whereas others concentrate on analyzing results, we are more concerned

---

20. For a sociological analysis of structures that reaches similar conclusions, see Starbuck's (1983) discussion of "behavior programs."

with examining efforts and their relation to re-sults. By this focus, we hope to provide man-agers with specific actions they can take to mar-ket better.

The MPA model combines our best sense of the previous literature on marketing productiv-ity and performance, Bonoma's research into the determinants of marketing implementation, and the more philosophical notes on perfor-mance given above as intricately intertwined with management's satisfactions from the re-sults of its efforts vis-à-vis the customer. Re-calling the three components of performance we described in the model preview, satisfaction, effort, and external factors, we reach the follow-ing base-level statement about marketing per-formance:

$$MP = \frac{SAT}{EFF} \times EXT, \qquad (1)$$

MP = marketing performance, or what others have called marketing pro-ductivity,

SAT = management's satisfaction from the results of marketing program efforts,

EFF = the effort expended to attain these results, and

EXT = the impact of actions external to the organization on marketing efforts.

This base model is our initial conception of marketing performance assessment. Not only do we believe this is the way managers often judge marketing programs in practice, but we maintain it is the way managers *should* judge marketing programs. In the next chapter, we develop a number of points about the base mod-el's rationale and assumption set, and then break down the model to its components.

Summary

This chapter drew lessons from the literature which we think are valuable, as well as critiqued its overwhelming emphasis on efficiency and its factoring out of the managers who must ulti-mately make performance analyses of market-ing. Second, we reviewed the theoretical bases of a six-year research program into the nature of marketing practices which appears to us to offer a good foundation for thinking about mar-keting performance analysis. From these two major avenues, we propose a novel model of MPA that employs both a marketing implemen-tation foundation and a psychological deriva-tion, as well as explicitly includes managerial judgments in the assessment of marketing per-formance. It remains to explicate that model.

Chapter 6

Rationale for the Model, and Assumption Set

Introduction

The assumptions about marketing performance assessment on which we base our initial model are sometimes counterintuitive but, we believe, nevertheless valid:

1. *The proper evaluation of marketing activities can only be performed at the level of marketing programs, which are synergistic and targeted concatenations of subfunctions in the service of a brand or segment.* The corollary of this assumption (cf., Bonoma, 1985a, for a fuller exposition) is that neither higher-level (marketing systems and policies) nor lower-level (marketing actions) analyses can yield estimates of marketing performance. By definition as well as formulation, MPA is based at the level of the marketing program.

Marketing's higher-level systems and policies, for instance, frame execution but do not engage it—it is the programs themselves that express either well or poorly, effectively or ineffectively, the general directions of marketing policies. Policy statements are far more useful in defining expectations than they are in assessing marketing performance. As to low-level measurement of marketing actions, we believe (and we read the literature to illustrate) that it is simply impossible to measure the effectiveness of say, selling efforts apart from consideration of the other subfunctions (price, promotion, etc.) with which selling effort is linked in the definition of a marketing program, and the objectives of that program itself. The best one can say about selling, or advertising, or pricing efforts evaluated devoid of a programmatic focus is whether they are efficient. Measuring cost per sales call, for example, in no way tells the sales manager or marketer whether personal selling is an effective method of vending the particular good in question; it only informs as to whether this subfunction is efficiently applied.

Therefore, to our way of thinking and as embodied in our model, marketing is reconstrued as a set of programs that are evaluated on both efficiency and effectiveness grounds, with our satisfaction measure attempting to get directly at marketing *effectiveness*, while our effort measure approaches traditional assessments of marketing *efficiency*.

2. It is not useful to evaluate marketing effectiveness and, hence, marketing performance apart from management's satisfaction with the results of marketing activities. All marketing programs and behaviors are and will continue to be executed and then evaluated by management, not only by the marketers who engage the program (and who are invested in its success), but also by higher-management levels seeking to evaluate the marketers and their endeavors. Basically, the ultimate test of whether a marketing program is "good," "bad," a "high performer," or a "low performer" depends on management's reaction to it. Otherwise, no matter how much revenue the program produces, or how much profit it generates, the program cannot be usefully evaluated except on efficiency grounds.

Effectiveness, by definition, requires a judgment about the results of a program against what the program was intended to achieve. It makes more sense to us to incorporate these judgments explicitly, learn to operationalize them, and deal with their limitations directly than it does to attempt useful commentary on MPA that does not incorporate the validity of managerial judgments in the evaluation of marketing acts.

This is perhaps the most controversial of our assumptions, and eventually will deserve some discussion along lines of method and philosophy. Among these is whether managerial satisfaction is a worthwhile conceptual variable for inclusion in an MPA model, or whether it is too "subjective"; whether satisfaction can be reliably assessed, once given its acceptance as a useful variable; and the all-important issue of precisely which managers are relevant to assess as to their satisfaction with marketing programs. These points are taken up below after our explication of the model.

3. Satisfaction (effectiveness) is weighted by effort (efficiency) to produce a measure of performance. Perversely, and in complete contravention of the Protestant ethic, performance is maximized from gaining the greatest satisfaction with the least effort. Low effort means higher performance. The base case

model's formulation argues that the most productive marketing program is not that which produces high satisfaction given high effort but, following Kurt Lewin's (1951) view of social power, that which produces the most satisfaction with the least effort. The overall relationship proposed between satisfaction and effort is shown graphically in Figure 4. The model predicts maximal marketing performance when effort is low and satisfaction high, and minimal marketing performance when effort is high but satisfaction low. We shall see below how the effort variable ties into the firm's "automatic pilot" of marketing structures and habits to make this possible.

4. Whether or not a marketing program is "productive" depends not only on management's satisfaction and efforts, but on factors in the external environment as well. This assumption relates to the many external modifiers we discussed in the literature review above. We believe the most important of these factors outside the company (but not the only one; see below) is the quality of competitors' response to a company's program. Whether or not marketing programs are high performers depends to a greater degree than most managers would like to admit, and most scholars have recognized, on the reactions, countermoves, and blocks put up by competition.

We next turn to each of the components of the base model in the remainder of this chapter; measurement concerns are addressed in Chapter 7.

Satisfaction and Expectations

Management satisfaction, as we use the term, is a compound psychological variable measuring the effectiveness of a marketing program as the congruity or incongruity between what management expects in terms of results from its marketing program, and the results that actually accrue from the program. Satisfaction, our effectiveness surrogate, is thus a joint function of results and expectations, as shown in Figure 5. Expectations for results and program results themselves interact, such that the lowest satisfaction is obtained when expectations are great but results meager, and the highest satisfaction when expectations are meager but results great.

To understand the relationship between standard measures of "objective" results and our

Figure 4 Marketing Performance: Satisfaction and Effort

Management's Perceived Effort Is

	Low	High
Management's Perceived Satisfaction with Results Is		
High	**Maximum Performance** Achieving the most results with the least effort, in complete contravention of the Protestant ethic. By definition, low effort is more easily achieved through, systematized or routinized procedures than through "exception management." $\frac{S t L}{S T R}$ — ↑	**Adequate Performance** High satisfaction is the "due consequence" of high effort. Effort, however, is costly, resulting in only adequate performance because much was expended to produce the results. Usually, effort is high when routinized systems and procedures cannot be delegated to do the job "automatically." $T?$ $\frac{S t L ↑}{S T R ↑}$
Low	**Adequate Performance** There is little to be satisfied with, but little effort was expended in achieving the low performance. The lack of effort is seen as justifying or explaining the lack of performance. $\frac{S t L ↓}{S T R}$ —	**Low Performance** Much effort was expended to little avail in terms of results. This is the worst possible state. $\frac{S t L ↑}{S T R ↓}$

Figure 5   The Determinants of Satisfaction: Results and Expectations

Results from Marketing Efforts Are

	Poor	Good
Management's Expectations for Results Are	High Dissatisfaction	Moderate Satisfaction
High	Results achieved do not live up to expectations. Management is unhappy with performance given prior expectations and promise.	Results match goals—which, after all, is only what should have happened. There are no surprises, either pleasant or unpleasant.
	Moderate Dissatisfaction	High Satisfaction
Low	Poor results match the low expectations held for the program. The poor results are only moderately unsettling because of the low expectations.	Good results far exceed what was hoped for or planned. Top management loves these kinds of surprises, despite its suspicion about being sandbagged.

psychological variables of management expectation and satisfaction, understand initially that there are results, and then there are results. In 1980, Frito-Lay, Inc. (FLI) decided to use its vaunted distribution system to expand from its traditional arena of salty snacks to single-serve, ready-to-eat cookies. Taking a regional brand it had recently acquired, GrandMa's Cookies, FLI rolled out nationally against large cookie manufacturers. The cookies met good acceptance from small FLI accounts nationwide. FLI built up a business with $50 million in revenues in under two years.

But management considered this effort a failure. The original GrandMa's plan called for significant penetration of large accounts and a $120 million business in two years; $50 million is great if your supervisor expects $50 million, but it is terrible if your supervisor expects $120 million. (Cf., Bonoma, 1984, for a full account of this episode.)

This type of outcome is not uncommon. Virtually any company with a formal budgeting/planning process or a financially oriented incentive system will report as a humiliating failure what another firm or another management might consider a raving success, and vice versa. A further example comes from a large financial services firm that eliminated a new ventures department when the department dramatically underperformed relative to its original revenue forecasts.

Expectations are more than management reaction to a set of numbers, however; they reflect the psychological environment of the organization. Here the "corporate culture" meets the "self-fulfilling prophecy." In a firm battling for survival, expectations are generally lower: surviving another day can be enough. For a firm with a high-growth history, nothing is beyond the organization's grasp. Concerning the latter, Allen Michels, former chairman of Convergent Technologies, describes this as the "dangerous conviction that we were always right" (quoted in *The Wall Street Journal*, December 15, 1986, p. 30). The firm's history dramatically influences its identity, and thus its expectations.

Stefflre (1985) raises a different but conceptually sympathetic set of internal environment problems in his discussion of organization size and bureaucratic decision rules (see above, pp. 48–49). Concerning management expectations, his findings suggest to us that a different set of criteria may govern larger organizations relative to smaller ones. For example, larger organizations may have more short-term and politically motivated expectations than small ones.

In any case, it is apparent to us that any measure of marketing performance must incorporate management expectations to reflect accurately managers' judgment of the program being executed. Some scholars and practitioners do this implicitly in their evaluation of performance. Hulbert and Toy (1977; see above, pp. 42–44), for example, compare performance relative to a budget that presumably bears some resemblance to management's expectations for a firm. The "pragmatic" productivity rule Zabriskie and Browning (1979; see above, p. 51) discovered essentially measures what Gross would call functional results (activities as opposed to financial results) compared to objectives rather than effort. Gilbert (1978; see above, pp. 49–50) takes this objectives-as-input approach to its logical extreme in his use of information, performance examples, and objectives as the motivators and the standards for performance.

The difference between our model and this work, or the fifty years of advances in psychology and the five in marketing which evaluate satisfaction in other settings, is that our model takes management satisfaction, a subjective measure, as its centerpiece. This departure is radical enough to merit some discussion of two criticisms of satisfaction as a measure.

Satisfaction Is a Subjective Measure; It Cannot be Assessed

One criticism of satisfaction as a variable measure that is repeatedly offered is that any possible operationalization of this concept is subjective, and hence not as useful as "harder" measures of financial or other results. We not only do not deny this, but in fact cheerfully affirm it, arguing that it is this very fact that permits the first useful and effectiveness-directed measure of MPA to be constructed.

All measures of all things are, of course, subjective, whether we mean the reading of a thermometer by a warm executive or measurement of his or her satisfaction with marketing results. What matters is whether these subjective perceptions of so-called "external reality" are replicable, constant, and valid across managers, settings, and situations. There is good confirmation in psychology (cf., e.g., Gergen, 1969; Berkowitz, 1969; McGuire, 1969; Simon and Stedry, 1969; Mischel, 1974; Locke, 1976) and marketing (Engel, Blackwell, and Miniard, 1986; Hawkins, Best, and Corey, 1986) that satisfaction measures, properly measured, meet this criterion. Hence, we do not consider it problematic that our model is based on a "subjective" measure of management satisfaction with marketing results. Indeed, management satisfaction with marketing outcomes is presumed in our model to be closely related to the expectations and objectives (or strategy) from which the firm is working. These objectives are, of course, the foundation of strategic marketing.

As to the preference for financial measures as opposed to a subjective one like satisfaction, it is important to note that the management satisfaction measure we propose uses financial results as one measure of satisfaction, but allows all results to be interpreted by management according to its expectations for them. Therefore, while satisfaction may be based on financial, market share, or sales results, it is not one with these measures but instead is an adjudged or interpreted "scaling" of results in units of expectation.

Further, we decompose the satisfaction variable into the discrepancy, or lack thereof, between results and expectations, which allows a quite simple and parsimonious measurement rubric to be developed for assessing and "triangulating" both the components and the summary variable of satisfaction. As will be seen below, expectations can be measured independently, as can results, leading to a summary measure of satisfaction. The beauty of the summary variable, however, is that satisfaction can also be assessed directly, then compared backward to the componential elements of validity assessment.

Whose Satisfaction Is Relevant?

Even if satisfaction is a useful and appropriate variable on which to base a model of MPA, critics say, the sticky question remains as to whose satisfaction, or expectations, in the management hierarchy represents an appropriate point for assessment. Clearly, marketing program managers themselves may be expected to experience different (and, possibly, characteristically higher) levels of satisfaction from achieved results than, say, a marketing vice president or corporation president. While we address this issue further in the methods section below, suffice it to say here that we intend the satisfaction measure to include an assess-

ment of both the program managers' estimations and also those of the management responsible for marketing performance across multiple programs. Depending on the size, organization, and nature of the firm under consideration, this second level of management may include general management or just top marketing management.

Results and Effort

Although using objectives or expectations as a comparison standard in a productivity measure obviously adds information for the managers involved, we do not believe that a measure of effort exerted as a useful surrogate for efficiency can be discarded. There is a big difference between meeting expectations while spending $1 million versus meeting the same expectations while spending $10 million. Therefore, we weigh results with an expectations factor, but retain the effort component. Rather than Results/Effort, as previous construals have expressed marketing productivity, we incorporate the traditional equation with our model equation, which is the unexpanded equation already given above:

$$MP = \frac{SAT}{EFF} \times EXT, \qquad (1)$$

where

MP = marketing performance, what others have called marketing productivity,

SAT = management's satisfaction from the results of marketing program efforts,

EFF = the effort expended to attain these results, and

EXT = the impact of actions external to the organization on marketing efforts.

Expanding the numerator to reflect our new understanding of satisfaction (SAT) as a joint function of results (RES) weighted by management expectations (EXP), we obtain Equation 2:

$$MP = \frac{RES/EXP}{EFF} \times EXT. \qquad (2)$$

Thus our model factors results by comparing them to expectations before adjusting for effort. It remains to expand the denominator of the equation, and to understand further what efficiency in marketing means.

Effort Decomposed: Management Skills and Marketing Structures

When the sum total of effort that management can bring to bear on a problem is considered, many simply think in terms of dollars. However, it is instructive to realize the various resources those marketing dollars can be used to buy. Following Bonoma's implementation model, one major resource that companies purchase is the skills of their marketing employees. The other resource a company has is the marketing structures the company has in place to support a program: information systems, order-processing systems, planning systems, firm-wide policies, and subfunction-specific rules of thumb, for example.

At any given point in time, an organization has a certain quality level for employee marketing skills, using the template given by Bonoma (1985b), and a certain quality level for marketing structures. (Compare this to the total-factor productivity measure of Beckman, 1961, discussed above on pp. 11–12.) The likelihood of producing a good (high-performance) program increases with the quality of skills and/or the quality of structures available. However, skills and structures are differentially useful depending on the situation in which the company finds itself.

One way to think about skills versus structures is in variable (skills) and fixed (structures) terms. The variable cost of producing a program is related wholly to the exception-management nature of exercising personal implementation skills in order to produce success from a program when it is feared or certain that the "semi-automatic" nature of the firm's habitual marketing structures will not or cannot take management to success. This construal of skills as "exception-management" is consistent both with Bonoma's (1985a) findings as he studied marketing-in-practice, and with the common-sense notion that allowing the structures to do most of the work requires less effort than a customized skill intervention program.

On the other hand, overall structures are already in place, and represent a fixed, sunk cost to the organization accrued over years of routinizing and finely honing the operations level of marketing to produce successful results with programs under usual, normal, and traditionally encountered situations. For example, Frito-Lay did not have to develop a distribution system for cookies from scratch; they already had

a strong system. Therefore, while the likelihood of producing a good program is the sum of skills and structures (SKL + STR), the cost is the quotient of these two elements: SKL/STR. To the extent that existing structures are adequate to the task, a lower level of management skill needs to be exerted on any given program, and therefore, less needs to be spent on personnel.[21]

From the perspective of the personnel involved, the firm's marketers need to exert less effort to achieve the same results. Figure 6 shows this relationship of skills and structures in the determination of effort. Note that when both skills and structures are strong, a conflict of sorts is engendered. It is in the rigid structures–weak skills area that effort is minimal and performance maximal. Bonoma's (1985b) research suggests this cell is most easily maintained by firms executing marketing programs in stable, low-change environments.

Expanding Equation 1 once again to incorporate our fuller understanding of the determination of effort, skills/structures, we obtain the following revision:

$$MP = \frac{RES/EXP}{SKL/STR} \times EXT, \qquad (3)$$

where the compound fraction expresses our beginning formulation of satisfaction/effort more precisely and clearly in the terms of Bonoma's previous implementation work. It remains to look at the external influences on the performance of marketing programs.

External Factors

Many companies evaluate their marketing managers explicitly on just internal types of measures, such as results or effort. Indeed, many managers seek to be compensated on financial return indices. From the organization standpoint, this often makes a great deal of sense. When a manager is faced with evaluation on the basis of a number over which he or she has only partial control, it is reasonable to assume that that manager will work very hard to make sure that he or she maximizes the results of the part he or she does control.

---

21. "Spent" is used here in the broad sense and refers to management attention, time, or money. We do not necessarily mean that fewer marketers will be required for structures-dominant programs than for skills-dominant ones, though that outcome is sometimes experienced.

Figure 6 The Determinants of Effort: Management Skills and Marketing Structures

Marketing Structures Are

	Flexible	Rigid
Management's Marketing Skills Are		
	Maximum Effort	**Moderate Effort**
Strong	Weak structures cannot help routinize repetitive decisions; all problems receive "custom" solutions from strongly skilled managers. While all get solved, the fixes are expensive and people-dependent.	Strong structures help routinize decisions, but strongly skilled managers come into conflict with structural constraints. Decisions with which the system cannot cope are handled on an exception basis by management. This is expensive but highly effective as long as systems and managers do not conflict destructively.
	Low Effort	**Minimal Effort**
Weak	Weak structures do not routinize well. Poorly skilled management does not or cannot exert itself to bridge the shortcomings between structural shortfalls and marketing requirements.	Strong structures routinize marketing decisions. Weakly skilled managers let the structure do the job, and are not compelled to intervene in its operation. This works superbly efficiently, and is effective as long as the environment remains stable.

Because of this, we have chosen to take a hybrid approach to MPA. Although we leave a results variable intact in our equation as a financial measure, we add a series of multipliers to reflect the influence of external factors on marketing performance. The three multipliers are the quality of competitive response (QCR), the quality of marketing partner response (PTR), and other variables in the environment, including legal, demographic, and technological factors (ENV). So far, we have illustrated but not discussed the first. In this section, we discuss all three external factors, then present the MPA model in its final form.

Quality of Competitive Response (QCR)

The effects of competition on the performance of marketing endeavors, as every manager knows, can be profound. Competitive proaction and reaction, of course, act to affect marketing program results; less well articulated is that they can also affect management expectations (and hence, satisfaction) as well as effort. Regarding expectations, the presence or absence of a strong competitor acts to decrease or increase, respectively, management's expected results from an ongoing or contemplated program. In the personal computer industry, for example, COMPAQ's management had lower expectations than they might otherwise have had concerning their universally praised 1986 introduction of a "next-generation" machine because COMPAQ, with its 5–7 percent share of market, had decided to innovate before giant competitor IBM by eight months. While no one, including COMPAQ management, felt certain of what IBM would do when it chose to announce machines using 80386 processors, many thought that COMPAQ sales would be suppressed until and unless such an announcement was forthcoming. This announcement, and only this announcement, could "legitimize" the technological move so boldly taken by COMPAQ.

Regarding effort, both the presence of a strong competitor or one known for quick and powerful reactions may cause management to allocate more time, money, or people to a marketing project than might otherwise be allocated, hence lowering performance. These management expectations about competition are built into the marketers' plans. Since our marketing performance index is a retrospective

measure, we are concerned only with *unexpected* competitive actions over the previous period. In Hulbert and Toy's (1977) terms, this is our way of attempting to sort out the planning variance (we expect certain actions but do not get them) from the performance variance (performance given what happened).

The QCR variable is designed as a multiplier on the base, internal MPA equation in order to "factor" the quotient of satisfaction over effort by the effectiveness and, essentially, the "toughness" of the competition. QCR can be greater than or less than 1.00, with smaller numbers indicating competitor absence or inability. The beginning of our final equation is thus

$$MP = \frac{RES/EXP}{SKL/STR} \times QCR. \qquad (4)$$

Quality of Marketing Partner Response (PTR)

With very few exceptions, most firms have outside partners in their marketing programs. These partners provide services to the firm or ultimate purchasers. The most common partners are other members of the distribution channel, such as wholesalers, and marketing service firms, such as advertising agencies. We call these two types of marketing partners independent and dependent partners, respectively. Independent partners are those who buy products or services from the firm, while dependent partners are those from whom the firm buys.

The distinguishing characteristic of independent partners, typified by distribution partners such as wholesalers and retailers, is that the partner is the firm's customer, to whom the firm must cater. With the exception of those firms that reach end-users through their own sales forces or by mail, most of what the manufacturing or middleman company does by way of marketing programs must be executed through middlemen, collectively called the distribution channel. A toy manufacturer, for example, may produce outstanding and timely toys, and support these with farsighted and internally productive marketing programs. But much of the marketing of the products themselves happens at the retail outlets, which for this industry includes two toy supermarket chains (Child World, Toys 'R' Us), discounters, and other channel partners. While the manufacturer's marketing programs may (or may not) act directly on the channel, the net impact felt by the end-user is clearly a joint function of how well the manufacturer handles the distribution channel as well as end-user marketing programs, and how well the channel carries through its functions of distribution and marketing. In the purchase decision, downstream members of the distribution channel, such as retailers, often exercise a great deal of power over upstream members such as manufacturers. Child World, for example, is large enough to influence the way toy manufacturers market their product. In addition, once a distributor purchases the product or service, it is very difficult for the manufacturer to control what the distributor does with it.

The power balance between firm and partner changes with dependent partners. Because the firm purchases the services of the dependent partner, it has more control, or at least final veto power, over the partner's actions. A firm may, for example, reject a proposed advertising campaign. Although once again the partner's performance of certain marketing functions is critical to overall performance, unlike an independent partner, there are no marketing actions directed at the partner. There is no equivalent of, for example, a trade sales promotion in the marketing service industry. Rather, the firm must concentrate on managing and monitoring the performance of its dependent partner to make it unnecessary for the firm to exercise its greater power.

To indicate this dependence of "internal" marketing performance on these all-important partners, we include a quality of partner response variable, called PTR, as a second multiplier on the MPA equation. It is represented thus in Equation 5:

$$MP = \frac{RES/EXP}{SKL/STR} \times QCR \times PTR. \qquad (5)$$

The PTR variable conceptually captures a number of efficiencies or inefficiencies. Some of these are structural. A packaged goods manufacturer that elects or is forced to market through a fragmented distribution channel in southern Italy, for instance, will experience more muted effects of its marketing programs and less marketing performance from a given amount of effort than one that focuses solely on the more industrialized north, with its hypermarkets and concentrated buying patterns. Other elements of PTR, however, are more directly affected by management's actions vis-à-

vis the channel. A manufacturer known for its poor trade relations, complete reliance on advertising and other "pull marketing" moves to bring the customers into the store, and an unwillingness to treat the channel to deal money, rebates, or other special incentives the trade feels it has coming, will also experience muted effects of its marketing programs compared to a more savvy channel partner, all other things being equal. Similarly, poor advertising or market research will diminish the power of other elements of a marketing program.

Environmental Factors (ENV)

Clearly, there are many other external factors in the environment which also can heighten or mute marketing performance. Government regulations, economic trends, and changing market demographics can all distort the impact of marketing programs. (Recall the many microeconomic mediating factors listed in Table 8.) One especially prominent factor, as reported by Bonoma (1981), is rate of market change.

When the rate of market change is high, Bonoma has observed powerful negative effects on the ability of the marketing structures of the firm to aid in economical program execution. These findings agree with those of Bucklin (1978), Anderson and Weitz (1986), and Ruekert et al. (1985). Lowered systems efficiency, according to our model, means heightened effort since management must substitute its skills for shortfalls in the structure. Heightened effort, in turn, means lower performance.

In measuring "environment," we advocate including only the broad market characteristics represented by the economic and demographic sections of Table 4 and the market characteristics of Table 8. We exclude product, customer, and task-specific environmental factors not because they are unimportant, but because we believe they are captured in the effort ratio, other external variables, and the expectations managers hold. The distinction we draw is similar to the macro versus task environment Kotler et al. (1977) discuss, and the task characteristics and environmental factors that Ruekert et al. (1985) use.

We explicitly make provision in the model to account for the market factors, otherwise unobservable in their effects, with a final variable, ENV, which denotes any and all environmental contingencies that might heighten or reduce marketing efforts, results, or expectations. Thus, the completed form of the MPA model is given in Equation 6 as

$$MP = \frac{RES/EXP}{SKL/STR} \times QCR \times PTR \times ENV. \quad (6)$$

Conclusion

This chapter explained the model's base assumptions and articulated its rationale. We began with an explanation of the psychological foundations of two of the model's key variables, satisfaction and expectations. Satisfaction, it was argued, is a joint function of what is expected and the results attained by a marketing program. It was explained how satisfaction is factored by effort, which is in turn a joint function of two variables, the structures the firm has in place to help automate the execution of marketing programs and the execution skills of its managers. This "major fraction" of satisfaction/ effort is itself modified by three external influences: the quality of the competition faced by the program; the execution of the program by the inevitable set of marketing partners, such as distributors, responsible for interpreting management's marketing program to the customers; and changes in the external environment.

The next chapter attempts to bring some of this heady theoretical work down to the level of measurable construct.

Chapter 7
Measurement Issues and Further Elaboration

Introduction

This chapter tackles directly the sometimes difficult methods issues involved in making the MPA model useful to both managers and researchers. We deal with these issues as they implicate quantitative and qualitative measurement decisions alike.

Quantitative Issues

Rather than measuring marketing performance using a set of specific terms, such as sales per employee, we have chosen to use an index-based measure, which we think is easier to calculate and to understand. It should also make comparisons across departments, firms, and industries simpler. However, each part of the equation raises some specific quantitative questions based on the arithmetic as well as the definitional issues involved.

Results

Results measurement is difficult only because various scholars and practitioners will find different terms appropriate. While we prefer a long-term, profit-related measure of results, such as a moving average of operating profits (Drucker, 1986), long-term cash flows (Buzzell and Chussil, 1985), or a measure of consumer franchise (Mehrotra, 1984), we realize this may be unrealistic given the short-term nature of performance evaluation at many publicly held companies. We suggest, therefore, that a company should examine its own business and decide the best set of terms for measuring the health of that business. This may be one measure or a combination of several.

The important point is to set up a comparison of expectations at the beginning of a time period (one year seems reasonable given the prevalence of annual operating plans) and the results at the end of the period.

The closest analogy in the current literature might be the variance analysis that Hulbert and Toy (1977) use. The numerical measurement technique we suggest would use 1.00 as the expectations base, and then results as a percentage of that base, similar to the calculation of the consumer price index. For example, if results exceed expectations by 5 percent, Results would appear numerically as 1.05, or 5 percentage points above expectations.

Expectations

The measurement of expectations is not as difficult as it first appears once researchers and practitioners overcome the attitude that there is something wrong, imprecise, or inadequate about managerial judgments on marketing programs.

That this barrier has not been surmounted in the past is, we believe, the single most prominent cause of why the effectiveness issues have been assumed, presumed, or simply ignored in past approaches to marketing performance assessment. In our opinion, however, it is simply not enough to measure efficiency and then to assert effectiveness. This is tantamount to saying that an executioner who dispatches multiple political prisoners per hour is productive without questioning the government policies that imprisoned these individuals, nor the judicial system that sentenced them. The former assessment requires counting; the latter, judgment.

The determinants of expectations as the driver of effectiveness judgments, or at least a guide for them, are no more difficult to measure than are the determinants of efficiency. It will be remembered that Bonoma's marketing implementation work proposed two high-level components to marketing policies: identity and direction. The former expressed management's sense and clarity about "who it is and what it does vis-à-vis the customer"—that is, its theme or vision (Bonoma, 1985a). The latter, policies of direction, are a combination of the firm's strategy and the strength of its leadership, which in turn serve as a directional indicator for all program efforts. In a sense, identity is the product of the organization's history and is thus "past-oriented," while direction explicitly addresses the organization's future. Combined, these two policy-level forces interact in predictable ways to determine expectations, as shown in Figure 7.

Following from the figure, when identity and strategy are clear, realistic expectations for marketing programs are engendered. When identity is clear but direction is not, there is a tendency to expect little from programmatic efforts, for it is not clear how they fit in with the firm's overall plans, nor indeed, what those plans may be. When strategies are unclear and identity is as well, conflicting expectations are engendered. On the one hand easy or vague goals lend little sense of direction to the programmatic marketing effort. On the other, conflicting or vague senses of identity among marketing management leads to highly conflicting expectations sets because there is no common framework within which to search for meaningful objectives.

Finally, the most unsatisfiable and unrealistic expectations for programmatic marketing efforts are engendered when strategies are clear but identity is not. Here tough goals coupled with able leaders give marvelous clarity to the strategic and directional policies guiding marketing execution. But managers carry very different senses of what the firm is about, leading in turn to the high expectations of top management being imposed on an operating marketing group that cannot temper these expectations with countervailing views because the group is too fragmented. The result is usually that top management's high expectations dominate.

Thus, whatever else is involved in the direct assessment of management expectations, policies of identity and directional clarity will also have to be assessed. When coupled with direct assessment, this suggests the following three-part measurement strategy:

1. Obtain direct assessments of expectations, either in the same units as employed for results, or directly, on a Likert-type scale. As noted above, these expectations measures should be obtained from both (a) marketing program management, and (b) the managers responsible for multiple marketing programs. In the smallest firms, this may well be the same individual. In medium-sized firms, it is likely to mean measuring the marketing manager's expectations and also those of general management, to whom marketing reports. In larger corporations, it may mean assessing the brand or product manager's expectations, and also those of

Figure 7 The Making of Expectations: Policies of Direction and Policies of Identity

Strategy and Leadership
(Direction Policies) Are

	Unclear	Clear
Marketing Theme (Identity) Is	Minimal Expectations	Realistic Expectations
Precise and Clear	Vague strategy and leadership direction ask little that is specific or tough. Clear identity as a lightweight in strategy or leaders depresses managers. They expect very little, just a continuation of "business as usual."	Tough, clear goals espoused by able leaders coupled with a clear idea of "who we are and what we do" provide both direction and identity to managers. No doubts; realistic expectations engendered.
	Conflicting Expectations	Unsatisfiable Expectations
Vague and Conflicting	Easy or vague goals propounded by weak leaders lend no sense of direction to marketing management. Conflicting or vague senses of identity reinforce the problem and lead to a series of wildly conflicting expectation sets.	Tough goals and able leaders propound clear strategies and direction. However, individual managers have very different senses of what the firm is about, leading to vastly different senses of what it can do and what can be delivered. Top managers' direction usually prevails, leading to unsatisfiable expectations.

the group product manager or marketing vice president.

2. Average the expectational measures so obtained to get a single overall expectations index, and compare it against results as a derived measure of satisfaction.

3. Assess thematic as well as strategic clarity directly on Likert-type scales in order to get cross-confirmation of the theoretically postulated relationships between these policies and expectations.

For instance, a company might decide that the best measure of the return a new product is making to the organization is unit sales. Expectations are then measured in the same units as results. Analysts would seek expectations for unit sales that managers had at the beginning of the time period being evaluated; otherwise, unanticipated external factors would be accounted for twice, once in the expectations variable and once in the external variables. Averaging the expectations of managers at different levels, the researcher would then have a base against which to compare results. The ratio can be in the form of a percentage increase/decrease from expectations, as suggested above, or it may also use actual numbers (e.g., 315,000 units sold when 300,000 were expected to be sold would be a ratio of 1.05, as above).

Skills and Structures

Assessing management skills and the strength of marketing structures requires judgments of adequacy and relative strength. While it is traditional to make such difficult measurements against an absolute or just undefined referent, we strongly agree with Gilbert (1978), who compares performance to the best existing performer (the "exemplar"). Thus, it is useful to have management (a) specify a common or at least agreed-upon exemplar with whom they wish to compare themselves, and (b) rate themselves against this exemplar in terms of percentage of best existing performance realized. For these measures, a company might decide that its management is at 95 percent of potential, while its systems are at 90 percent of potential, where potential is understood as the level of management skills and marketing structures adjudged to be present in the company's best competitor, as identified by management itself. In such a scenario, a firm's evaluation of its own management skills and structural adequacy would thus be .95/.90 against the best

competitor, and the equation as a whole so far would equal $(1.05/1.00)/(.95/.90) = .99$. Note that our hypothetical organization's performance index has been *reduced*, not enhanced, because skills are stronger relative to potential than systems with regard to the marketing program under consideration. This is a correct and necessary consequence of the model's derivational form. To the extent that highly skilled managers must intervene to make programs work, and to the extent that the firm's automatic marketing systems do not suffice to produce program success with only some management oversight, then effort is increased to that degree. Note that this means the model will be somewhat biased against new programs or programs in unstable industries because there will be little action that managers can structure.

The skills of marketing managers, as opposed to production managers or marketing support staff, are measured for two reasons. Pragmatically, the marketing program's managerial group is a clear identifiable set. Theoretically, it is reasonable that a program's marketing managers are the strongest determinant of the program's marketing performance. While this approach excludes the efforts of support staff and other departments, it is the most feasible way of assessing the skill variable.

As with expectations, it is necessary to obtain multiple measures, both from marketing program management and also from the general management to which this former level reports, in order to avoid over- or underestimation of these variables. In the absence of better procedures, data across individuals can be averaged in order to obtain the necessary summary index.

Because we assume that skills are a variable cost, as explained above, the 5 percent overperformance in results is offset by the roughly 5 percent dominance of skills over systems. The message here is that we are doing well in our market, but that we require stronger, presumably more expensive, managers to achieve this performance. The computations so far do not inform us why this is the case, only that it is so.

External Modifiers (QCR, PTR, ENV)

QCR is in some ways a comparison to expectations. Any good marketing plan contains some expectations as to what competitors will do and how competitors will fare in response to the planned actions. If all goes according to plan, QCR is a flat 1.00 because the reaction has presumably been anticipated, which leaves the base equation unchanged. QCR will vary when a company is surprised, which in our experience happens distressingly often. A competitor might repackage an old product. A new company might enter the industry. On the other hand, a competitor might suffer a strike. To the extent that competitive response is stronger than expected, the multiplier increases; to the extent that it is weaker, the multiplier decreases.

This measurement prescription is somewhat counterintuitive in that stronger competitive response produces *higher* marketing performance. In this context, the important thing to remember is that our marketing performance index is a retrospective measure that looks back over a specified period of time and evaluates how well a marketing program performed. QCR (and PTR and ENV) as we construe it attempts to explain some variation in the results measure. Any program that produces superior satisfaction in the face of strong competition has obviously performed better than a program that produces superior satisfaction in the face of weak competition. Thus, we reward the former program with a higher performance index than the latter. This is our attempt to distinguish between the performance and planning variances that Hulbert and Toy (1977) discuss. By identifying unanticipated external events, these variables allow top managers to assess performance—how programs should have been expected to perform given the events that actually occurred. More roughly, as we suggested in the model preview, this separates the lucky from the smart—those who succeed or fail from fortune rather than merit.

Prospectively, of course, it is usually a better strategy to attack weak competitors, or rather, those that turn out to be weaker in actuality than plans predicted. This raises the longitudinal issue that the correct strategic decision (attack weak competitors) may eventually produce lower marketing performance (because weak competition lowers the MPA index).

Assessment methods recommended for QCR are exactly the same as those indicated for expectations, which is to say, a Likert-type assessment of the "surprise value" of competitive actions generated from two management levels, marketing and general management, and then averaged. In our hypothetical case, let us assume an unexpected new entrant in the industry, and a corresponding QCR of 1.05. The message here is that our performance index will be higher because we achieved our results in the face of unexpectedly strong competition. We had a planning variance, in Hulbert and Toy's (1977) terms, because we did not anticipate our competition accurately, which modified our performance.

Partner response (PTR) and environment (ENV) behave similarly to QCR, and the recommended measurement methods are identical. To the extent that their actions unexpectedly diminish our chances of success in the measurement period, the multiplier increases (because our results have been achieved in the face of adverse conditions, meaning our program had higher quality than the results indicate). Unexpectedly improving our chances decreases the multiplier (because it means our results were achieved with the aid of good conditions we did not create, meaning or program had lower quality than the results indicate). In this case, let us imagine unusual trade enthusiasm for our program (PTR = .95), but new government packaging regulations that damage our distribution during the year (ENV = 1.05). Substituting as with the QCR variable, our sample calculation is completed as follows:

$$MP = \frac{RES/EXP}{SKL/STR} \times QCR \times PTR \times ENV;$$

substituting for the variables, we obtain

$$\frac{1.05/1.00}{.95/.90} \times 1.05 \times .95 \times 1.05 = 1.04.$$

The individual number 1.04 is obviously meaningless by itself. It must be compared to the indices for other programs within the same company and, if possible, against the programs of competitors. Management will find it useful to examine the components of the measure as well. In our sample calculation, we have learned a great deal about the hypothetical firm's performance just by specifying the variables in the equation. For instance, the marketing program in question exceeded expectations by about 5 percent, but required more skilled managers to do this relative to structural adequacy. In addition, uncontrollable factors hurt us over the course of the year, with stronger competition and an adverse environment offsetting trade enhancement of our program. This makes our performance all the more impressive.

Sample Calculations and Interactions among Variables

To illustrate better the calculations that comprise the index, Table 11 lists sample MPA outcomes for twenty hypothetical marketing programs. Program 1 is the base outcome: the company achieved the results it expected, skills and structures are in balance, and there were no external surprises over the course of the period. Programs 2 and 3 simply alter the results variable, demonstrating that, all other things being equal, a certain percentage change in RES will produce an identical change in the marketing performance index.

Programs 4 through 6 examine the components of effort (EFF = SKL/STR). As we discussed, dominance of skills over structures, as in program 4, is expensive and thus produces lower marketing performance. Dominance of structures over skills, as in program 5, means little management intervention was required in the program, thus producing higher performance. Note that it is not the absolute level of structures and skills that the model considers

important, but their levels relative to each other. Program 6 has the same marketing performance as program 1, despite its lower-quality skills and structures. This is a problem for the model in theory, since program 1's effort obviously costs more than program 6's, but in practice we think an exact balance is unlikely to hold. Strong managers contending with strong systems will either get bored and leave or have their skills erode from lack of use. Weak managers contending with weak systems will become stronger or the program will not survive.

Programs 7 and 8 illustrate the impact of unexpected competitive response (QCR) on marketing performance. As with RES/EXP, a given percentage change in QCR will produce an identical percentage change in the performance index. This logic also applies to partner response (PTR), environment (ENV), and the overall external part of the model (EXT).

Programs 9 through 12 illustrate off-setting interactions among the model variables. All four programs achieved an overall performance index of .99, but this value was attained in very different ways. Program 9 produced expected

Table 11 Hypothetical Outcomes from the MPA Model

$$MP = \frac{RES/EXP}{SKL/STR} \times QCR \times PTR \times ENV$$

Program	RES	EXP	SKL	STR	QCR	PTR	ENV	MP
1. All normal	1.00	1.00	1.00	1.00	1.00	1.00	1.00	1.00
2. ↑ RES	1.20	1.00	1.00	1.00	1.00	1.00	1.00	1.20
3. ↓ RES	.80	1.00	1.00	1.00	1.00	1.00	1.00	.80
4. ↓ STR	1.00	1.00	1.00	.80	1.00	1.00	1.00	.80
5. ↓ SKL	1.00	1.00	.80	1.00	1.00	1.00	1.00	1.25
6. ↓ STR and SKL	1.00	1.00	.80	.80	1.00	1.00	1.00	1.00
7. ↑ QCR	1.00	1.00	1.00	1.00	1.20	1.00	1.00	1.20
8. ↓ QCR	1.00	1.00	1.00	1.00	.80	1.00	1.00	.80
9. ↓ STR, ↑ QCR	1.00	1.00	1.00	.90	1.10	1.00	1.00	.99
10. ↑ RES, ↓ QCR	1.10	1.00	1.00	1.00	.90	1.00	1.00	.99
11. ↓ RES, ↑ QCR	.90	1.00	1.00	1.00	1.10	1.00	1.00	.99
12. ↓ SKL, ↓ QCR	1.00	1.00	.90	1.00	.90	1.00	1.00	.99
13. ↑ RES, ↑ QCR	1.20	1.00	1.00	1.00	1.20	1.00	1.00	1.44 — *winner*
14. ↓ RES, ↓ QCR	.80	1.00	1.00	1.00	.80	1.00	1.00	.64
15. ↑ RES, QCR ↓ SKL	1.20	1.00	.80	1.00	1.20	1.00	1.00	1.80
16. ↓ RES, STR, QCR	.80	1.00	1.00	.80	.80	1.00	1.00	.51 — *beyond help*
17. V ↑ RES	1.30	1.00	1.00	1.00	1.00	1.00	1.00	1.30
18. V ↑ RES, ↓ QCR	1.30	1.00	1.00	1.00	.80	1.00	1.00	1.04 — *compet died*
19. V ↓ RES	.70	1.00	1.00	1.00	1.00	1.00	1.00	.70
20. V ↓ RES, SKL	.70	1.00	.75	1.00	1.00	1.00	1.00	.93 — *Too little mgt attention*

↓ = Low
↑ = High
V = Very

results in the face of unexpectedly stiff competition, but required extra management skill intervention to do this. Program 10 displayed better than expected results, but only because competitors proved unexpectedly weak. Program 11 produced results below expectations with strong competition. Finally, program 12 had weak competition, but also produced its results through structures rather than skills, and thus was less expensive.

Programs 13 through 16 show compounding interactions. Here performance was higher or lower, as the case may be, than looking at results alone would indicate. Program 13, for example, not only exceeded expectations for results, but did this despite stronger than expected competition, whereas program 16 was not just bad, but spectacularly bad, failing to meet expectations despite weak competition, and doing the whole thing with management intervention rather than systems.

Finally, programs 17 through 20 reveal the variances beyond simple results measures in performance assessment. Programs 17 and 18 were both very successful in terms of management satisfaction with results, but in the case of program 18 results were easier to produce because competition rolled over and died. Programs 19 and 20, on the other hand, were both unsatisfactory, but program 20 at least did not absorb much management skill.

The outcomes for programs 9 through 20 once again demonstrate why we believe management must examine the values for components of the model as well as the overall performance index. Finer analysis will produce better prescriptions for improvement. Concerning program 20, for example, one might argue that it received too little management attention; more care might have altered its disappointing results. A program like 13, on the other hand, appears to be a winner; management might now try to routinize some of the effort that went into 13, reducing the necessary level of management skill involvement and improving its performance even further. Program 16 may be beyond help. Despite management efforts, it could not even capitalize on the opportunity of weak competition. In general, we believe that a performance index achieved because of unexpectedly favorable external factors ($QCR \times PTR \times ENV = EXT$) is less promising than an index in which EXT is neutral or unfavorable because there is no guarantee in the former case

that we will benefit from the same external largess in the future.

Indeed, comparing the results/expectations ratio to external factors can shed light on the interaction of planning and performance variances that Hulbert and Toy (1977) propose. For example, it is reasonable that if competitive reaction is stronger than expected, results will be weaker (see program 11). This is a planning variance; if the company had known its competitors would react the way they did, the company would have lowered its expectations or changed its effort, thus bringing results more into line with expectations. The performance index, which is higher than the results figure alone, reflects this. Program 2, however, appears to be a performance variance; it simply beat its forecast. Very high results relative to expectations (program 17) or repeated moderately high ratios (program 2) with no external surprises can give a third message indicating poor forecasting or intentional underforecasting.

Although comparing programs within a given time period is useful, comparing the quality index across time periods will provide more information as firms accumulate data longitudinally in the MPA format. Over time, logic suggests two general trends in the variables. Most will gravitate toward unity as management forecasting ability improves or markets stabilize. The gap between results and expectations should diminish, for instance, as management's understanding of the market improves. This trend toward stability, however, provides opportunity for the second trend to emerge. As management forecasting improves or the program's market stabilizes, management should be better able to systematize marketing operations. Program managers will understand their market well enough to decide which behaviors are useful to routinize. As they systematize these behaviors, the requisite SKL level will decrease, and the STR level will increase. This in turn will drive the effort equation down, and thus push the performance index up. Thus in a program executed for a long period of time, the index should move toward the situation in program 5, in which management gets the results it expects with no external surprises and low skill relative to structures.

On the other hand, measurement over time can be more difficult because of the interactions among the index components. Obviously the skills and structures a program has available affect the accuracy of expectations (and vice versa). What is needed is an instrument that allows the relevant information to be gathered without too much effort regularly. We address that issue below.

Comparing Performance Indices

One of the criticisms that may be made about the model as we present it is that we are vague about specifying measurements. This is intentional. The choice of what to measure for results, effort, and external factors is not trivial, and indeed is one of the great learning experiences managers can have (and researchers can study) in using the model. We *expect* that different items will be part of the index in different firms.

However, our preliminary research indicates that measures may not differ widely (see Chapter 8). Data on over thirty programs suggest four basic popular measures: sales, market share, profit, and number of customers served. But the use of different measures by different firms might make cross-industry comparisons of performance difficult with our approach.

Even where terms of measurement do differ, there is some precedent for comparing performance measures. On a quantitative basis, the technique of data envelopment analysis (DEA) does this by allowing each decision-making unit analyzed to have its inputs and outputs weighted to maximize the efficiency score of the unit. Each unit is given the highest possible score by maximizing its relative performance score, even though the weights for different units will be different. (See Lewin and Minton, 1986, for their account of using DEA in assessing organizational effectiveness.) Similarly, MPA lets top managers choose the weights and measures that are important for their programs, and then compare programs in light of how well they reach their potential, whatever that may be.

Within firms, comparing programs will reveal information not only about the programs themselves, but about the firm as a whole. If, for example, all programs within a company show many unanticipated external events, either a planning problem or a program portfolio problem (for financial stability alone, a firm should probably have some stable programs) is implied. Similarly, analysis may reveal that a com-

panywide structure, say an order-processing system, is inadequate to the needs of several departments, and that it is time for an overhaul.

Within an industry, firms may be able to gain a competitive perspective. If done by an outside agent, the MPA index may provide more sophisticated information than the type of market share data many consultants and trade associations currently collect. Even if there is no outside agent, calculating a rough index for competitors may suggest management priorities in another firm.

Across industries, comparisons become more problematic because criteria can differ wildly. Still, relative industry stability, structural adequacy, competitive intensity, or dependence on marketing partners to execute programs should be assessable. The danger here is that uninformed users of such data might make conclusions about strategies based on information about short-term execution.

Qualitative/Process Issues

Obviously there is a great deal more judgment involved in quantifying the components of the market performance index than, say, in many of the efficiency measures posed above. At this stage in our research, we have used case studies to establish the general validity of the index's variables. To this point, the general model has had good confirmation from anthropologically designed investigations into its plausibility in large and small firms,[22] but correspondingly, this type of case investigation does not allow parameterization of the measures proposed. At this writing, therefore, we can offer only general comments; although we believe we have uncovered some important considerations in a number of the model's components that deserve mention.

Results come largely from the existing information systems of the organization, unless the measures management uses are not available on this system. This seemingly innocuous point is important, for it appears to us that managers of marketing manage the data input to the information system much as they manage any other

---

22. We have completed three case clinical studies to date in order to determine the plausibility of the base model. These are, respectively, LifeSpan, Inc., Gillette Personal Care Division, and Hurricane Island Outward Bound School. They are discussed in Chapter 8, and included in their entirety in Appendix A.

function on which they are measured and, possibly, paid. That is to say, it is by no means uncommon to see, for example, sharp fourth-quarter sales increases that might not otherwise have occurred, especially if end-of-year bonuses are computed in a manner that gives high attention to late as opposed to early sales. It is probably important to use a medium-term (one year or more) measure of results, so that biases and other "blips" have a chance to straighten themselves out.

Expectations present a problem in that there is the question of whose expectations are the important ones, and it is tempting not to perform the multiple measurement we think necessary to get a good view of program expectations. One tactic is simply to take the plan or budget numbers as the appropriate set of expectations, but these numbers are often the subject of intense and undocumented negotiations among various groups. The budgeted numbers may represent a compromise solution to strongly held opposing views. We prefer not to use them.

According to our research, expectations are the product of five factors: (1) the overall strategy of the company, (2) the leadership quality of top management, (3) the marketing theme of the company (high-quality and consumer-oriented, for example), (4) the company culture as discussed above, and (5) the information that management has available. While the budget numbers are easy to find, these factors lead us to believe that the most relevant expectations are those of the highest-ranking executive who receives information on the individual program involved. This might be a division president who receives information on many individual brands, while his or her superior might receive information only on groups of brands; the division president would have informed expectations, and the superior would not. We have found that interviewing the person with informed expectations as to what will "really" happen can work, but some managers resist the exercise on the grounds that the budgeted expectations are the real expectations. Note as well that revelation of dramatically different expectations held by senior executives can be divisive in that program managers might become confused about which expectations (budgeted or executive) they should concentrate on meeting. Despite this early finding, our recommendation at this point remains consistent with the

one we made above—measure the program manager and the division manager, and average the expectations.

Management skills are a function of program managers' abilities and, as such, are best measured either by naturalistic observations, by peer ratings, or by some other interpersonal evaluation technique. We do not endorse using personnel records to assess marketing implementation skills, for many of the skills that make a manager a good marketer are "subversive" in nature, and not the stuff of glowing personnel reports (cf., Bonoma, 1986).

Marketing structures vary across companies, and thus require judgment as to what a structure is and whether it is adequate; again, there is no substitute for naturalistic observation. A steel manufacturer, for example, requires very different marketing structures from a financial services company. Still, Bucklin's (1978) division of marketing services into logistical, informational, and product-functional seems applicable here as well. Every company needs structures in these areas. Of course, finding an exemplar against which to judge structural adequacy will still be difficult.

Competitive information is available from a number of sources. Many companies keep files of such information. In addition, one may survey other channel members to discover competitive activities. The press and trade associations are often useful sources. Channel response quality is best estimated by talking with the organization sales force for information on wholesalers and retailers, and with the people who purchase materials for information on suppliers. Marketing service firm work is best judged by the program managers. Environmental information is available from much the same sources as is competitive data.

This is a tremendous amount of data to collect and interpret. The categories may also appear familiar; they are basically the same as those we examined in marketing audits (e.g., the audit outline in Kotler et al., 1977). Indeed, we believe the ideal time to prepare a performance index is in the course of an audit, largely because the audit will gather most of the information the person composing the index will need. However, we also believe it is possible to do some thoughtful self-evaluation via questionnaire, and to this end, have prepared the instrument and instructions in Appendix B for both researchers and managers interested in pursuing the topic further. We are presently preparing to establish a national-level database on marketing quality with this instrument in order to generate the kind of large-sample data necessary to make normative statements.

Summary

We outlined in this chapter a set of beginning methodological issues encountered when translating the MPA model from theory to operational measures, and suggested some ways in which to resolve those issues. The components of satisfaction, results, and expectations are relatively easy to measure, although some thought must be given to whose expectations are to be measured and how the expectations of different managers at different levels in the hierarchy are to be reconciled. Effort is measurable with somewhat more difficulty as the compound function of the quality of marketing structures for "automatic" execution of programs, and the execution skills of the program managers. External variables, such as quality of competitive response, distribution channel efficacy, and environmental change, can also be made to submit to our measure, even if with some difficulty.

The important point here is not so much that elegant measurement systems can be constructed for the MPA model, but rather that the model appears to be methodologically robust whether complicated measures or simple self-report scales are used to assess its parameters. This may allow it to be used in both management and research endeavors, though the former depends on whether the model generates "right-sounding" predictions for managers, while the latter revolves around whether disconfirmable propositions can be constructed. But before we look at the implications of the model in both management and research, we first present the available evidence about its plausibility.

Chapter 8
Early Data: Clinical Evidence

Introduction

One of the first steps we took in refining the model was to conduct preliminary field research. The result has been three case studies (reprinted in full in Appendix A): Gillette Personal Care Division: Marketing Planning and Control; LifeSpan, Inc.: Abbott Northwestern Hospital; and Hurricane Island Outward Bound School. We have also conducted a handful of structured interviews and a small test mailing using earlier versions of the questionnaire printed in Appendix B, which together gave us anecdotal data on over thirty marketing programs. Finally, we discussed the model extensively with selected executives and academic colleagues. We do not dignify these approximately 250 discussions with the term "interview," for they were either unstructured or else followed a presentation of the rudiments of the model to a group of executives followed by a discussion and critique of its parameters. The overall intent of the case studies, questionnaire, and discussions was simply to do a "plausibility check" on the relatively different path we chose to follow in constructing the MPA model.

We had two specific goals in doing clinical field research. First, we wanted to discover whether the variables we considered important in marketing performance appraisal were important to others, reflecting how operating managers thought about their marketing programs as they evaluated them in an everyday context. Second, we wanted to learn whether, within the constraints of the clinical method, such evidence as we could gather would roughly confirm that the variables interacted in the way we postulated. If these two confirmations could be made, we would take encouragement from the clinical data and informal discussions. More important, we would take away data that might help us develop a more scientific measurement instrument for future information gathering.

Although all the variables considered theoretically important in the MPA model did appear in various ways throughout our cases and interviews, the use of the variables in performance assessment in each of the cases shows some deviations both from the model as postulated and from each other. For now, the observations in this chapter must be called speculative and exceedingly preliminary; the next phase of our research will produce more solid data to answer the questions raised here.

Summary of the Cases

The Gillette case examines the marketing planning and control systems of a major packaged-goods manufacturer, using the examples of a recent new product launch (White Rain shampoo and conditioner) and a "restage" of an established brand (Right Guard deodorant). The former program had been judged highly successful by Gillete managers, while the latter was scaled back after one year.

For LifeSpan, Inc., we show the efforts of a major nonprofit hospital's marketing department to evaluate its contribution to the hospital's recent success. At the case's beginning, the department manager's budget request has been turned down because LifeSpan's president confesses he sees no link between marketing's efforts and actual improvement in performance.

The Hurricane Island Outward Bound School investigation illustrates a conflict over goals and actions within a small nonprofit service organization as it plans its marketing in the wake of a financial crisis. Financial concerns clash with long-held service values as the new marketing director contemplates his first annual marketing plan for the organization.

Importance of the Variables

Results

Results are important to performance judgments in each of the three case studies, but one of the things that has struck us in the field is that, despite the four general measures we mentioned at the end of Chapter 7, these measures were calculated and weighed differently by different organizations, and sometimes by different managers within the same organization.

This might be expected in nonprofit organizations such as LifeSpan or Outward Bound. Kanter and Summers (1987) point out, and we agree, that defining performance measures for nonprofits is especially difficult because such organizations typically evaluate themselves against their service mission rather than a financial return, and these services are "notoriously intangible and difficult to measure" (p. 154). Some administrators at Hurricane Island, for example, measure success in terms of the number of students served and the demographic mix of the student body; others look at revenue figures. At LifeSpan, managers examine such standard business measures as market share, profit, and awareness, but are also concerned with such service-specific issues as bed utilization and the number of patient referrals received from rural doctors.

As we suggested above, one of the reasons that marketing effectiveness measures receive so little scrutiny in for-profit organizations is that "everyone knows" sales and/or profit are the critical barometers. In looking at the Gillette data, however, we were surprised at the diversity of answers we received in response to a question we routinely asked: "How do you know if a marketing program is good?" The "Informal Measures" section of the case demonstrates some of this variety both in differing measures and in relative emphases on agreed-upon measures.

Expectations

Beyond doubt, the question of the role of expectations in marketing performance appraisal provoked the most discussion and received the strongest confirmation from case clinical data, interviews, and questionnaires. In discussion, general managers adamantly insisted that their own and program managers' expectations, whether formalized in the budget submission or not, were key to their resulting determination of whether a marketing program was effective. The case data show not only this same power of expectations, but a recurrent kind of goal conflict that produced muddled program expectations in several instances.

The Hurricane Island Outward Bound case is a good example of the evolution of expectations from policies of identity and policies of direction, as we discussed in Chapter 7. Led by a founder repeatedly referred to as a "visionary," the school retains a powerful core mission of serving youth and the underprivileged. Unfortunately, these populations are unable to pay the costs of providing the services from which they can benefit. Stagnant enrollment figures in the late 1970s, combined with growing operating deficits in the early 1980s, led to a formal upgrading of marketing within the school, and eventually, a corporate reorganization. The sense of identity at the school remains a service one, but the new direction is a financial one. The desire for growth, to serve more and more students, contends with the fact that the areas in which the school would most like to grow are not self-financing. Therefore, marketing looks elsewhere to generate revenues. As predicted by the model, this conflict leads to conflicting goals and expectations, especially as demonstrated in the case's "Evaluating Marketing Tactics" section. This, in turn, makes program evaluation a difficult business, for it is possible for any one program like expanding executive education to satisfy one set of objectives (profit) while it grossly fails at another (serving disadvantaged populations).

LifeSpan's Abbott Northwestern Hospital, on the other hand, had more focused goals: while it has a service ethic, the organization prides itself on its size and expertise in the Minneapolis/St. Paul (Minnesota) area, and wishes to become an even more potent regional force in health care. Already the largest private hospital in the Twin Cities, the organization's immediate marketing goal is to increase market share further in its specialty areas. As one executive puts it: "While the party line is human service, it is vital that we meet the bottom line." This makes program evaluation easier, for there is a more generally agreed-upon yardstick against which to measure, for instance, Medformation. There is goal conflict as well, however. The case does not give us much idea of physicians' viewpoints, but these health care vendors, a prime customer group for the hospital, might on the whole not agree with this bald an assertion about health care's purpose.

Among the three organizations, it is at Gillette that managers are most explicit about the role of expectations. We heard the following sentiments in interviews there: "A lot depends on expectations," one marketing manager notes; "one of the reasons White Rain has been

such a success is that no one expected it to do so well." Agreeing, White Rain's current manager remarks, "For all the excitement, it's still only a 3 [percent] share in the total market. A 3 share is not much."

These expectations arise from both an elaborate planning process and ongoing interpersonal negotiations about what should be expected from brand management's actions. As part of the planning and budgeting process, brands are placed in strategic categories somewhat similar to the Boston Consulting Group scheme described in Chapter 3. This decision is in turn partially based on sometimes intense negotiation among the marketing, sales, and market research departments. These three departments develop unit volume forecasts that are a major component of the marketing plan. As one manager explained it, "The brand knows the programs, [Market Research] knows the division history with similar products, and Sales knows the current environment." There is, as another manager notes, a great deal of "reasoning by analogy." Brand history and division experience with similar products play great roles in setting expectations. Eventually, the expectations incorporated in the plan are at least the basis of the ones against which results are evaluated.

Gillette was one of the organizations where we encountered the question we mentioned in Chapter 7 of whether expectations as codified in budgets were the same as management's real expectations. Because of the negotiations and differences of opinion about the prospective performance of brands, it seemed reasonable that expectations might differ as well. In asking various Gillette managers about this, we received three different answers: (1) "The budget is the real number, the best number available against which to evaluate results"; (2) "The budget is in a range of reasonable numbers for the brand, and so is good enough"; and (3) "I don't think the budget numbers are right, but we can't manage without some agreed-upon budget number."

This difference of opinion over whether budget expectations were the "right" ones to measure was paralleled in a broader executive concern over measuring individual managers' expectations. We received feedback from a number of executives who thought that if the MPA model could delineate a range of expectations rather than a point estimate, it would better mirror the program expectations held by different executives in the firm. We agree that a range of expectations is probably a more accurate way of operationalizing the expectations variable, but we do not think we do grievous harm by averaging point estimates to get a sense of the range for measurement purposes. As to budget numbers, it remains our inclination not to use them in measuring expectations unless no more direct measure is available. We think it better to assess program expectations directly, free of the politics and jockeying that budgeting processes engender.

There is a question, too, of what one executive called the "gaming style" of the managers involved. Some managers "never oversell," while others are less disciplined. After a while, senior managers get a feel for whose numbers they can trust, and whose include a "fudge factor." While this makes measurement more difficult, it is a good illustration of why we think simple measurements against budget are suspect.

Another comment we received was that "wrong" or "bad" expectations would lead to suboptimal performance no matter what the marketing department did, according to our model. An organization that was "fat, dumb, and happy" would have expectations that were too low relative to actual opportunities in its environment. Performance indices would be lower because there would be no push to exceed inaccurate expectations, while vulnerability to competition would be high. Overly optimistic expectations, on the other hand, would lead to lower performance indices as results could not achieve the level that expectations dictated. Both these propositions are true, and both illustrate why we call the model an implementation-based assessment of marketing performance. Inaccurate expectations are the result of vague policies of identity and direction, particularly strategy. This model does not measure the efficacy of strategy; rather, it measures the efficiency and effectiveness of marketing programs in light of strategy. Thus, the marketing performance index will often not reveal an organization that is "fat, dumb, and happy," except in the sense that it will show its marketing performance to be moderate at best.

Finally, interviews and discussions suggest that cross-time comparisons of expectations would be difficult because of the effect past expectations have on current ones. One senior manager described this kind of interaction as "a snake with its tail in its mouth."

Both the case data and our executive discussions seem to indicate that expectation level is a powerful component of marketing performance assessment.

Skills and Structures

Obviously, companies have marketing managers with some level of skills, and marketing support structures to help these managers. The higher the degree of structural adequacy relative to a program, we hypothesize, the less management skill will be needed. We can see the evolution of structural adequacy in the course of a product life cycle. On a new product launch in a new company (the proverbial "start-up"), for example, the need for management skill will be high because there will be no structures or rules in place upon which management can rely. Everything is done manually rather than automatically. Because successful behavior patterns are not known for either the firm or the new product, there is literally nothing to routinize. Basically, whenever a company does something new, the task will require more skilled management because structured patterns of behavior will be unavailable. In more established companies, even new product launches are not terribly demanding, for the firm has over the years built numerous systems to help routinize the launch task, which becomes simply a matter of management's doing the job "by the numbers." Most of our cases fell somewhere between these two extremes.

In the Gillette case, for example, the structures were not fast enough to get White Rain launched on time. J. D. Grinnell personally shepherded the White Rain launch through the company to make the scheduled launch date. That required more effort for him and his managers, but the time pressure made the extra effort worth it. One can argue as well that LifeSpan illustrates an organization's attempt to define useful behaviors (in the form of advertising expenditure guidelines) so they can be structured in the future.

As a product matures, the organization begins to learn the useful marketing behaviors for that product. The organization develops system-level structures such as distribution networks. It promulgates subfunction rules such as a discount for retailers of "40 percent off retail price" rather than "subject to negotiation." Thus Philip Chin, who manages the marketing for $5 million in sales in the Hurricane Island Outward Bound case, is stretched thin, while Pat Flaherty and three assistants smoothly administer a $70 million business in the Gillette case; Chin has few support structures, whereas Flaherty has many. It is particularly telling to compare the exhibits in the Hurricane and Gillette cases. In the former, the school's marketing information is quite limited, while Gillette managers, some students have suggested, have more information than they need. Somewhere in between in capability, LifeSpan has few rules or structures for marketing, but has a complex financial capability that allows marketers to know their sales and costs intimately.

When we decomposed the model to its parts in Chapter 7, we remarked that while the cost of a program was the quotient of skills/structures, the likelihood of developing a good program would be the sum of skills and structures. We came to this realization as we talked with managers in the course of our case research. Managers were wary of the idea of maximizing structures and minimizing skills. While they agreed in theory that the direct cost of a program could be skills/structures, they were concerned that anything other than maximum skills and maximum structures would produce less satisfactory results. Managers were wary of experimenting in this area, regardless of the model's predictions. As one put it:

> Here, if we think there are six factors that might affect results, we try to maximize all six rather than use one and hold all the others constant to see if that one might be important. . . . I want them to experiment on someone else's brands.

Some managers felt as well that effort, as measured by expenditure, was simply a less important variable than management satisfaction with results. Said one, "I wouldn't get any extra points for doing it [making planned results] with less money. I wouldn't lose any points for doing it with more." Another manager at the same company cautioned further, "Never volunteer to cut [expenditures] . . . then they'd want more profit next year." Maximizing results/effort ran a distant second to maximizing results/expectations in this manager's mind for his organization. A preliminary questionnaire

tentatively supported this view. Whether this is an insight of more general merit awaits better data.

Quality of Competitive Response

That competitive actions are important is beyond question, and both the case and executive data indicate this is so. That companies account for competitive surprises in evaluating marketing programs is much less certain. This is particularly evident in the Gillette case. Both White Rain and Right Guard were significantly affected by competitive surprises, but these surprises appear to have been largely ignored by general management in evaluating the success of the programs. In White Rain's case, the shampoo's regional test market was buoyed by an unexpected price increase on the part of chief rival Suave from Helene Curtis. Right Guard, on the other hand, was buffeted by unexpectedly intense competitive activity, including a 45 percent increase in advertising by its main competitor, Mennen. However, these elements of good and bad fortune did not appear to reduce marketing performance evaluations for White Rain or increase it for Right Guard. Remarked one senior executive, "Even though some of the things are beyond [the manager's] control, we believe most are under his or her control."

The absence of competitor information in the Hurricane Island case is marked, but not all nonprofit organizations are so hampered. LifeSpan at least has information on market share and image on many of its competitors, and is aware of competitor price policies. Still, competitive reaction to specific programs at LifeSpan's Abbott Northwestern Hospital, such as Medformation and WomenCare, goes unnoted insofar as the case reports the data in management's thinking about the evaluation of the Medformation programs.

Partners: Channel Response

There seems little doubt that the strength of distribution channel partners has increased relative to manufacturers in the last ten years. Sophisticated financial modeling, increasing consolidation of distributors and retailers in many industries, and growing use of scanners that read universal product codes have all passed both information and power to the downstream members of the channel. Manufacturing company marketing executives mourn the old days:

It used to be that manufacturers had a lot more power. They were big, and they had information. We would go into accounts and tell them what was selling. Now all the retail chains are gobbling up the independents, so they're bigger. And, with scanners, they have the information. We go in and they tell us what's selling.

Agreed another:

It used to be you could get away with many more facings than a brand might have earned because the brand was established and retailers thought it was big even if it actually wasn't. Now, with scanners and DPP [direct product profitability] models, when your sales drop, your shelf space disappears like that.

In the LifeSpan case, we see a hospital caught in the midst of a dramatic change in the distribution of health care. Whereas health care was once distributed primarily by physicians in private practice who maintained relationships with local hospitals, by 1985 health maintenance organizations (HMOs) had grown to account for 41 percent of the Minneapolis/St. Paul market, nearly four times the national average.

Obviously, trade relations are crucial to any company that does not distribute its own products or services. Executives at Gillette frequently use the word "trust" to characterize the most important measure of channel response. Good experiences with previous marketing programs from an organization can smooth entry of a new program. Bad experiences can doom it.[23]

In Gillette, however, the channel's reaction is considered neither an obstacle nor an enhancement to marketing efforts. Rather, some of what we see in the Gillette case suggests that it is considered marketing's job to make the channel an enthusiastic partner. One of Right Guard's failures was not generating trade enthusiasm for the restage, for example. The implication is that when the trade doesn't "jump for joy" at the sight of the program, it is the program's fault. We think this is unnecessarily harsh—channel members may have many reasons for not pushing a company's product—but it does fit with the idea that managers are sometimes responsible for things over which they have little control.

Channel importance in LifeSpan depends to a great degree on how the channel composition

is construed. If it is construed narrowly, to mean only HMOs, then there is middling but very unimpressive evidence of channel importance affecting the evaluation of marketing programs such as Medformation. If, however, the channel is construed broadly to include Abbott's physicians and other primary health deliverers, then the channel is seen of exceeding importance, and indeed, the entire reason for Medformation's existence (physician referral). In fact, Medformation itself could be called a channel-directed program, and in this sense, one would believe that physician reactions to Medformation loomed large in management's mind in calling the programs effective.

Environment

Case research and common sense both suggest that unexpected environmental changes can wreak havoc upon (or strongly support) marketing programs. The many products now aimed at so-called baby boomers, for example, pin their hopes for success on the demographic phenomenon of a "bulge" moving through the population structure of the United States. The power of the environment was confirmed by numerous interviewees and questionnaire respondents as well.

Of the cases, LifeSpan demonstrates most dramatically the effect of environmental changes on a marketplace. As we noted above, the distribution channels for health care are changing rapidly. The major reason for this distribution change is the revolution in health care financing caused by the Medicare and Medicaid reforms of the early 1980s. Cost containment concerns of major private insurers played a role as well. The low-cost operations of HMOs won approval from these major health care financiers, and were also tremendously popular with consumers. The dramatic growth of HMOs pushed a restructuring in the health care industry, linking doctors, hospitals, and insurance plans in "managed health care systems." In addition, an oversupply of physicians has changed the role of doctors. These events were beyond the power of LifeSpan's marketing managers; indeed, one may argue from the case that the changes are what provoked the need for marketing managers in the first place. In this sense, management was very responsive to our ENV variable.

Once again, though, LifeSpan seems not to have a way of incorporating environmental impact in a formal performance measure for marketing. The president's objection at the case's

---

23. For an interesting economic analysis of trust networks, see Wintrobe and Breton (1986).

beginning suggests that the organization has little feel for how marketing affects its overall performance, which is perhaps not surprising given that marketing is a recent phenomenon in the organization. Perhaps the best that can be said about the ENV variable is that there is good reason from the case data to continue to believe that it is important, but that the model of MPA we have derived may overstate management's current practices in taking it into account when evaluating its marketing programs.

Interaction of the Variables

Do interactions between variables implied by the model seem to apply in the real world? Case and other preliminary research cannot supply the answer to this question, but based on these limited data the answer is maybe. The clearest supporting evidence is available for the results versus expectations interaction, which case subjects universally cite and interviewees report as accurate, even if they are sometimes uncomfortable about its implications. Gillette shows one program wildly exceeding expectations and being hailed by management, while the other achieves mixed results and is denigrated. Likewise, Philip Chin in the Outward Bound case is definitely responsible for meeting a set of objectives.

Indeed, the big difference between the model and what we have explored in the field so far is that the results/expectations variable (satisfaction) dominates other variables in the minds of management as a key to program evaluation. Some managers do not care whether the effort expended is high so long as the program "makes the numbers." And competition, channel response, and the environment are often seen as "no excuse" for poor performance. One might hypothesize from this that the other variables are less important, and that we will need a system of empirical weights to adjust the model as necessary. We will test this in the next phase of our research.

An Illustrative Calculation

The information in the Gillette case is sufficient for us to perform a rough and completely illustrative calculation of marketing performance indices on White Rain and Right Guard. The exercise is instructive both in analyzing the case and in showing the assumptions that can

underlie such a calculation. In the absence of rigorous data on some variables, we make educated guesses. Clearly, we encourage neither academics nor managers in this practice, but rather recommend the more rigorous type of assessment we have proposed in our methods chapter and embodied in our questionnaire (Appendix B). The only purpose of the calculation here is to provide more information on how the various variables estimated by our model may be combined to support better judgments of marketing performance.

Starting with Right Guard's 1983 performance, we find that the first decision we have to make is which set of results and expectations to use. Exhibit 8 provides several possibilities, including share, shipments, sales, and contribution; because of the emphasis the division put on the declining market share, we choose it. Therefore, RES = 7.6 percent (from the actual 1983 figures) and EXP = 8.1 percent (from the 1983 plan forecasts—probably not a reflection of "real" expectations, but the only numbers available). Note that this is the most pessimistic set of figures regarding the program.

There is no particular evidence in the Right Guard situation to suggest either that managerial skills dominated structures or that marketing structures dominated skills, although one does get the feeling the relaunch was done "by the book." The restage arose through the normal planning processes and was based on an existing brand with which the organization had extensive experience, but it also required a fair amount of effort to plan and implement because it was a wholly new program with some complicated components. We thus leave SKL and STR in equilibrium with each other, say at 90 percent potential each.

There is strong evidence, however, that Right Guard faced unexpectedly adverse competitive conditions, especially the huge advertising campaign put out by chief competitor Mennen. Let us say, then, that QCR is 1.20, or 20 percent stronger than expected. Partner and Environmental effects seem largely insignificant, so we leave them at 1.00. This gives us a marketing performance of

$$MP = \frac{RES/EXP}{SKL/STR}$$

$$\times\ QCR \times PTR \times ENV$$

$$MP = \frac{7.6/8.1}{.90/.90} \times 1.20 \times 1.00 \times 1.00 = 1.13.$$

For White Rain's 1985 national rollout, we have fewer measures in Exhibit 9 than we had for Right Guard in Exhibit 8. For results and expectations, we use "total brand shipments." Once again, this is a more pessimistic measure than using shampoo and conditioner results and expectations alone. Since the case suggests that the shampoo also helped the hair spray, including hair spray shipments seems appropriate. We therefore have 41.6 million units actually shipped in 1985, while the brand expected only 31.4 million units.

Unlike Right Guard, White Rain obviously had a dominance of skills over structures as J. D. Grinnell personally negotiated the launch through the system to get it out on time; the structures were too slow to help very much. So, let us say SKL = 1.00, while STR = .90.

We will also assume that any favorable effect from Suave's price increase in 1984 has dissipated in 1985, making QCR = 1.00. PTR and ENV remain at 1.00. This gives us

$$MP = \frac{41.6/31.4}{1.00/.90} \times 1.00 \times 1.00 \times 1.00 = 1.19.$$

Thus, while White Rain is a success by MPA standards (assuming 1.00 is standard or neutral), so to a lesser degree is Right Guard. This fits management's retrospective views on the Right Guard program—senior Gillette managers today do not call Right Guard a failure. Rather, they claim that there were other opportunities in 1984 that deserved money more than Right Guard did. The interpretation that Right Guard's restage was simply a failure is better supported by a simple RES/EXP measure, in this case 7.6/8.1 = .94. (White Rain is even more of a success if RES/EXP is examined alone: 41.6/31.4 = 1.32.)

These sample calculations demonstrate that the model, while elegant, is sensitive to changing assumptions. Changing educated guesses or the measures of results would produce different performance indices. Of course, MPA should be done not on educated guesses by outsiders, but by measures and judgments of managers.

We think the preliminary data indicate that there is some question as to whether the full model, or just the satisfaction measure, best explains marketing performance *as currently construed by managers*. Survey research (see Appendix B for a copy of our preliminary research instrument) should reveal whether the full model or the RES/EXP component best describes performance assessment for marketing. The fact that the initial data do not necessarily point to the importance of trade, competitor, or environmental variables as clearly as they do to the managerial judgment variables should not be surprising, given the tentative nature of the preliminary data we used to check the model's plausibility. Managers we interviewed were unanimous in their support of the external variables as posited. However, it remains a matter for empirical determination just how important these external modifiers are to marketing performance. Should they turn out not to be in favor, it is a fascinating empirical task to see if their inclusion can improve marketing performance assessment.

Conclusion

Overall, we take both the clinical case data and returns from our interviews and test mailing as strong confirmation of the thrust of the overall model, generally strong confirmation of the presence of the variables postulated by it, and mixed or just "no comment" on some of the important interactions postulated by the model. It remains, with this generally encouraging preliminary plausibility check, to do the difficult spadework that may allow the first cross-firm, cross-industry database of marketing performance statistics to be constructed. That is the task before us.

Chapter 9

Some Preliminary Research Propositions, Managerial Implications, and Hypotheses from the MPA Model

Introduction

This section explores the preliminary implications and hypotheses that follow from the MPA model and our initial case research. It is divided into a set of research propositions for further research, and a set of managerial guidelines that arise from the model propositions. The section concludes with some specific implications of the model for managers.

Research Propositions

The research ideas presented here represent straightforward propositions that come from a derivational analysis of the MPA model, expanded ones that follow from the marketing implementation framework within which the model has been built, and speculative propositions about possible nonorthogonalities between the model's components that might be predictively useful.

Derivative Propositions. Table 12 shows some of the model's more straightforward predictions. These are broken down into single-factor and interactive effects. Along with the following propositions, the table simply derives from the model's formulation. Of course, both need independent confirmation.

Proposition 1. The stronger the results of any given marketing program, all other things equal, the higher the marketing performance.

This proposition is simply a necessary consequence of our derivation, which places results in the numerator of a complex fraction defined as marketing performance. Clearly, the larger the numerator, the higher the marketing performance.

Table 12   Factors Affecting Marketing Performance (Derived from the MPA Model)

Factors Increasing Performance	*Factors Decreasing Performance*
Single-variable factors	
• Strength of marketing results	• Need for strong execution skills
• Modesty of expectations	• High or unrealistic expectations
• Structural adequacy	• Weak or overly flexible marketing structures
• Strength of competitive response	• Weak competitive response
• Poor channel response	• Good channel response
• Unfavorable environment	• Favorable environment
• Stable environment (allows better structures)	• Unstable environment (requires more skill)
Interactive variables	
• Results exceeding expectations	• Expectations exceed results
• Results exceeding effort	• Effort dominates results
• Structures dominate skills	• Skills dominate structures

[handwritten annotation: flexible does not imply weak]

Proposition 2. The higher management's expectations for a given marketing program, the lower the adjudged marketing performance of that program, all other things equal.

This proposition is again implied by the placement of expectations in the denominator of the fraction defining satisfaction. However, the hypothesis is in no way intuitive, and is one of the more provocative implications of the model as proposed. As noted above, the model and its predictions explicitly incorporate management's goals for its programs as one important baseline against which results, and hence satisfaction, will be measured.

Proposition 3. Results divided by expectations is a good proxy for management's satisfaction with its marketing programs. The higher the satisfaction with a marketing program, the higher the adjudged performance.

This proposition can be read to suggest two different and important implications for marketing performance assessment. The first is that managerial satisfaction with marketing program outputs is a joint function of results factored by expectations, a derivational necessity of the model. The second is that operationally, it is possible to find good correlations between the quotient of results and expectations and any independent measurement of management satisfaction obtained by more direct means. Clearly, both implications of this proposition are eminently disconfirmable and in need of the kind of cross-industry and cross-management testing we proposed above.

To the extent that these implications are confirmed by evidence, however, a powerful joint construct of satisfaction is validated for use in MPA. Essentially, satisfaction is the "gap" between what was desired, expected, and planned for and management's evaluation of the results of a given marketing program. The model is explicit in its predictions that the more results exceed expectations, the higher the adjudged marketing performance.

Proposition 4. Effort, the denominator of the marketing performance equation, is measurable as the joint function of the adequacy of marketing's routinizations or "structures" and the skills of the managers doing the marketing job. These two factors operate in a kind of hydraulic tension, such that greater structural adequacy allows for less of the customized management by exception, problem-solving program management that occurs when implementation skills are regularly exercised by marketers. Structural solutions are always cheaper than skill solutions. As a result,

Proposition 4a. The lower the effort expended in achieving a given level of satisfaction, the higher the adjudged performance of a given program.

Proposition 4b. The higher the structural, systemic, or routinizable elements of a marketing program relative to skills, the lower the effort and the higher the marketing performance.

Proposition 4c. The higher the need for management's continual and constant intervention in programmatic concerns to produce results by the exercise of "exception skills," the higher the effort and lower the marketing performance.

These propositions make a number of assertions and carry some provocative implications, all of them testable and all needing confirmation. As to assertions, effort is held to be a joint function of structural adequacy and the skills of the managers doing the marketing job. Also, the model claims that structural engagements of a marketing program are cheaper and, hence, easier to effect than the kind of "exception management" that occurs when marketers must constantly exercise their personal execution skills to keep a program on track. Among the implications of these propositions is the notion that situations of high uncertainty, such as when the rate of environmental change is great, or when a product is new, will produce lower marketing performance because more management intervention will be necessary in the face of situations that are impossible to systematize. The penalty for new products is an example of why we call the model an evaluation of execution relative to strategy rather than of long-term strategy itself. A company may elect to suffer lower performance for some time in the interest of building a position in a market. The MPA model will reveal the level of performance, but will not show the ultimate effectiveness of the strategy.

A second implication of this concept of effort is that it is possible that there may be a difference in the personnel found in companies with strong and adequate structures versus weak and flexible ones—in firms with strong structures we might expect to find, for instance, more junior, lower-paid, or less experienced (i.e., less skilled) managers than in the latter.

Additionally, the positive correlation between strength of structures and skill levels of marketing management needs independent confirmation despite Bonoma's (1985a) strong clinical evidence that this relationship holds. What he found, paradoxically, was that strongly structured companies tended to have the most, not the least, skilled managers, a result in some conflict with our speculative implication about managerial skills and structural dominance. One possible explanation of Bonoma's clinical findings is his contention (1986) that the best managers "subvert" marketing structures when necessary. Presumably the stronger the structures, the more skill a manager needs to subvert them.

Proposition 5. Not only internal marketing factors, but also factors external to the firm affect marketing performance.

Proposition 5a. Higher quality of the competitive response, QCR, increases performance because program results are achieved despite strong competition.

Proposition 5b. Marketing partners are powerful factors enhancing or detracting from management's marketing efforts. More receptive or higher-quality partner response decreases marketing performance because results are achieved partly through the good fortune of having enthusiastic or skilled partners rather than through the firm's efforts.

Proposition 5c. The general color and character of the environment affects marketing productivity as well, in two ways. First, unanticipated environmental changes affect marketing performances beneficially or detrimentally (usually the latter). Beneficial effects lower marketing performance, while detrimental effects heighten performance. Second, high rates of environmental change will cause this variable and performance as a whole to vary more widely, because predictions of environmental impacts on marketing will be more difficult.

Again, these propositions are derivative from the model itself; their logic has been explained at greater length in the derivation and measurement sections. However, it is useful to note here that the MPA model suggests *marketing* performance, at least, is most stable in a monopoly, for there is no competitor with whom to be concerned, and few environmental changes that can act as negative surprises for the manufacturer. In addition, the model reaffirms the importance of the channel and other service firms as marketing partners that can mute or intensify management's best-laid efforts to reach the customer.

Implications from a Marketing Implementation Framework. Table 13 shows a much more complete decomposition of the model to its base of marketing implementation constructs, and how each factor is presumed to affect marketing performance.

Regarding satisfaction, Bonoma's marketing policies of direction and identity are presumed to be implicated in the expectations levels that management sets. Policies of direction, in Bonoma's (1985a) terms, relate to the strategy that the firm sets for itself and also to the quality of leadership with which the marketing effort is run. Unclear or inappropriate strategies, obviously, lead to either unclear or wrongly set expectations, which are in turn likely to be at variance with produced results and hence to lead to lowered marketing performance. (Our experience suggests that unpleasant surprises are much more likely than pleasant ones.) Less obviously, weak or inadequate leaders in the marketing function, where that function has its own leadership, or in general management for smaller companies, leads to exactly the same thing. Hence,

Proposition 6. Policies of direction (strategy and leadership) are directly implicated in the setting of expectations for marketing programs. Specifically,

> *Proposition 6a.* Unclear or inappropriate strategies result in unclear or inappropriate expectations, and the gap between expectation and results is thus maximized.
>
> *Proposition 6b.* Weak or ineffective leadership has the same effect as unclear or inappropriate strategy.

Similarly, policies of identity affect marketing performance. Identity, as we discussed above, represents the theme and culture of the marketing organization. These in turn arise from the history of the organization and the attitudes of the managers who run the organization. Vague or conflicting identity leads to vague or inappropriate expectations, leading to (probably) poorer marketing performance.

Proposition 7. Policies of identity (theme and culture) are directly implicated in the setting of expectations for marketing programs. Vague or conflicting identities result in vague or inappropriate expectations, which maximizes the gap between expectations and results.

Looking down Table 13 to the effort variable, it can be seen that Bonoma's previous work on marketing implementation allows both structures and skills to be decomposed further than the global variables we have been working with might suggest. Specifically, structural sufficiency is seen as a joint function of structural soundness at each of Bonoma's four "levels of marketing" in the firm: subfunctions or actions, programs, systems, and policies. Managerial marketing skills can likewise be decomposed into the four "implementation skills" that Bonoma identified as being critical to getting the marketing job done: interacting, allocating, monitoring, and organizing.

Proposition 8. Structural sufficiency is definable as an equally weighted sum of action, program, system, and policy sufficiencies. Higher

levels of routinization in each of these increases structural sufficiency, which in turn lowers effort and increases marketing performance. Lower levels increase effort and decrease marketing performance.

Some may wonder why we believe that subfunctional sufficiency, in particular, contrib-

Table 13 Productivity Effects of Each Model Component, Expanding the Model Consistent with a Marketing Implementation Framework

Factor	Level	Effect
Satisfaction	High	Raises
	Low	Lowers
Results	High	Raises
	Low	Lowers
Expectations	High	Lowers
	Low	Raises
Policies of direction	High	Depends
	Low	Depends
Policies of identity	High	Depends
	Low	Depends
Results/expectations	High	Raises
	Low	Lowers
Effort	High	Lowers
	Low	Raises
Structural sufficiency	High	Raises
	Low	Lowers
Subfunctions	High	Raises
	Low	Lowers
Programs	High	Raises
	Low	Lowers
Systems	High	Raises
	Low	Lowers
Policies	High	Raises
	Low	Lowers
Skills	High	Lowers
	Low	Raises
Interacting	High	Lowers
	Low	Raises
Allocating	High	Lowers
	Low	Raises
Monitoring	High	Lowers
	Low	Raises
Organizing	High	Lowers
	Low	Raises
External factors	Positive	Lowers
	Negative	Raises
Quality of competitive response	Positive	Lowers
	Negative	Raises
Quality of partner response	Positive	Lowers
	Negative	Raises
Environmental	Positive	Lowers
	Negative	Raises
Stability	High	Raises
	Low	Lowers

utes to lower programmatic effort, and hence, to heightened marketing performance, especially in view of our insistence that no subfunctional questions about effectiveness can be asked. There is no inconsistency in this view because, first, the model's derivation incorporates subfunctional routinizations into the effort denominator of the equation, which, it will be remembered, is concerned with marketing efficiency. Second, "good habits" about advertising, for example, will be reflected in all the programs the firm engages which call upon that subfunction, again meaning that higher subfunctional sufficiency of structure lowers programmatic efforts and hence heightens the adjudged performance of marketing programs.

Basically, proposition 8 simply restates what has been said earlier about structural sufficiency, but decomposes this overall construct into the elements of marketing's execution structures uncovered by Bonoma in previous work. It may or may not be valuable to measure structural sufficiency at levels below that of the overall construct, however.

Proposition 9. Marketers' management skills are defined as an equally weighted combination of interacting, allocating, monitoring, and organizing abilities. A higher usage level of each and any skill acts to increase effort and decrease marketing performance.

Looking at the skills lines in the table, the marketing implementation foundations of the model suggest that marketers' skills fall in four categories, and that each of these contributes to the marketing quality equation in the same manner. Clearly, this proposition is as commonsensically unrealistic as it is theoretically valid. Like everything else management does, any given marketing program has a character requiring more of the exercise of some skills, and less of others. Some programs with equal structural sufficiency, for instance, will be politically unacceptable for some managers in the firm, and may require more interacting than (say) monitoring skills for success. Other programs, such as one designed to take a retail optical vendor toward new "superstore" formats, may be only indifferently funded by the formal budgeting system, and may require many allocating adjustments by line management if they are to have a chance of success. While it is theoretically true that each marketing implementation skill should contribute equally to the chances of success for any program, in practice we might

expect that some skills will dominate in one program and others in another. Nonetheless, it is useful to make a beginning decomposition of the rather grand term "skills" into something more narrow and measurable.

One strong advantage of the MPA model is its foundation in years of clinical research work into the determinants of marketing implementation. As we have noted time and again, this work does not comment on the causes of effective marketing practice, but it has been useful in identifying (1) a framework within which to think about problems of marketing practice, and (2) some correlates of effective marketing practice, both of which mightily enrich the present model.

Speculative Relationships and Propositions. After the derivational and foundational propositions are mined, the MPA model still remains a rich lode of further propositions, admittedly more speculative but by the same token more interesting. Many of these arise because of probable second-order-and-beyond interactions between the variables thought to be implicated in judging marketing performance. Figures 8, 9, 10, and 11 graphically present four major areas in which some interesting interactional thinking about MPA might be captured. They are, respectively, the interaction of effort and expectation with outcomes, the interaction of the consumption of resources and performance, the relationship between strategic promises and results, and the relationship between marketing plans and management efforts.

An explicit attempt has been made in this section to go beyond the usual kinds of predictions made by academics in two directions. The first is to make predictions that we believe have immediate utility to managers, who have to do or to supervise the marketing job, as opposed to academics, who only have to study it. The second is to go beyond the model to take into account those things we have observed, both in the marketing implementation development work and in our clinical work leading to the development of the MPA model, about managerial judgment, psychology, and reaction to various effort, reward, expenditure, and outcome conditions. Some of the propositions offered here, therefore, are much more tenuous than those given above. All are consistent with the model's derivation and implications.

Effort and Expectation. Figure 8 shows the hypothesized triple interaction of effort, expectation,

Figure 8 Effort and Expectation under Two Outcome Conditions

High Outcomes

Management's Expectations Are	Perceived Effort is High	Perceived Effort is Low
High	Expected Plan and execution are okay	Expected Superior planning credited
Low	Gratified Superior execution and line management credited	Suspicious Low-ball plan is suspected; or, management is elated

Low Outcomes

Management's Expectations Are	Perceived Effort is High	Perceived Effort is Low
High	Disappointed Plan or strategy is suspected	Disappointed Execution is suspected
Low	Expected Plan and execution are okay	Expected Execution is suspected

and results as two two-by-two matrices, one under high outcomes (top) and one under low outcomes (bottom). The two matrices can be summarized in the following propositions:

Proposition 10. Under high outcome and high expectations conditions, management will report that the outcomes were expected regardless of management's perceived effort. But the locus of causality for those expectations will vary according to perceived management efforts:

> *Proposition 10a.* When outcomes and expectations are high, the perception of high effort by management in the marketing program will lead management to credit superior execution as the cause of the success.
> *Proposition 10b.* When perceived effort is low under these high outcome, high expectations conditions, however, management is likely to credit superior planning for its successes, for it cannot perceive the difficulty of the effort exerted by marketing.

With lower expectations, the outstanding results achieved must truly be regarded as a surprise by top management. Here again, perceived effort is believed to parcel the causal attributions:

Proposition 11. Under high outcome but low expectations conditions, management will either be grateful for the unanticipated success or else highly suspicious of the marketer's planning skills. Specifically,

> *Proposition 11a.* When outcomes are high, expectations low, and perceived effort high, management will credit marketers' superior execution, line management, and "exception management" skills with the successes attained.
> *Proposition 11b.* When outcomes are high, expectations low, and perceived effort low, management will suspect the marketers' plan of being a "low-ball" or "sandbagged" set of projections artificially lowering expectations to maximize satisfaction.

This set of propositions describes half of a theoretically complex interaction that is known to every line manager—the problem of managing the boss's expectations, the amount of effort

exerted and perceived by management,[24] and (to the extent possible) the results obtained. Overall, however, the top half of Figure 8 shows that the problems of high outcomes are welcome ones for most managers.

The bottom half of the figure explains what happens to these three variables under conditions of low outcomes. Specifically,

Proposition 12. When marketing outcomes are low and management's expectations high, disappointment (dissatisfaction) occurs regardless of the degree of perceived marketing effort. But, again, the causal attributions will differ depending on perceived effort:

> *Proposition 12a.* Under low outcome, high expectations, and high perceived effort conditions, management attributes marketing's program failure to the plan or strategy.
> *Proposition 12b.* Under low outcome, high expectations, and low perceived effort conditions, management attributes marketing's program failure to its execution of the program.

Again, the problem here is one of managing against expectations with effort, given unrewarding results.

We are not confident enough of our thinking here to assert with certainty that satisfaction will be heightened or lowered in each or any of these cells, but the choice of the terms "disappointment," "gratified," and suchlike is intended to indicate that we do believe each of the cells in the top and bottom half of the figure could be rank-ordered on satisfaction, and hence, marketing performance grounds. For example, in the bottom half of the figure, cells LB (left-bottom) and RB certainly produce higher satisfaction than LT (left-top) and RT. Furthermore, we believe that cell LB will produce more satisfaction than cell RB, and cell LT more than cell RT, since management values effort over less effort in its determination of satisfaction.

Consumption of Resources and Performance. Figure 9 shows a nine-cell matrix relating the consumption of resources to delivered outcomes. The entries in the matrix describe, *ceteris paribus,*

---

24. What is exerted is not always what is perceived. Many hourly laborers are not unfamiliar with the first-line supervisor's frequent admonition "Quick! Look busy—the bosses are coming!" during a slow period on the loading dock. The preceding discussion does not attempt to take into account the impression management process engaged in by all workers and indeed, by all individuals (see, e.g., Tedeschi et al., 1973, for a theoretical exposition).

Figure 9 The Consumption of Resources and Results

Resources Consumed Are

	Few	Moderate	Heavy
Results Delivered Are **High**	Suspicion or elation	Joy	Satisfaction
Medium	Joy	Satisfaction	Disappointment
Low	Satisfaction	Disappointment	Despair

Figure 10 The Relationship Between Strategy and Results

Management Delivers	Strategy Promises		
	Weak results	Industry historical average	Strong results
Strong results	Suspicion or elation	Joy	Satisfaction
Industry/historical average	Joy	Satisfaction	Disappointment
Weak results	Satisfaction	Disappointment	Despair

management's rough degree of satisfaction with the outcome states on the borders of the matrix: the amount of resources consumed by marketers and the results obtained. Three propositions describe the conclusions:

Proposition 13. The major relationship between consumed resources and delivered results is an equity one. Low resource consumption with low results, middling consumption with middling results, and high consumption with high results all produce an equivalent and positive amount of satisfaction in management.

This is best seen in the symmetrical entries on the main diagonal of the matrix.

Proposition 14. Moving northwest from the center of the matrix produces satisfaction-heightening outcomes; that is to say, reducing resource consumption or enhancing delivered results maximizes satisfaction.

This is another way of stating our "most with the least" derivation about satisfaction and effort above, here though restricted purely to results and to consumed resources.

Proposition 15. Moving southeast from the center of the matrix produces dissatisfaction. This is the obverse of proposition 13: heightened resource consumptions with lowered results is dissatisfying to those managing the marketing effort.

Note the "Suspicion or elation" entry in cell 1,1 of the figure. This entry suggests that there is a limit to what management is willing to believe, and functionally, that there is an asymptote to minimizing resources in the interests of maximizing management satisfaction. It is possible to go too far in one's striving to maximize revenues while reducing expense, as most marketers know.

Strategic Promises and Results. Figure 10 shows another nine-cell matrix, this one crossing the promises of marketing's program strategy against the results delivered in the program. The matrix is identical to that described for results and resource consumption, which in itself is quite interesting but should not be surprising as strategic plans also normally propose some realistic level of resource consumption for their realization. The following propositions are similar to the foregoing:

Proposition 16. As in proposition 13, the relation between results and strategic promises is an equity one. Low promises and low results, industry average promises and industry aver-

age results, and high promises and high results all produce an equivalent and positive amount of management satisfaction.

Proposition 17. Moving northwest from the center of the matrix produces satisfaction-heightening outcomes. That is to say, reducing strategic promises or enhancing delivered results maximizes satisfaction. Instead of concerning itself with the resource dimension, however, the strategic promises columns of the matrix are concerned with the grandiosity of marketing's promises to management. Again, synergy dominates the satisfaction-formation process.

Proposition 18. Moving southeast from the center of the matrix produces dissatisfaction. This is the obverse of proposition 17: heightened objectives or expectations with lowered results is dissatisfying to those managing the marketing effort.

In some ways, this set of propositions is a variant on the "under-promise and over-deliver" advice usually given to every starting manager. There is a real incentive, in this way of thinking, for formulating strategies that do not promise too much, and then over-delivering on them to general management. However, the difference between our model and other attempts to think about MPA is that we (1) account for these quite real-life psychological distortions in the MPA process, and (2) are willing to measure them and explicitly incorporate them in the determination of MPA.

Marketing Plans and Management Efforts. The final speculative set of predictions is shown in Figure 11. It formalizes the rank-ordering of general management satisfaction derived from various explicit targets promised in the marketing plan, and management's estimates of the effort that marketers expended to attain them. It is interesting to note that our model finds the usual under-promise, over-deliver cliché reconfirmable in a new form: under-promise, then over-commit. That is to say, we explicitly note that general management will credit effort even if it cannot attain results in assessing its satisfaction with the marketing program under consideration. Since this appears to be a flat contradiction of the model's derivation, which presumes that lowered effort leads to heightened marketing performance, it is useful to explore this potential nonorthogonality directly:

Proposition 19. Effort may enter the MPA

Figure 11 The Relationship Between Marketing Plans and Management Effort

Management's Execution Efforts Are	Marketing Plan Is: Conservative	Marketing Plan Is: Ambitious
Undercommitted	3* Self-fulfilling failure	4 Over-promise and under-deliver
Overcommitted	1 Under-promise and over-deliver	2 Over-promise and deliver

*The numbers in each cell rank-order that cell in terms of satisfaction.

equation in two forms. The first is the formal one, as the denominator of the compound fraction used to determine marketing performance. The second, however, is in an informal and more provocative way—as an enhancer of management satisfaction. That is to say, higher rather than lower levels of effort may make general management more comfortable with any perceived gaps between results and expectations, in effect acting to reduce any existing gaps because of the intensity of the attempt.

We are in no way certain, or even insistent, about this set of speculative propositions. However, our case clinical experience in both MPA development work and in the marketing implementation project convinces us that it is plausible to propound this dual role for effort, even though we do not and have not formally incorporated it in the numerator of the satisfaction-determination procedure. The matrix summarizes our current thinking on this variable.

Managerial Implications

To the extent that the research propositions generated by the model are validated, numerous managerial implications arise. These can be divided into insights for senior managers who supervise a number of programs, and for program managers themselves. Again, these are most tentatively advanced here only for their thought value—it is impossible to say if they are correct, or even likely, at the present time.

Implications for Senior Managers

As managers responsible for evaluating the results of many programs, senior managers can learn much from assessing programs using the MPA framework. As we suggested in Chapter 7, analyzing the patterns of the performance index's components can reveal a great deal of context that results measures alone do not demonstrate. Compiling data over time also offers insights. Managers may elect to do this using their own personnel or outsiders, as in a marketing audit. Even on a qualitative level the questionnaire in Appendix B may provoke some questions managers would want to ask themselves and their subordinates.

On a more abstract level, the thrust of MPA is that managers need to be aware of the context of program performance. One wants to know which programs were truly successful both to reward those programs' managers and to make allocation decisions for the future. Evaluating results versus expectations may show the performance and planning variances Hulbert and Toy (1977) suggest. Seriously examining effort may provide new insight for allocation improvement; as we noted in Chapter 8, a surprising number of executives seemed to care little about effort as long as results were adequate. Looking at external factors, and asking whether the same conditions or volatility are likely to hold in the future can be extremely useful; it is fine to be lucky once, but one cannot rely on continued fortune, and an unlucky program may be able to recover if it is given more resources.

It is also good to be aware of the evaluative biases and management pitfalls that some of the research propositions suggest. Some suggestions:

1. Make sure strategies are clear and leadership firm. Following research proposition 6, this suggests that the way to minimize the gap between results and expectations is to make sure everyone understands the strategy and to hew closely to it. Clarifying strategic goals not only assures that there will be something against which to compare results at the end of the period, but also tends to flush out any latent doubts concerning the wisdom of the strategy in the first place.

2. Be aware of the marketing themes and cultures affecting a program. This is especially important to managing a program with which the manager is unfamiliar. Following proposition 7, if a program or its parent company sees itself one way and the supervising manager sees the program differently, conflict can easily develop. Sometimes this is good—cultures can be dysfunctional, too—but the important thing is to not be surprised. By harmonizing differing views of the program's identity, or at least being aware of conflict where conflict exists, senior managers have clearer, more realistic expectations about program performance.

3. Routinize what can be routinized with sound systems and structures. According to the model, less effort is required when managers and systems have standard procedures to deal with management issues than when programs require continual interventions and exception-management. Systematizing what can be structured frees managers for the nonroutine tasks that always remain.

4. Managers should validate the accuracy of their perception of the relationship among expectations, results, and effort. Following propositions 10–12, senior managers should be aware that it is easy to misattribute the causes of performance, because the complicated relationship among expectations, outcomes, and perceived effort may bias their evaluation of programs. Knowledge of these potential biases should mitigate against such misattributions, allowing a clearer understanding of actual performance.

5. Do not worry too much about measures such as advertising effectiveness or sales efficiency as you go along; think instead in whole-program chunks. As long as the program as a whole is meeting or exceeding objectives, measures of individual components of the marketing mix are unimportant and in fact likely to be misleading. The true focus of MPA is at the program level, where all the mix elements come together in the service of a target market of the product. Individual pieces, like sales call frequencies or advertising intensity, can provide some piecemeal explanations about program efficiency, but they are inadequate measures of program effectiveness.

Implications for Program Managers

In many cases, especially at smaller firms, the program manager may be the senior manager for evaluative purposes. In those cases, the program managers would obviously be concerned with the above insights. For program managers who are part of a larger hierarchy, the model suggests several additional rules to follow in managing programs.

1. Set expectations correctly. Whether or not senior managers think as we do about MPA, our research shows that expectations are the single most important thing for marketers to manage. The best expectation for a marketing manager to plant in a senior manager's mind is something slightly less than the marketer thinks he or she can deliver. This gives the program some reserve in case of disaster, and some pleasant surprise value regularly.

2. Calibrate external modifiers carefully. Monitoring marketing channels, or partners, the competition, and the environment closely is not only sensible but paramount for effective marketing response. Competitors might not work on a firm's timetable, for instance, and may decide to mimic an especially effective pricing move midyear. Moreover, the channels may not be executing program plans, or may execute them in such a manner as to make original expectations unrealistic without some fast exception management. And, when markets move, they do so with the suddenness and lack of warning of mountain avalanches.

3. Routinize what can be routinized with sound systems and structures. As discussed above.

4. Always pick on weak competition when possible. Competitive reaction will almost always hurt a program; therefore, managers should pick on competitors who have little power to hurt them.

5. Choose supportive and pliant marketing partners. Although managers of individual marketing programs sometimes have little choice in making distribution selections, wherever possible they should find partners who will give their all to a program. This is likely under only one condition—if the partner needs the program desperately. The program can help assure this in a variety of ways, among them providing such central services that partners cannot do business without the program, or having an exclusive channel policy (where possible) that makes the program's choice of the partner an important competitive advantage. Sometimes this means you should not pick the industry leader for a partner; you may be more important to a smaller, hungrier company.

6. Be cautious in unstable markets. The more unstable the market, the lower a program's expectations should be for results. This is a simple rule which is often violated by program managers. Clearly, the more unstable the market, the higher the likelihood of pleasant surprises we all want, to make results really beat expectations. But it also follows that the more unstable the market, the higher the likelihood of unpleasant surprises that make even meager promises made a few quarters before look like the ravings of a lunatic.

7. Recast expectations as frequently as top management will allow it, and always in light of unanticipated external events. When something material happens externally, the marketing manager should immediately reassess the expectations set for the time period in question. In the case of a bad surprise, this allows the marketer to prepare senior managers for lower results or for a request for more resources to bring in the plan. In the case of a good surprise, the marketer can think about resource reallocation in light of the new information.

8. Do not worry too much about measures such as advertising effectiveness or sales efficiency as you go along; think instead in whole-program chunks. As discussed above.

9. Always try to do the most with the least. There is a real trend in larger firms toward "extravaganza management," where the most important program manager is he or she who commands the most resources, the highest staff count, and the like. This is madness from the point of view of effective program performance. The most powerful manager is not the person who spends the most or has the biggest revenue stream, but the one with the best results achieved at the *least* effort.

Conclusion

We have derived a number of propositions, many of them empirically testable without further operationalization, from the MPA model. These fall into three categories: (1) derivational propositions, (2) propositions resulting from further decomposition of the MPA model using its marketing implementation theory base, and (3) speculative, interactive, and especially relevant managerial propositions that the model appears to imply, but about which we are not convinced until they are submitted to rigorous testing.

Clearly, a number of other propositions, hypotheses, and putative empirical links could have been drawn. We have restricted ourselves to the most prominent, provocative, and we hope, useful ones in the hopes of stimulating management attention as well as marketing research. The reader interested in extending these propositions is invited to examine Appendix A, which contains three clinical case studies we performed while refining the model's parameters in order to do some "reality checking" on both the model parameters and relationships. They provide a rich lode of materials for independent derivation of principles about MPA.

In addition, we have explored several managerial implications of the model, assuming the model is accurate. These guidelines will also be tested as further clinical and survey work is done.

Chapter 10
Further Materials and Next Steps

This chapter represents not an ending, neat edges, or tied knots, but a beginning, with all the roughness and unconnected paths of any preliminary theoretical statement. It also serves as an introduction to our preliminary MPA survey instrument and the text of the clinical case studies used in developing the MPA model, which are presented in the appendices.

What Has Been Done, and What Remains

This book has attempted to review the massive amount of directly and tangentially targeted material that has appeared in a number of disciplines over almost half a century relating to marketing productivity and marketing performance. It has pointed out certain inadequacies in those attempts, one important one stemming from our belief that marketing performance assessment cannot and must not rule out the very managers, management processes, and management practices it is intended to measure. It has also reviewed several pieces of work from the newly emerging subdiscipline of inquiry into marketing practice *as* practice as a potential baseline for the development of a new view of MPA, which was then derived in a model format. The measurement, quantification, and operationalization implications of that model were pursued, and it was noted that, while measurement will be difficult, it is by no means impossible. Finally, the derivational, foundational, and speculative implications and hypotheses generated from the model were presented in the form of preliminary propositions for management attention and research engagement.

What remains to be done is to validate, refine, and revise the model in the field, a task in which we are now engaged more formally than our initial investigations allowed. The research program has had several steps, including (1) development of a self-report instrument on MPA incorporating the model's parameters in a usefully operationalized way; (2) doing preliminary validation of the model in a structured interview setting; and (3) conducting a national-level sample designed to give some parameter point estimates, or at least confidence ranges, to the model's components. At this writing we are preparing the national survey.

Instrument to Measure MPA

Appendix B presents our current pilot instrument in a form suitable for response as well as criticism and commentary. We invite all marketing executives who are interested to respond, and will in return make respondents part of the database, including readministration of the instrument if it changes significantly during further development. We invite comments, criticisms, and aid from our academic colleagues as well.

It is important to note that this version of the instrument, the first "production" version, reflects certain choices and methods compromises. We very much wanted to create a pilot instrument of perhaps more interest to managers than to academics, and therefore elected not to decompose the model's parameters as far as theory allows for fear of fatiguing even the most sympathetic respondents. But the instrument as it stands is serviceable for testing the model, and will allow a good start on further refinements. As to validation, the instrument should be regarded by academics warily, for it is currently unvalidated. However, we are now engaged in final preparation of the instrument for national mailing.

Assuming this process proceeds as planned, we will have a national-level sample across industries and companies to validate the model and, we hope, to provide a "first-round" set of generalizations about MPA, such as those advanced in Chapter 9.

Case Clinical Data

We also provide in Appendix A the full text of the three clinical case studies we developed during the model's formulation and early testing. The Gillette case was written by Clark under Bonoma's supervision, and is a quite bald attempt to compare a very successful and a failed program while holding company and

even divisional context constant. The LifeSpan, Inc., case, written by Professor Melvyn Menezes of the Harvard Business School, is a fascinating examination of a nonprofit institution vending medical care. The marketing vice president attempts to justify to his board of directors why the latter body should grant him a large increase in the marketing budget for what is essentially outbound and inbound telemarketing of health services. He asserts the programs are effective, and the board asks him to demonstrate this. Finally, the Hurricane Island Outward Bound case, also written by Clark, assesses marketing performance issues in still another kind of organization, a place that attempts to transform people's lives. Value conflicts are overlaid on program comparisons, and economics competes with organizational mission, making the establishment of marketing performance criteria an especially chancy business.

As the model is refined, the authors expect to do further case clinical work to explore relationships that appear in data generated by the survey program and comments and criticisms the model generates.

Annotated Bibliography

Finally, Appendix C presents as a service to other researchers and interested managers an annotated bibliography of our sources on marketing productivity and performance. We hope it is useful to those who will go further with this important topic.

Conclusion

We do not believe that much of the work that remains to be done will be easy, or that MPA is a topic that lends itself easily to empirical inquiry and cross-company measurement. Yet it is our view that researches into such thorny, complicated, and murky topics as MPA must be engaged with ever-greater frequency in marketing, perhaps gaining in boldness what they lose in precision. The reason for this is our more fundamental belief that marketing academics have allowed the rift in interests, relevance, and practicality that separates them from the managers their discipline claims to serve to become a veritable chasm. It is important to build bridges continually, not only because the discipline is intended to serve and advance management practice, but because it is often the case that the best practice outstrips theory, making the practitioner one of the best "colleges" in which the academic can matriculate.

Research Appendices

Gillette Personal Care Division: Marketing Planning and Control

LifeSpan, Inc.: Abbott Northwestern Hospital

Hurricane Island Outward Bound School

Gillette Personal Care Division: Marketing Planning and Control

Bruce H. Clark, *Associate for Case Development, prepared this case under the supervision of Professor* **Thomas V. Bonoma** *as the basis for class discussion rather than to illustrate either effective or ineffective handling of an administrative situation. Certain information in the case has been disguised.*

Nursing a cup of coffee one morning in October 1986, Bill Ryan, president of the Gillette Company's Personal Care Division (PCD), contemplated the recent success of the White Rain shampoo and conditioner launch. At the same time, Ryan was considering the division's planning and control system for marketing. This system consisted of an elaborate set of formal procedures and reports designed to help the division develop good marketing plans and then evaluate the plans' results. On the planning side, the division's marketing department carried out a year-round sequence of activities to gather information from the field, rethink brand strategies, and develop detailed sets of marketing actions. On the control side, managers received a wide variety of reports on their business, from daily sales reports to annual consumer surveys. These reports told managers whether their plans were producing the desired results, and also provided the foundation for the next year's planning process.

The link in Ryan's mind between White Rain and the planning and control system was that while White Rain had been a spectacular success, the launch had been accomplished by taking numerous shortcuts through the system. Meanwhile, new product launches and revitalizations ("restages") coming through the formal planning and control system still faltered sometimes;

Ryan recalled the Right Guard restage in 1983 as a good example of a thoughtful strategic plan which came through the traditional system and had not produced the expected results. These facts led Ryan to wonder whether the system was as good as it could be.

Gillette Company and the Personal Care Division

The Gillette Company, founded in 1901 by inventor King C. Gillette, was a leading international manufacturer of consumer products ranging from electric razors to ballpoint pens. In 1985 the company recorded sales of $2.4 billion and a net profit of $160 million. U.S. operations accounted for 42% of Gillette's 1985 sales and 44% of its operating profit. These sales came from three divisions: the Safety Razor Division (blades and razors), the Paper Mate Division (writing instruments), and the Personal Care Division (toiletries and cosmetics).

PCD was responsible for Gillette's U.S. entries in hair care, skin care, and deodorants/antiperspirants (known within the company as "deodorant/AP"). Bill Ryan reported to Derwyn Phillips, executive vice president in charge of Gillette North America. Phillips in turn reported to the Gillette Company's president Joseph Turley.

PCD's marketing function was organized in a product-manager system. (See *Exhibit 1* for a partial organization chart of PCD.) Reporting to Bill Ryan was the vice president of marketing, Bob Forman. Four marketing managers worked below Forman to develop groups of company products, such as hair care or deodorants. Product managers for individual brands reported to the marketing managers.

The marketing function was supported by and in turn supported sales and the marketing research division (MRD). These groups worked together to produce and implement marketing plans.

The Planning and Control System

Planning

Each April the sales planning department and the brand managers organized a field sales and marketing manager meeting to discuss potential changes in marketing plans for the next year. Before the meeting, district sales managers gathered information from their field representatives based on an agenda developed by sales planning and the brand managers. In the week-long gathering, representatives from marketing and sales discussed the effectiveness of the previous year's trade and consumer promotions. (Over 85% of PCD's volume was sold in association with some kind of promotion.) The director of sales planning compiled a summary of the meeting for both marketing and sales. Much of this summary was eventually incorporated into the brand fact books.

Fact books were the most important documents covering the activities of PCD and its competitors. Written in the spring by the brand groups, these 200-page books reviewed the previous year, using information from four sources: the sales/marketing meeting, MRD, outside market research, and brand management. Each brand's fact book reviewed the category in which the brand competed (shampoo and conditioner, for example), and then the activity and results of the brand itself. The books provided (1) historical perspectives on the category and the brand, (2) competitor profiles, (3) actions in advertising, promotion, pricing, and product, (4) consumer attitudes and behavior, and (5) quantitative results (sales, market share, shipments, contributions, and so forth).

With their fact books in hand, brand managers developed marketing plans over May, June, and July. (See *Exhibit 2* for a representative marketing plan table of contents.) The plans fulfilled needs for both brand managers and top management. From the brand's perspective, the plan established general strategic direction and specific marketing programs for the next year. From top management's perspective, plans allowed senior managers to evaluate their current portfolio of products and consolidate profit-and-loss statements for financial planning.

A key goal at the marketing plan stage was to develop an accurate forecast for the brand's annual volume of sales. This forecast strongly influenced the amount of program money the brand would receive. The volume numbers were the subject of negotiations among the brand's managers, sales planning, and MRD. One manager noted:

Marketing tends to lobby high because their expenses are based on the number.

Sales lobbies low because they want quotas that are achievable. Marketing Research takes a more mathematical approach and tries to act as the honest broker.

Pat Flaherty, Right Guard's product manager, looked at the process positively:

We end up with better numbers because of the negotiations. The brand knows the programs, MRD knows the division history with similar products, and sales knows the current environment.

J. D. Grinnell, White Rain's product manager, emphasized the qualitative side of the process:

There's a lot of reasoning by analogy. Someone will ask, "How did our last hair care launch go?" You get this mass of data that you put into the "intuitive machine" and come out with something that feels comfortable.

Through the late summer and early fall, brand managers reviewed the volume numbers and the accompanying plans with their superiors: first the marketing managers, then Bob Forman, and finally the Operating Committee. Plans were continually polished at the lower levels; once a plan reached the Operating Committee, further modifications were rare.

The Operating Committee consisted of Bill Ryan as chairman, the division controller, and the vice presidents of marketing, sales, manufacturing, market research, research and development, and personnel. Ryan identified four factors he looked at in judging the quality of a marketing plan at the Operating Committee review. First, a plan had to be strategically consistent with the brand's objectives—a growth plan for a growth brand, for example. Second, the plan had to make "investment sense," given the division's available resources and priorities. Third, the plan needed to make "component sense," by emphasizing marketing-mix elements that the division believed would work with the brand (consumer promotions for a price-oriented brand, for example). Finally, Ryan liked to see innovative plans.

The quantitative forecasts from the marketing plans were incorporated in the division budget in October. Finance used the budget numbers to plan for cash inflows and outflows. The budget allowed for necessary mid-year expense corrections through Marketing Authorization Change Forms (MACFs, pronounced "Mac-ifs"), which the Operating Committee had to approve.

Profit shortfalls were a more complicated matter. Each level of management had its own profit responsibility. As long as a manager made the profit number, he or she was allowed great flexibility in methods. Therefore, marketing managers would sometimes juggle contributions, offsetting a low contribution from one brand with unexpectedly high contributions from others. Marketing vice president Bob Forman could also do this across brand categories, using surplus contribution from one marketing manager's group to help others. Groups thus aided were said to have been granted "profit relief." Managers avoided asking for such grants if at all possible, fearing that it would reflect badly on them.

Based on the marketing plans and the division's overall expected profit contribution to the Gillette Company, the marketing managers and Bob Forman developed category and division strategic business plans in November, December, and January. These long-range plans covered the next five years of business for PCD. The first year came directly from the budget that was finalized in October. The second year was a detailed estimate of future business. The division put particular emphasis on providing an accurate estimate of pretax profit contribution to the Gillette Company. Years three, four, and five were less precise and detailed in projection.

As part of developing the strategic business plan, brands were divided into four rough categories: Build, Hold, Harvest, and Withdraw. Each category had a general mandate. Build brands were supposed to build market share. Hold brands were expected to maintain share and profit levels. Harvest brands maximized cash flow. Withdraw brands attempted to make a painless exit from business.

Strategic categories were strongly tied to resource allocation. "It's sort of like venture capital," explained Carole Johnson, deodorant/AP marketing manager. "The division has so much profit they have to contribute to Gillette, and therefore only so much they can spend."

Bill Ryan expressed dissatisfaction with the labels themselves because he felt they carried inaccurate connotations. "I think they're of limited utility. They sound too much like that old Boston Consulting Group portfolio theory."[1]

---

1. In the early 1970s, the Boston Consulting Group advocated what they called portfolio management. They di-

As part of their plan reviews with the marketing managers and Bob Forman, brands "made their case" as to what category they should be in. The determining factors influencing this decision included perceived opportunity, the importance of the brand to the overall business (in terms of profit and place in the division product mix), and the quality of the plan. Bob Forman and the marketing managers made the category decisions, which were then reviewed by the Operating Committee.

A brand's strategic category strongly affected the planning and execution of its marketing. Division sales priorities followed brand priorities, with build brands at the top. Category designation also could make a difference in the ability of a brand to maintain the integrity of its program should business conditions change. Pat Flaherty explained his approach to this phenomenon:

> I'm a hold brand. My job is to provide profit to the rest of the company. If I see from the reports that one of the build brands is having trouble, I'll give finance a call and see if they're looking at cutting back on money for me to make up for it. If they're going to take money out of my media budget, they do it a quarter in advance. Then I can try to change my plans.

Category changes were common, particularly from hold to build (on a restage, for example). Build brands could be demoted just as quickly. One manager remarked: "I would say our corporate management is very financially driven. I think they would like to see every new brand make money after the first year. People are very quick to decide."

Once the strategic business plans were approved by the Operating Committee, they were reviewed with Derwyn Phillips for Gillette North America, and then Joseph Turley for the Gillette Company as a whole.

Control

Each marketing plan included the brand's objectives for market share (dollars and units compared to total consumer sales), unit shipments, sales, and net contribution (sales minus cost of goods sold minus direct marketing expenses minus other assignable department expenses). An intermediate profitability number that marketing management considered very important was "direct marketing contribution," which added back the "other assignable expenses" to the net contribution figure. (See *Exhibit 7* for an example of calculating direct marketing contribution.) To measure their performance against these goals, PCD managers relied on a number of regular reports. Pat Flaherty described the reports as creating an "information build" that, when combined, gave a clear picture of a brand's performance.

The Daily Sales Report was the report that managers followed with the greatest interest. Every morning the 20-page report first summarized three activities: (1) division activity for the month through the previous day, (2) activity that corresponded to the organization of the sales force,[2] and (3) activity by major brand and form of brand. The eye-catching cover of the report was a simple chart showing actual division sales in dollars versus scheduled (budgeted) sales (see *Exhibit 3*).

The next page of the report graphed actual versus scheduled orders for the Toiletries and Toni divisions, by promotion cycle. PCD divided the year into nine cycles. These were the calendrical units to which promotions (such as off-invoice discounts) were assigned.

The third page charted major brand sales versus scheduled sales for the month to date. The remaining pages presented the numbers that supported these charts, with an emphasis on original forecast, current schedule, and actual orders for the previous day and the month to date.

Product managers also received a Monthly Sales Forecast, which showed actual results by month for the year to date and estimates by month for the remainder of the year. (See *Exhibit 4* for a sample page from the Monthly Sales Forecast.) Each product manager received data on the various stock-keeping units (SKUs) in his

---

vided a company's businesses into four categories, based on current company share and overall market growth: *question marks, stars, cash cows,* and *dogs.* Funds from cash cows (high-share, low-growth businesses) were used to develop question marks (low-share, high-growth) into stars (high-share, high-growth). Dogs were low-share, low-growth businesses, considered hopeless programs ripe for termination.

---

2. Until 1978, PCD had been divided into the Toiletries and Toni divisions. Sales representatives were still assigned to a division's products, thus allowing them to better focus their sales efforts. Toiletries consisted of most of the deodorant/AP brands, shave creams, facial care, and some hair care products; Toni covered most hair care products, some body sprays, and Dry Idea antiperspirant.

or her brand (for example, the 18-ounce size of White Rain shampoo or the 10-ounce size of Right Guard deodorant). Copies of the forecast were usually covered with handwritten numbers as managers reorganized the information on the chart.

The Daily Sales Report and the Monthly Sales Forecast provided information on factory sales (i.e., sales to the trade rather than sales to consumers). For consumer information, PCD relied on both internal reports and reports by outside market research houses.

Each month, product managers received "Management Action Charts" on their product category from Selling Areas-Marketing, Inc. (SAMI) (see *Exhibit 5* for a sample page from the SAMI report). The report covered sales in food stores, which accounted for 40% to 45% of overall division sales. It emphasized dollar market share information, and gave figures by brand, region, and form, as well as overall.

Bimonthly, managers received the Nielsen Two-Outlet Flash Report, which provided information on sales in food stores and drug stores. These two channels combined provided 55% to 60% of division sales. Like SAMI, the Nielsen report concentrated on market share, enumerating dollar and unit share by form, product, and overall. Nielsen offered more detailed sales information than SAMI.

Using the Nielsen data and the Monthly Sales Forecast, MRD produced the Merchandise Flow ("merch flow") report. The merch flow tied together factory sales and consumer sales to depict the amount of product in the trade pipeline monthly over a three-year period. (See *Exhibit 6* for a sample page from the merch flow.) Managers used trade inventory knowledge to identify trends in distribution.

MRD also provided managers with internally generated research reports. Annually, they performed the National Consumer Study (NCS), which surveyed consumer attitudes and awareness for each brand category. Every five years, MRD did segmentation studies for individual brands, which provided much more detail on attitudes for particular segments of the market. They also did irregular studies at the request of specific managers.

For profit information, managers relied on the Monthly Update. Its cover page was a summary of variances in shipments, sales, and direct marketing contribution. (See *Exhibit 7* for a sample page from the Monthly Update.) Within, the report broke down sales, expenses, and profits by SKU and promotion cycle, and it analyzed variances in those measures. The report told a manager if a brand was on target for its budgeted profit contribution.

The analysis of these reports eventually became a major part of the next year's brand fact book and marketing plans. MRD also kept extensive records on program results from past years.

Informal Measures

In addition to formal reports, managers used a variety of personal measures to determine marketing effectiveness. Deodorant/AP's Carole Johnson tried to assess the "likability" of her programs, both internally and externally. She looked at purchase intention after sampling and at whether consumers liked the advertising campaign. She also sought out trade reaction to programs, both through the sales force and on her own. "Trust" was a word Carole used frequently; if the trade had a good experience with a brand's programs, she felt it was more likely to accept that brand's programs in the future. Finally, Carole followed a philosophy of "ask the nonexpert." She recalled one example when a chemist told her that a package design didn't seem quite "right." A consumer test of different designs confirmed that a modification of the original would significantly improve consumer attitudes toward the product.

White Rain's J. D. Grinnell kept a personal spreadsheet of information he gleaned from the monthly sales forecast. The spreadsheet organized shipments data by promotion cycle and product, and it compared data from year to year. One figure Grinnell watched closely was the proportion of goods sold on promotion to total goods sold. If the proportion consistently increased, that meant he was more frequently having to sell White Rain through lower pricing, which suggested that the other elements of his marketing mix might need adjustment.

Right Guard's Pat Flaherty counted his brand to be more successful if, over the long term, he was consistently providing "product news" to the trade and consumers: new forms, brand extensions, new packaging, and new formulations. He also tore ads out of newspapers and posted them on his wall to keep track of competitive activity that might affect Right Guard.

In addition to these informal measures, different managers assigned different emphases to the formal measures the system produced. Pat Flaherty tended to focus on profit. Carole Johnson watched share, unit shipments, and unit sales, although she felt the division as a whole cared more about profit. Linda Keene, hair care marketing manager, felt the best formal indicator of a new brand's strength was share, particularly the stability of share growth. J. D. Grinnell, in a build situation, looked most closely at share and shipments. Bill Ryan studied sales, shipments, and share, calling them the ultimate predictors of profit.

Using these formal and informal measures to feed back into the planning system, managers developed marketing programs that formed the centerpiece of PCD's business. Two examples of these programs were the 1983 Right Guard restage and the 1985 White Rain launch.

The 1983 Right Guard Restage

Background

Right Guard had been one of Gillette Company's flagship brands for over two decades. Introduced in 1960, Right Guard pioneered deodorants for male users and by 1967 was the premier deodorant/AP in the United States, with a unit market share of 26%. Then, in the mid-1970s, the fluorocarbon scare burst onto the national scene.[3] Right Guard, like most other antiperspirants at the time, was an aerosol, but its aerosol image seemed more entrenched than the images of its competitors. The brand had great difficulty expanding outside of the aerosol form to solids and roll-ons. Right Guard lost its overall market leadership in 1976; the late 1970s and early 1980s saw many new competitors and new products, some from within Gillette itself. By mid-1982, Right Guard's position had slipped to number five in the market, and its

unit market share was down to 8.5% from 9.9% in 1981. In mid-1982, the brand lost its 20-year market leadership among males to the Mennen Company. Right Guard's aerosol heritage still dominated the brand's sales in 1982, with 72% of revenues coming from aerosol products. Meanwhile, consumers continued to move to nonaerosol forms, particularly sticks and solids.

Despite the brand's low share, PCD could not afford to lose Right Guard. It was the division's largest brand, accounting for approximately 15% of division sales and 25% of division operating profits. Right Guard had managed to maintain its budgeted profit contributions by curtailing marketing expenses, but by mid-1982, Ryan recalled, the division concluded that "Right Guard needed a massive shot in the arm or it would continue in a downward spiral."

The Plan

The brand group proposed, and PCD accepted, a radical restage. Right Guard was moved to build status. The brand received a complete makeover. Two new chemical formulations and a new fragrance were put into consumer-use testing. The tests revealed substantially improved efficacy in the new products. New graphics were developed for all brand packaging, modernizing and unifying the line's appearance. Advertising was reduced for the remainder of 1982 to maximize immediate profit and make room for an entirely new campaign in 1983. A price increase in October 1982 also added a profit cushion.

The restage was scheduled to run for three years. The first year was called the "phase-in." (See *Exhibit 8* for plan financial projections.) Right Guard began 1983 with an inventory-management program that used consumer promotion to drain the old products off trade shelves. Meanwhile, the new packaging and product improvements moved through manufacturing. The brand continued to hold advertising to a low level through the first five months of the year. Introductory trade promotions were grouped together during the second-quarter seasonal peak, and the full line was promoted together to maximize restage impact. Rich deal terms encouraged the trade to accept the new products, while trial generation programs placed them directly into consumers' hands.

---

3. Well-publicized scientific studies in the early and mid-1970s suggested that chlorofluorocarbons (CFC), widely used as propellants in aerosol sprays, were damaging atmospheric ozone, which shields the earth from ultraviolet radiation. Partly due to U.S. consumer boycotts, the proportion of U.S. deodorants and antiperspirants sold in aerosol form dropped from 80% of the total market in 1974 to 45% in 1977. In March 1978, the U.S. government banned nonessential CFC-propelled aerosols; most manufacturers developed non-CFC propellants.

The new products came to retail shelves during the second quarter, followed closely by Right Guard's $12.7 million advertising campaign (slogan: "You work hard, you need Right Guard"). In the second and third quarters, Right Guard was the largest media spender in the product category.

The Results

The year 1983 turned out to be more active than expected in the deodorant/AP category. The 1983 category overview noted:

> Consumer reluctance to switch brands, coupled with slower market growth, has led to intense competition among existing brands. Given the very high price of entry into the category, major manufacturers have been reinvesting in their existing franchises to hold or build share.

Overall market volume increased over 2% to 506 million units, slightly more than the brand's original forecast of 503.4 million.

After years of media-spending increases between 4% and 10%, 1983 saw a 13.2% increase. A competitive surprise was that Mennen, one of Right Guard's chief competitors for male users, increased its advertising of male brands by 45% to $12.8 million, surpassing the Right Guard campaign. Despite Right Guard's spending advantage in the second and third quarters, its share of category advertising for the year was only 10.5%, well up from the artificially low 5.1% in 1982 but below 1981's 12.4% figure. The category overview also noted "innovative" media selection on the part of PCD's competition.

Other competitive activities during the year included Procter & Gamble's introduction of major packaging and formulation changes to Secret Roll-On, and additional product sizes for both Secret and Sure. In June, Mennen launched Lady Speed Stick, which was a resounding success, reaching a 2.2% share by mid-1984.

Right Guard missed its unit share goal by .5%, achieving a 7.6% share for the year rather than the forecasted 8.1%. (For a comparison of this and other quantitative measures, see *Exhibit 8*.) In addition, trade and consumer reaction to the restage appeared weak. In retail stores, Right Guard's status—as shown by brand ranking in retail displays, special prices, in-ad coupons, and local advertising—declined slightly, showing either stable or lower rankings on all measures.

For consumers, year-end market research revealed that Right Guard's share of consumers' "last brand purchased" had continued its decade-long decline. In addition, male users ranked Right Guard well below chief competitors Mennen and Old Spice on key factors such as product effectiveness, application aesthetics, value for the money, and fragrance/male orientation. The one top performance Right Guard achieved, its extraordinarily high brand awareness (66% unaided and 100% aided for men, 42% and 97% for women), was viewed with mixed feelings. Some managers feared that such strong awareness would make Right Guard's old aerosol image that much harder to modify.

In 1984's division plans, the original plan was modified downward in light of 1983 results.

The Present

Despite the initial disappointment, PCD managers saw some positive results from the restage over the long term. The brand's decline in shipments, share, and consumer sales slowed appreciably between 1983 and 1986; aerosol sales stopped declining altogether. Direct marketing contribution from the brand rebounded to the highest levels in 10 years, aside from 1982. Managers also noted that the program did create some excitement among both the sales force and the trade, important factors in maintaining the brand's distribution.

Still, 1986 found Pat Flaherty managing Right Guard as a hold brand. Its target market had been refocused on males aged 12–24 because the limited advertising budget that the brand's sales justified was no longer sufficient to support a mass-consumer appeal. Flaherty had not had any new products in over a year; he was running an image campaign as part of the new focus on younger males. (One of the facts that MRD's attitudes/awareness survey consistently showed was that Right Guard was still heavily associated with the aerosol form and was considered old-fashioned.)

While his current business was not robust (Right Guard was down to a 6.5% share in mid-1986), Flaherty had hopes for the future. In 1987, Right Guard would be introducing a series of product improvements. Successful test-market results might allow another national restage: "The window of opportunity for Right

Guard is 1988. But we have to prove we're better. If we do a good job in '87, then we might be a build brand in '88.''

The 1985 White Rain Launch

Background

Bill Ryan described the White Rain shampoo and conditioner launch as "an opportunistic foray into a new business." In 1983, Ryan noted that PCD business had begun to erode slightly. While dollar sales were still up, PCD's unit share of the toiletries business had declined marginally. The division had excess factory capacity. MRD and the Nielsen reports suggested that "value" (low-price) brands were becoming a growing force in the market. With most Gillette brands positioned as "premium" (high-price) brands, Ryan felt that PCD was missing an opportunity by not fielding any strong price-value brands. He set in motion a number of projects to develop that type of product. One of these was White Rain shampoo.

White Rain had had a shampoo as recently as the 1970s. The shampoo had been introduced in 1952 as a low-price brand. In 1962, a hair spray had been added to the line with a similar value position. However, the brand never developed sustained national distribution. The shampoo was phased out in the late 1970s. The hair spray had an extremely strong regional skew, selling well in the Southern and Central states, but very poorly in the Northeast and the West.

Bill Ryan spoke to PCD's Southern regional sales manager. The manager reacted enthusiastically to the idea of a new White Rain product. (White Rain hair spray had a 10% market share in the region.) PCD decided to do a test market of a shampoo in 1984.

"The key was that there was no up-front expense," explained Ryan. "We would try it in White Rain's strong region. If it sold, then we would think about rolling it out. If it didn't, we hadn't really lost anything."

The Test Market

The White Rain brand group was given the responsibility of developing and executing a plan that would take the shampoo into test mar-

ket by mid-1984, much sooner than PCD's normal product development process would allow. To achieve this, the group did an "end run" around the standard system. For example, once safety and effectiveness tests had been performed on a new shampoo in the laboratory, MRD usually conducted consumer-use tests (CUT) to assess consumer attitudes toward the new product. White Rain tried to shorten this final step. "We told R&D we wanted a shampoo so good that we wouldn't have to test it," recalled J. D. Grinnell. Eventually the brand compromised and did some attitude testing. Testers ran the shampoo through a "gross negative screen." The screen involved a sample that was one-third the size of a full test, and looked only for major negative reactions rather than the more detailed information on attitudes that a CUT provided.

Bill Ryan's name was invoked frequently to push the project through on time. Grinnell remembered quelling another department's concerns about a lack of documentation by saying, "Look, Bill wants this program executed; we don't have time to prepare a real MACF. If you need an official notification, we'll issue documentation, as long as you understand it will mostly be white spaces." In general, the group avoided the extensive documentation that went into a traditional marketing plan, and instead "backfilled" written information later while talking the project through the various departments necessary to complete the preparation for the test.

White Rain shampoo was rolled out in the Southern region in May 1984. The object of the test was to see if a price-value shampoo with no advertising would be accepted by the trade. Ryan was convinced the brand would succeed nationally, so the test was designed as much to refine the marketing plan as anything. The new shampoo's chief competitor was Helene Curtis's Suave shampoo, so White Rain came out with an 18-ounce bottle for the same price as Suave's 16-ounce bottle.

Just as White Rain went into test market, Suave increased its prices. White Rain decided not to follow; having a lower price would be one more argument the sales force could use to convince the trade to stock the product. The results were very encouraging. The shampoo surpassed its goals on both shipments and consumer sales, and reached a 2% share in parts of the region.

The Rollout

The results of the test reinforced Ryan's perception that White Rain would do well nationally. The growing importance of national chains like K mart made a regional rollout difficult at best. A national rollout was approved for mid-1985.

Again under time pressure, Grinnell continued the "low documentation" style that had worked so well in the test market. "I tried to avoid writing a marketing plan at all. It was tough enough to execute what I was trying to do." Instead, he relied on his and Linda Keene's presentations at the Operating Committee's monthly meetings. "I tried to keep them up to date on what was happening. Then when we got to the last monthly update where I said 'This is the go/no-go point,' they had been briefed well enough all along to say 'go.'"

White Rain had learned some things from the test market. First, having no advertising was a significant barrier to gaining shelf space with many retailers. The brand therefore authorized a minimal advertising campaign for the rollout. Second, two-thirds of consumers surveyed had not learned about White Rain until they saw it on store shelves. In response, the brand developed special shelf displays. Third, the success of the hair spray and shampoo together convinced the brand to develop a conditioner for the rollout.

Using this modified marketing effort and success stories from the Southern region, PCD's sales force began national distribution of White Rain shampoo and conditioner in May 1985. A further modification at this point was the decision to do a joint promotion of all three White Rain products (hair spray, shampoo, and conditioner), pricing them so that any one could be sold for $.99 at retail. An unforeseen result of this promotion was that White Rain hair spray gained distribution in areas where it previously had not been carried. At the same time, sales of the shampoo and conditioner also dramatically exceeded forecasts. (See *Exhibit 9* for a quantitative comparison of White Rain's budgeted and actual results.) In addition to the quantitative success, communications from field sales were enthusiastic. "The basic message from sales," Bill Ryan said, "was 'Hurry up, we can sell this stuff.'" In light of the success, White Rain added a mousse to the line in February 1986.

The Present

By late 1986, it was apparent that White Rain would exceed its sales forecasts again. The brand was given more resources to work with, and its build status continued into 1987. Grinnell, however, tried to put the success in perspective: "White Rain is the largest hair care brand in PCD, but for all the excitement, it's still only a 3 share in the total market. A 3 share is not much."

Linda Keene added her own caution for the future:

A lot depends on expectations. One of the reasons White Rain has been such a success is that no one expected it to do so well. This year we'll exceed our expectations by less, and next year we'll probably be right on. Somewhere around that point, management begins asking, "When are you going to start making money?"

Comments on the System

Managers at Gillette generally regarded the planning and control system positively, although with qualifications. One important benefit was the amount of communication the system fostered. Pat Flaherty remarked, "If you stay with a brand, there's enough communication and information flow to allow you to keep the brand up to date."

Another positive outcome was that the system required managers to step back and examine the relevant variables in their programs *and* the interactions between variables. J. D. Grinnell commented, "The system protects us from making mistakes. Sometimes we solve the problem we see without considering all the ramifications. Systems make us look at the ramifications." Linda Keene felt the brand strategic-planning process was often as valuable for the long-term thinking it provoked as for the plan it produced.

The system also provided powerful historical perspective in the fact books and plans that it generated. Grinnell commented, "If you don't have a system like this, you lose the ability to go back and look at the documents. Then if you change people on a brand, you lose a lot of knowledge with the people who leave."

A common negative view was that the process took too long. Carole Johnson remarked,

"We develop the ideal plan in July, and by the time we reach the budget in October, things have changed." Grinnell agreed, but added:

I think Gillette is pretty middle of the road in planning and control. There are a lot of things we don't have, like central control mechanisms. For example, there is no one place to go where you can find out the status of all the different projects going on in the division. But if you had that, it would slow you down even more. At the other extreme, we don't allow individual managers to continually go off into their personal "skunk works" to develop programs.

A second negative view dealt with commitment. Compromise solutions to strongly held opposing views sometimes resulted in a lack of enthusiasm from all quarters. This problem was exacerbated by the movement of people from brand to brand.

The most controversial outcome of the system was its effect on resource allocation. One manager noted:

Anytime you have a resource-allocation process like this, you are going to suboptimize a lot of things. S. C. Johnson Company will lose money for two or three years on

Edge shaving cream because it [Edge] is important to them. That kind of competitor is very tough for a Gillette to go against.

Bill Ryan admitted that the system was in some ways unfair:

Frankly, in this kind of system some triage goes on. What we do is take our top priority brands—and there aren't many of them—and make sure they have 100% of the funding they need. After that, you try to give enough to the other brands, concentrating on spending on the element—say, advertising—that matters most to the brand.

Ryan wondered again whether his triage was identifying the right programs and opportunities. Another manager framed the issue somewhat differently:

A system is required for normal business to maintain control and accountability, but companies and markets change, and you eventually end up serving the system instead of your market. So when you go around the system, in the short term it's more efficient. But in the long term you can't run a business that way.

Exhibit 1 Partial Organization Chart—Gillette's Personal Care Division

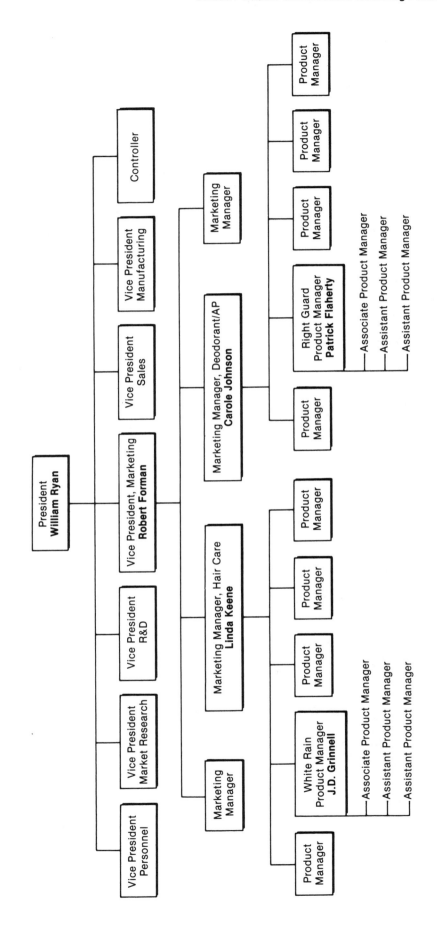

Exhibit 2   Marketing Plan Table of Contents

Overview
- I.   Brand Perspective
- II.   Key Issues
- III.   Plan Assumptions
- IV.   Objectives
- V.   Marketing Strategy
- VI.   Long-Range Plan

Marketing Plan
- I.   Overview
- II.   Product
- III.   Packaging
- IV.   Pricing
- V.   Advertising—Creative
- VI.   Media
- VII.   Promotion
- VIII.   Public Relations
- IX.   Distribution
- X.   Marketing Research

Summary
- I.   Financial Summary
- II.   Plan Summary

Appendix
- I.   Issues
- II.   Financial Detail
- III.   Share Goal Justification by Form
- IV.   Promotion Detail
- V.   Merchandise Flows

Source: Gillette Company

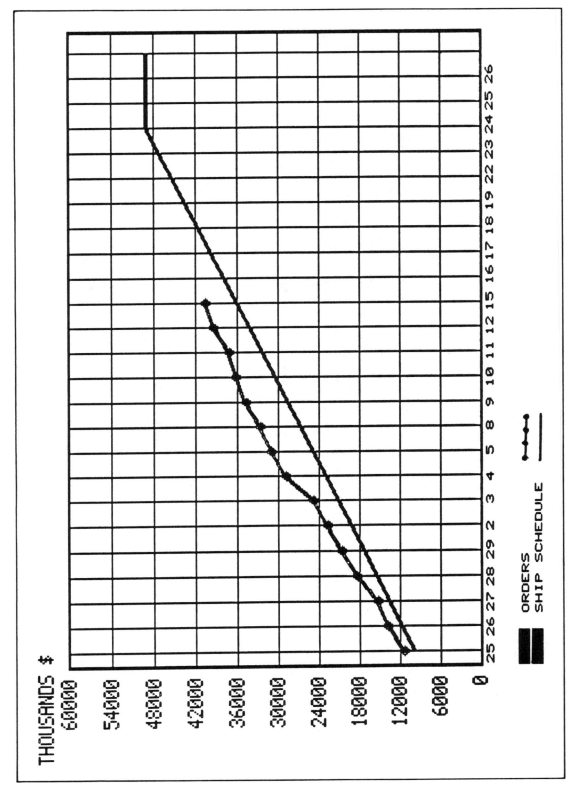

Exhibit 3 Cover, Daily Sales Report

Exhibit 4 Sample Page, Monthly Sales Forecast

[Handwritten annotations: "July Pre-Shipment Meeting", "22 days of 24", and various circled figures throughout]

05/29/86   13:46:56   1986 JUNE ESTIMATES

WRS18	JAN	FEB	MAR	APR	MAY	JUN	JUL	AUG	SEP	OCT	NOV	DEC	TOTAL
CIVP	731	1449	3154	781	1670	3209	1082	1680	2640	1200	1920	1920	21436
CIVOS	69	124	58	90	55	40	100	120	95	100	110	130	1091
GOVOS	12	25	17	6	14	0	0	0	20	0	0	0	94
GOVP	3	12	37	42	25	40	60	60	0	30	40	40	389
MISC	0	0	0	0	0	0	0	0	0	0	0	0	0
TOTAL	815	1610	3266	919	1764	3289	1242	1860	2755	1330	2070	2090	23010

TOTALS	JAN	FEB	MAR	APR	MAY	JUN	JUL	AUG	SEP	OCT	NOV	DEC	TOTAL
CIVP	731	1449	3154	781	1670	3209	1082	1680	2640	1200	1920	1920	21436
CIVOS	69	124	58	90	55	40	100	120	95	100	110	130	1091
GOVOS	12	25	17	6	14	0	0	0	20	0	0	0	94
GOVP	3	12	37	42	25	40	60	60	0	30	40	40	389
MISC	0	0	0	0	0	0	0	0	0	0	0	0	0
TOTAL	815	1610	3266	919	1764	3289	1242	1860	2755	1330	2070	2090	23010

[Handwritten calculations in left margin: 9) = 4; 334 = 1; 34 D = 2; 364 = 12; 604 = 2712; 614 = 464]

Exhibit 5 Sample Page, SAMI Report

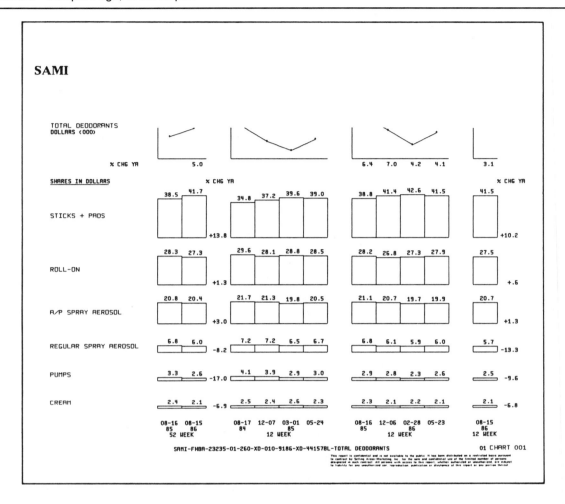

SOURCE: Reprinted by permission of SAMI/Burke, Inc.

15

Exhibit 6 Sample Page, Merchandise Flow

RIGHT GUARD AERO DEOD

09/14/86 2

	TOTAL MARKET RETAIL UNIT SALES (MM)	BRAND SHARE	NET FACTORY SHIPMENTS TOTAL	MILITARY & MISC	CIVILIAN PROM	CIVILIAN NON-PROM	TOTAL	CONSUMER SALES	TRADE INVENTORY	MONTHS SUPPLY	CHG. TRADE INVENTORY
JAN84	37.6	3.6	865	66	707	92	799	1344	6129	4.6	-545
FEB84	39.5	3.7	1068	82	825	161	986	1470	5645	3.8	-484
MAR84	40.8	3.5	1755	102	1211	442	1653	1418	5880	4.1	235
APR84	41.7	3.5	1066	67	790	209	999	1477	5402	3.7	-478
MAY84	45.0	3.7	1549	87	1248	214	1462	1660	5204	3.1	-198
JUN84	46.1	3.8	2618	135	2118	365	2483	1729	5958	3.4	754
JUL84	48.0	3.7	1152	86	775	291	1066	1778	5246	3.0	-712
AUG84	47.5	3.8	2006	73	1607	326	1933	1786	5393	3.0	147
SEP84	46.3	3.6	3346	114	2887	345	3232	1683	6942	4.1	1549
OCT84	43.9	3.8	1645	72	1313	260	1573	1711	6804	4.0	-138
NOV84	43.0	3.7	1255	77	1077	101	1178	1609	6373	4.0	-431
DEC84	42.0	3.6	2503	116	2246	141	2387	1518	7242	4.8	869
TOTAL	521.4	3.7	20828	1077	16804	2947	19751	19183			568
JAN85	38.5	3.6	759	74	602	83	685	1397	6530	4.7	-712
FEB85	40.7	3.4	972	85	764	123	887	1374	6043	4.4	-487
MAR85	42.9	3.6	1300	117	1010	173	1183	1541	5685	3.7	-358
APR85	44.1	3.4	898	117	571	210	781	1495	4971	3.3	-714
MAY85	44.9	3.5	1714	96	1367	251	1618	1568	5021	3.2	50
JUN85	46.3	3.6	3554	165	3060	329	3389	1658	6752	4.1	1731
JUL85	48.8	3.9	1246	161	866	219	1085	1896	5941	3.1	-811
AUG85	48.1	4.0	1916	83	1564	269	1833	1915	5859	3.1	-82
SEP85	47.6	3.8	3010	184	2536	290	2826	1800	6885	3.8	1026
OCT85	45.2	3.8	1348	122	1048	178	1226	1718	6393	3.7	-492
NOV85	44.3	3.3	941	106	737	98	835	1476	5752	3.9	-641
DEC85	43.3	3.4	1937	157	1635	145	1780	1488	6044	4.1	292
TOTAL	534.7	3.6	19595	1467	15760	2368	18128	19326			-1198
JAN86	39.6	3.4	713	51	533	129	662	1354	5352	4.0	-692
FEB86	41.9	3.2	1466	64	1255	147	1402	1346	5408	4.0	56
MAR86	44.3	3.5	2238	134	1781	323	2104	1531	5981	3.9	573
APR86	45.6	3.4	1095	94	956	45	1001	1562	5420	3.5	-561
MAY86	46.5	3.4	1458	85	1309	64	1373	1592	5201	3.3	-219
JUN86	47.6	3.5	2182	103	1790	289	2079	1680	5600	3.3	399
JUL86	49.0	3.8	957	62	729	166	895	1860	4635	2.5	-965
AUG86	48.8	3.9	2035	96	1650	289	1939	1880	4694	2.5	59
SEP86	48.0	3.7	2355	100	1940	315	2255	1780	5169	2.9	475
OCT86	45.9	3.7	1140	77	923	140	1063	1710	4522	2.6	-647
NOV86	44.8	3.3	1207	64	998	145	1143	1480	4185	2.8	-337
DEC86	43.7	3.5	2152	58	1974	120	2094	1520	4759	3.1	574
TOTAL	545.7	3.5	18998	988	15838	2172	18010	19295			-1285

Exhibit 7 Sample Page, Monthly Update

	1985 ACTUAL	% FRS	1986 BUDGET	% FRS	1986 MID-YEAR	% FRS	SEPTEMBER ESTIMATE	% FRS	ACTUAL VAR.	%	BUDGET VAR.	%	MID-YEAR VAR.	%
TOTAL MARKET (DOLLAR)	941,336	---	983,288	---	983,440	---	0	---	(941,336)	---	(983,288)	---	(983,440)	---
(UNIT)	406,372		411,768		413,288		0		(406,372)		(411,768)		(413,288)	
SHARE OF MARKET (DOLLAR)	5.8		5.5		5.5		0.0		(5.8)		(5.5)		(5.5)	
(UNIT)	5.2		5.0		4.9		0.0		(5.2)		(5.0)		(4.9)	
QUANTITIES:														
CONSUMER SALES	27,791		27,341		27,007		26,712		(1,078)		(629)		(295)	
MILITARY SALES	2,160		1,847		1,682		0		(2,160)		(1,847)		(1,682)	
CHANGE IN TRADE INVENTORY	(2,008)		(1,448)		(1,932)		0		2,008		1,448		1,932	
TOTAL SHIPMENTS	27,943		27,740		26,757		26,712		(1,230)		(1,028)		(45)	
FULL REVENUE SALES $	56,933	100	57,277	100	55,791	100	55,342	100	(1,591)	(3)	(1,935)	(3)	(449)	(1)
COST OF SALES:														
DIRECT COST	14,307	25	14,002	24	13,898	25	13,812	25	518	4	306	2	26	0
DIRECT COST VARIANCES	(349)	(1)	0	0	(116)	(0)	(116)	(0)	(233)	67	116	0	0	0
TOTAL COST OF SALES	13,958	25	14,002	24	13,782	25	13,696	25	285	2	422	3	26	0
PROFIT CONTRIBUTION	42,975	75	43,275	76	42,009	75	41,646	75	(1,306)	(3)	(1,513)	(3)	(423)	(1)
DIRECT MARKETING EXPENSES														
LOST REVENUE	7,822	14	7,090	12	7,032	13	6,949	13	873	11	141	2	84	1
SALES PROMOTION	2,863	5	3,374	6	3,588	6	3,564	6	(701)	(24)	(189)	(6)	24	1
ADVERTISING:														
MEDIA	5,204	9	5,322	9	5,355	10	5,355	10	154	3	228	4	0	0
PRODUCTION	460	1	532	1	560	1	560	1	(100)	(22)	(28)	(5)	0	0
OTHER	339	1	935	2	1,142	2	1,142	2	(803)	(237)	(207)	(22)	0	0
TOTAL ADVERTISING	6,003	11	6,789	12	7,057	13	7,057	13	(749)	(12)	(7)	(0)	0	0
TOTAL DIRECT MARKETING EXPENSE	16,688	29	17,253	30	17,677	32	17,569	32	(576)	(3)	(55)	(0)	108	1
DIRECT MARKETING CONTRIBUTION	26,287	46	26,021	45	24,332	44	24,077	44	(1,883)	(7)	(1,568)	(6)	(315)	(1)
NET SALES $	49,111	86	50,187	88	48,759	87	48,393	87	(718)	(1)	(1,794)	(4)	(366)	(1)
PERCENT PROM FRS TO TOT FRS	79		77		80		81		(2)		(4)		(1)	
PERCENT PROM EXP TO PROM FRS	24		24		24		23		0		0		0	
PERCENT PROM EXP TO TOT FRS	19		18		19		19		(0)		(1)		0	

17

Exhibit 8 Right Guard Restage Objectives and Results (units and dollars in millions)

	1981 (actual)	1982 (fall forecast)	1983 (est.)	1984 (est.)	1985 (est.)
I. 1983 Plan Forecasts					
Market size (units)	491.0	498.4	503.4	508.4	513.5
Market share[a]	9.9%	8.5%	8.1%	9.0%	9.7%
Shipments (units)[a]	45.7	37.6	36.4	41.7	45.3
Sales	$74.1	$65.5	$69.6	$82.1	$94.0
Direct marketing expenses	25.3	17.2	26.9	31.6	30.9
Direct marketing contribution	$29.2	$32.2	$22.8	$27.6	$36.3
	1981	1982	1983	1984	1985
II. Actual Figures—1981–1985					
Market size (units)	491.0	495.3	506.0	521.4	534.7
Market share[a]	9.9%	8.7%	7.6%	7.0%	6.8%
Shipments (units)[a]	45.7	39.9	37.7	35.4	33.5
Sales	$74.1	$70.8	$72.3	$70.1	$68.2
Direct marketing expenses	25.3	17.5	26.4	21.4	20.3
Direct marketing contribution	$29.2	$36.2	$25.7	$31.8	$32.7

Note: A "no restage" financial forecast in the 1983 plan projected the following figures for 1983–1985, assuming a continuation of 1981–1982 trends.

	1983	1984	1985
Market share[a]	7.3%	6.6%	6.0%
Shipments (units)[a]	31.8	30.5	28.0
Sales	$60.5	$62.1	$60.8
Direct marketing expense	19.9	20.5	20.0
Direct marketing contribution	$24.4	$24.9	$24.5

Source: Gillette Company

a. All market share figures are calculated from consumer sales. Shipments are calculated from factory sales.

Exhibit 9 White Rain Launch Objectives and Results (all units in millions)

	1982 (actual)	1983 (actual)	1984 (actual)	1985 (est.)	1986 (est.)
I. 1985 National Launch Forecasts					
Hair Spray					
Market size (units)	244.0	252.1	268.3	272.8	279.3
Market share[a]	7.4%	6.6%	7.1%	7.1%	7.7%
Shipments (units)[a]	18.5	17.1	24.0[b]	20.5	22.4
Shampoo					
Market size (units)				630.5	639.1
Market share[a]				1.0%	1.5%
Shipments (units)[a]				7.6	10.5
Conditioner					
Market size (units)				339.4	342.1
Market share[a]				.5%	1.4%
Shipments (units)[a]				3.3	5.4
Total brand shipments	18.5	17.1	24.0[b]	31.4	38.3

	1982 (actual)	1983 (actual)	1984 (actual)	1985 (actual)	1986 (est.)
II. 1986 Mid-Year Forecasts					
Hair Spray					
Market size (units)	244.0	252.1	268.3	283.4	326.8
Market share[a]	7.4%	6.6%	7.1%	9.0%	9.6%
Shipments (units)[a]	18.5	17.1	24.0[b]	26.2	32.3
Shampoo					
Market size (units)				612.5	618.4
Market share[a]				1.6%	3.4%
Shipments (units)[a]				11.2	23.0
Conditioner					
Market size (units)				339.9	343.3
Market share[a]				1.1%	2.8%
Shipments (units)[a]				4.2	10.6
Total brand shipments (includes mousse in 1986)	18.5	17.1	24.0[b]	41.6	71.3

Source: Gillette Company

a. All market share figures are calculated from consumer sales. Shipments are calculated from factory sales.
b. Includes test-market shipments of shampoo.

LifeSpan, Inc.: Abbott Northwestern Hospital

*Assistant Professor **Melvyn A. J. Menezes** wrote this case as the basis for class discussion rather than to illustrate either effective or ineffective handling of an administrative situation. Certain names and data have been disguised. Special thanks to Professor **Thomas V. Bonoma** for his support.*

It was Thursday, January 2, 1986. Steve Hillestad, vice president of marketing for LifeSpan, Inc. (the parent holding company of Abbott Northwestern Hospital), was thinking about the next morning's special budget meeting with the Abbott Northwestern Hospital board. Earlier that day at the regular budget meeting, Hillestad had presented what he thought was an excellent review of the progress made by Abbott Northwestern Hospital during 1985 in a number of marketing areas. He had requested a substantial increase in the 1986 advertising budget—from $717,000 to $1.25 million. But Gordon Sprenger, president of LifeSpan, had expressed some concerns:

> Steve, Abbott Northwestern Hospital has come a long way in 1985. But many of us are unconvinced about the role of marketing in this performance. Show us that marketing did in fact play a major role in our improved *performance*—not just awareness or public relations—and we will be better able to evaluate your request for a 75% increase in your 1986 budget. Also, while you are at it, please tell us more clearly how those increased resources might get allocated across different programs. I know you've pondered these issues, and would appreciate your presenting them to the board members tomorrow at 9 A.M.

The Health Care Industry

The health care industry was among the largest in the United States. National health expenditures had grown very rapidly, reaching $425 billion in 1985. Health care expenses as a percentage of the nation's gross national product (GNP) had doubled during the previous 25 years; by 1985 they accounted for as much as 10.7% of the GNP (see *Exhibit 1*).

Employment in the private health industry had grown three times as fast as that of the total private nonfarm economy, reaching over 7.2 million employees in 1983. The unemployment rate for health care workers was lower than rates for comparably skilled workers in other areas. Viewed over time, the data described an industry that was large, strong, and insulated from business-cycle swings.

National health expenditures were divided into the following categories: personal health care, program administration, government public health activities, noncommercial research, and construction of medical facilities.

Personal health care included a number of different goods and services: hospital care, nursing home care, physicians' services, dentists' services, drugs and medical sundries, eyeglasses and appliances, and other health services. It was the biggest category of health care expenditure—accounting for approximately 88% of total industry expenditures. In 1985, $371.4 billion was spent on personal health care ($166.7 billion of this went to hospital care alone).

Financing Health Care

Health care was financed either by direct patient payments or by "third-party payors" who could be classified into (1) government and (2) private insurance companies. The health care market differed from the market for most other goods and services in that it was dominated by these third-party payors. According to industry analysts, third-party coverage of health care may have contributed to a healthier population, but it had increased prices as well. The analysts believed that most consumers did not care very much about price since they did not directly pay for health services at the time of consumption.

The main third-party payor—the government (federal, state, and local)—spent $174.8 billion in 1985, accounting for 41.4% of all health care expenditures. The advent of Medicare and Med-

icaid programs had dramatically changed government funding of personal health care.[1]

Rapid growth of health care expenditures in recent years placed an increasing financial strain on government programs such as Medicare and Medicaid. To control Medicare costs, a series of major reforms had been enacted since 1981. Despite these reforms, Medicare spent $70.5 billion in 1985. Considered together, Medicare and Medicaid financed 29% of the personal health care expenditures in 1985 and expended $110 billion in benefits to 48 million people (see *Exhibit 2*).

The other major third-party payor—the private health insurance industry—had been attracting an increasing number of consumers, and paid $113.5 billion in medical benefits in 1985. The main third-party payors—government and private health insurance—were not independent, but shared a complex relationship. For instance, when Medicare and Medicaid were established in 1966, hospital care spending increased dramatically, and the portion paid by private insurance, although growing in dollar terms, dropped from 41% in 1965 to less than 34% by 1967. Since then, however, private third-party payments of hospital care had grown to 37% because consumers sought more depth in their hospital coverage.

Third-party payments accounted for 71.6% of the total U.S. health care expenditures, and the balance (28.4%) was borne by consumers paying directly for health services. However, the share of direct consumer payments varied by type of service. For example, direct payments accounted for 26.3% of physicians' services expenditures, but for only 9.3% of hospital care expenditures.

Hospital Systems

Expenditures on hospital care had increased from $52.4 billion in 1975 to $166.7 billion in 1985—a growth rate of 13% per year.[2] The total

---

1. Medicare was a federal program that provided hospital and medical insurance benefits to persons 65 years and older and to certain disabled persons under 65. Medicaid was a joint federal-state program that provided medical assistance to certain categories of low-income people. Both programs were established in 1966.

2. Hospital care included all inpatient and outpatient care in public and private hospitals, and all services and supplies provided by hospitals.

supply of hospital beds had increased substantially. By 1985, there were 6,148 hospitals with about 1.3 million beds. Industry observers generally agreed that the supply of beds exceeded the demand by as much as 20%. The 67% bed-occupancy rate of hospitals in 1984 supported this contention.[3]

Hospitals could be characterized in a number of different ways, including ownership, type of patients treated, and whether they were teaching or nonteaching hospitals. According to the American Hospital Association, 305 of the 6,148 hospitals in the United States were owned by the federal government, 1,723 were owned by state and local government, 3,363 were non-profit "voluntary" hospitals, and 757 were proprietary (investor owned).

Changes in the Industry

Historically the health care industry had functioned as a decentralized cottage industry with a multitude of individual operators—physicians, hospitals, pharmacies, other services—offering fairly homogeneous services, differentiated mainly by their geographic distribution. However, after World War II and more strikingly in the 1975–1985 period, the industry was reshaped by social policy, technology, scarcity of capital resources, and an increased number of physicians as well as health care facilities. It resulted in the emergence of several centralized and well-structured organizations—often with regional or national scope—designed to compete effectively and efficiently with other medical organizations in the marketplace.

Health maintenance organizations (HMOs) represented one of the significant changes occurring in health care. HMOs required a fixed payment for each person enrolled, and delivered comprehensive, coordinated medical services—usually with 100% coverage of hospital and physicians' services, including routine physicals. An attractive feature of HMOs was that they offered preventive health care services.

HMOs were priced competitively. They provided no incentive for a physician to institute extra procedures to augment his or her fee, as might occur in the "fee-for-service" cases. Many studies also showed that hospitalization rates were lower for customers of HMOs than for

those of private physicians in traditional practice. As cost-consciousness increased, health planners and government payors increasingly endorsed HMOs. The number of HMOs in the United States grew from 39 in 1971 to 431 in 1985, with 16.7 million people enrolled in those 431 HMO plans. However, some consumers resisted joining because HMOs offered a limited choice of physicians and hospitals.

Toward the end of 1985, the health care industry was undergoing further restructuring. An emerging organizational structure involved the linking of doctors, hospitals, and an insurance plan. These organizations, referred to as "supermeds" or "managed health care systems," offered a full range of vertically integrated services within one structure. For example, Hospital Corporation of America had purchased an insurance company to enable it to develop managed health care systems. Industry experts believed that by 1990 there would be 10 to 20 managed health care systems delivered by very large organizations which operated on a national basis with regional affiliates.

The role of physicians also was beginning to change. Historically, there had been too few doctors for too many patients. Physicians' success depended on their reputation among their peers; they built their practices in a year or two; and information about their medical skills spread by word of mouth from one patient to another and from one doctor to another. In addition, there existed few specialists, and their offices were so crowded that they had trouble catching up with their appointments. As in many professional service organizations, advertising was taboo.

However, all this had changed in the 1980s. The supply of physicians had increased substantially, and there was no dearth of specialists. Major contributing factors were (1) the increase in medical schools (from 79 in 1950 to 126 in 1980), and (2) aid from the government in terms of grants to medical schools and loans to medical students. The number of medical students graduating each year rose from 7,000 in 1960 to 15,000 in 1980. By 1980 the consensus was that there were too many physicians.

Company Background

LifeSpan, Inc., a Minneapolis-based, not-for-profit corporation, was the parent holding com-

---

3. Bed-occupancy rate is the percentage of total staffed beds that are actually utilized.

pany of a diversified health services corporation consisting of three hospital corporations, a nursing home, a major rehabilitation center, two product and equipment corporations, a home health services corporation, and a foundation. It was incorporated in 1982 when Abbott Northwestern Hospital (ANH)—a regional medical center in its one-hundredth year of operation—underwent a corporate restructuring, creating LifeSpan, Inc., as its parent corporation. The primary function of LifeSpan was to direct the overall strategic planning and new business development for members of the LifeSpan family. It also provided its members with support services such as financial planning, marketing, human resource administration, internal audit, management, and information systems.

LifeSpan's long-range goal was to develop a comprehensive regional system of the highest-quality health care services in the Midwest, focusing both on a metropolitan area (Minneapolis/St. Paul) total care network and on referral relationships with physicians and hospitals outside Minneapolis/St. Paul. The operating revenues for LifeSpan and its combined affiliate organizations were $211 million in 1985 (see *Exhibit 3*). LifeSpan's net income increased by over 25% to $9.8 million in 1985, from $7.8 million in 1984. This increase in net income was achieved, according to Gordon Sprenger, "through a combination of cost containment and improved productivity further supported by low price increases, all strategically positioned to enhance growing market share." In its most recent debt offering, LifeSpan received an AA credit rating from Standard and Poor. LifeSpan was a founding member of Voluntary Hospitals of America (VHA), a national organization of 650 large hospitals representing 20% of the country's inpatient market share. VHA was created to be a national health care delivery system of preeminent institutions; it included organizations such as Johns Hopkins and Massachusetts General Hospital.

Abbott Northwestern Hospital

Abbott Northwestern, an 800-bed hospital in South Minneapolis, was the largest private hospital in Minneapolis/St. Paul (Twin Cities), with a high market share in many key medical services. For example, its share of medical surgeries was 18.8% in 1985 (see *Exhibit 4*), yet in its own backyard (South Minneapolis), its share was very low.

Abbott Northwestern had seven "Centers of Excellence"—cardiovascular, neurosciences, rehabilitation (in conjunction with the Sister Kenny Institute, a LifeSpan organization), cancer, perinatal (in conjunction with another LifeSpan hospital, Minneapolis Children's Medical Center), low back, and behavioral medicine. Its cardiovascular program, for example, was unique in that it provided truly comprehensive services, from diagnostics through heart replacement. In 1985, ANH performed nearly 1,000 open heart surgeries—more than any other hospital in the area. On December 17, 1985, the first woman ever to receive an artificial heart had one (a mini Jarvik 7) implanted at ANH. The cardiovascular program at ANH was viewed as the premier one in the upper Midwest and served portions of the five-state area. This was an important market for ANH, since more than 50% of its cardiac patients came from other parts of Minnesota and out of state—primarily Wisconsin.

ANH's patients could be classified into inpatient and outpatient categories. Inpatients were admitted to the hospital by a physician and were resident in one of the hospital's beds. Outpatients used the services of the hospital without being admitted. The latter included both former inpatients who required follow-up treatment and patients referred by their private physicians to have day surgery or laboratory or diagnostic tests performed.

Management. The ANH management philosophy was to render high-quality service with emphasis placed on taking care of the patient's needs. Although a not-for-profit organization, the objective of various policies was twofold: to support the corporation's long-range goal and at the same time maintain strong financial viability (represented by a fair return on equity) to finance appropriate growth of quality health care services. Therefore, in order to assure corporatewide commitment to necessary asset maintenance, enhancement, and expansion, management set key business ratio targets for liquidity, leverage, and profitability. As one executive noted: "While the party line is human service, it is vital that we meet the bottom line."

The management team was young (average age, 34), including the marketing group, which was beginning to have an increasingly high profile within ANH. Richard Kramer, executive vice president of LifeSpan, had received an M.S. degree from Syracuse University and a master's degree in hospital administration from the University of Minnesota. He had been with the organization for 15 years and was very active in developing LifeSpan's hospital mergers, physician joint ventures, and strategic plans. Kramer started the LifeSpan marketing department in 1982. He was involved in various industry associations, and in 1985 was a member of the Government Relations Committee of the Minnesota Hospital Association.

Steven Hillestad, vice president of marketing, had a double master's degree in health administration and public administration from the University of Wisconsin. Hillestad, who had been involved in health care marketing since 1974, had served as executive director of corporate marketing for another hospital in Minneapolis prior to joining LifeSpan in October 1983. Hillestad had published several marketing articles in journals such as *Modern Healthcare* and *Journal of Health Care Marketing*. He also was a co-author of a book entitled *Health Care Marketing Plans: From Strategy to Action*.

The Minneapolis/St. Paul Health Care Market

The health care industry was the largest employer in Minneapolis/St. Paul. In addition, the Twin Cities had one of the most fiercely competitive health care marketplaces in the United States, with as many as 26 hospitals and 6 HMOs. During 1980–1985, HMOs in the metropolitan area had experienced an annual growth rate of 80%, reaching a level of 865,000 members. In 1985, HMOs controlled as much as 41% of the Twin Cities marketplace, compared with just 11% on a national basis.

Industry experts believed that this dominance by HMOs had caused the inpatient market to shrink. During the five-year period 1980–1984, hospital utilization had declined by approximately 29% (see *Table A*).

As inpatient days declined, many hospitals had lower occupancy rates. Richard Kramer commented on the shrinking market size:

> Some hospitals experienced declines of over 50% in the number of inpatient days during the 1980–1985 period. In those hospitals, occupancy was down to less than 50%. Many hospitals were under severe financial pressure and "business as usual" was no longer feasible.

To survive with HMOs, hospitals were undertaking cost containment measures and changing practice patterns—shifting more care to an outpatient basis. During 1981–1985, ANH's outpatient surgery volume increased from 13% to 44% of all surgical procedures performed at the hospital. Hospitals also resorted to using more temporary personnel. For example, full-time permanent professional staff such as nurses were often replaced with part-time employees.

Despite the fact that total admissions and inpatient days were declining, the number of physicians was increasing. The result was a decline in the admissions per physician. In 1985 there was a surplus of doctors in the Twin Cities, and their average income had declined by 25% from 1984 to 1985. Consequently, the Twin Cities began witnessing intense rivalry between doctors. Competitive pressures were transforming the industry and pushing hospitals, HMOs, and doctors into a struggle for survival.

Table A   Twin Cities' Hospital Utilization

Year	Discharges	Inpatient Days	Average Length of Stay (in days)
1980	361,421	2,794,810	7.73
1981	353,220	2,647,065	7.49
1982	343,716	2,486,505	7.23
1983	333,933	2,298,459	6.88
1984	316,695	1,989,466	6.28

Source: LifeSpan, Inc.

The Buying Process

In 1982 ANH management conducted a survey of 1,800 consumers and 400 physicians in the Twin Cities. The survey found that increasingly of late, it was the *patients* who selected which hospital to enter, once the physician decided that hospitalization was required. Previously, the patients had depended on their physicians to select the hospital. (*Table B* presents the summary of the responses to the question, "Who is the key decision maker in hospital selection?")

Various factors were found to influence consumers' hospital choice. Most important among patients with recent hospital experience were proximity to home, quality-related attributes, and presence of a particular physician.

The survey results also indicated that

(1) consumers believed that most hospitals were of good and similar quality, and
(2) consumers had no marked preference for any hospital—with the exception of the University of Minnesota Hospital, which was perceived as the hospital to go to if one was very sick.

With respect to ANH, the survey indicated the following:

- Two out of three consumers did not recognize the name *Abbott Northwestern Hospital*.
- Less than 10% of consumers had a clear image of Abbott Northwestern Hospital.
- Approximately 30% of ANH's patients came from outside the seven-county metropolitan area.
- Those who had used ANH were very satisfied with their experience.

- Of the consumers that did recognize the name *Abbott Northwestern Hospital*, over 80% believed that ANH was located in a part of Minneapolis in which a disproportionately large amount of crime took place.

Marketing at Abbott Northwestern Hospital

The goal of the marketing group at ANH was to increase ANH's market share. To achieve this goal, a three-pronged approach was adopted:

(1) Provide potential customers with an incentive to visit the hospital when they were not sick. (The marketing group believed that once consumers had contact with ANH through one of its various programs, they would be so satisfied with the service quality that they would be more likely to use ANH when they needed hospital facilities and services.)
(2) Identify potential customers who did not have a physician, and recommend an ANH physician to them. (This would please not only the potential customer, but also the physician, who, it was hoped, would then send the patients to ANH whenever hospital facilities and services were needed.)
(3) Ensure that patients were very satisfied with their experience at ANH and that they felt they were treated as individuals. The marketing group believed that patients who had a positive feeling about their experiences at ANH would probably choose ANH again if they needed a hospital. Also, in relating their hospital experiences to relatives and friends, their positive word-of-mouth would help ANH's image.

Table B   Key Decision Maker in Hospital Selection, 1982 Twin Cities Survey (%)

| | Consumer's Views[a] | | | Physicians' Views[b] | |
	Men	Women	Total	Inpatient Stay	Outpatient Surgery
Patient alone	36	26	30	7	7
Patient with doctor	24	28	26	49	38
Subtotal	60	54	56	56	45
Physician alone	37	42	40	40	51
Emergency room	3	4	4	4	4
Subtotal	40	46	44	44	55
Total	100	100	100	100	100

a. 1,800 consumers
b. 400 physicians

6

ANH management believed that this strategy was consistent with the culture at ANH, which encouraged all employees who had contact with customers to exhibit a warm, tender, and caring attitude. For example, patients who arrived at ANH early in the morning for the popular one-day surgery program were received with a warm welcome between 5 A.M. and 7 A.M. by a hospital manager and a senior executive such as Robert Spinner, executive vice president of ANH, and Steve Hillestad, vice president of marketing. Also, free valet parking was introduced, primarily to assist the elderly and handicapped. Richard Kramer felt that "all this was a customer orientation never before seen in the health care industry."

To make ANH more attractive to out-of-Minneapolis patients and their families, a 123-room hotel-like facility called Wasie Center was set up in the ANH complex. Accommodations in Wasie Center, though not fancy, were very clean, comfortable, and secure. The center was run on a break-even basis, and rooms for patients and their families were priced at $28–35 per day. This encouraged nonlocal patients to pick ANH when selecting a hospital in Minneapolis.

Product Management

At ANH each medical service, such as cardiology, radiology, neurology, cancer, chemical dependency, and emergency services, was treated as a "product" or department. ANH management kept a close watch on the progress made by each product. Management felt that while some products (e.g., cardiology) were doing very well, some others (e.g., urology), though profitable, were not receiving adequate attention. To focus attention on products that were profitable but not being given much attention, product management was introduced in May 1985. Five nonphysician product managers were appointed—one for each of the following products: neurology, urology, orthopedics/rehabilitation, low back, and chemical dependency.

The primary objective of product managers was to increase the market share of their product. They interacted with concerned physicians, made sales calls, talked to patients, worked on special programs to promote the product, and were responsible for pricing. Product managers were evaluated on the basis of their performance with respect to targets which were set for gross dollar sales as well as number of operative procedures. A product manager's compensation consisted of a base salary (approximately $35,000) and a bonus linked to accomplishment of previously set targets.

Most ANH managers felt that the product management system worked very well. An indication of its success was the large number of requests for product managers received by Hillestad from various departments. For instance, emergency room services wanted a product manager to increase ANH's share of the emergency room business. As one executive put it:

> If the emergency room product manager could put together a program directed at neighborhood groups, neighborhood schools, and ambulance drivers, our emergency room business will shoot up and so will our revenues and profitability. For instance, we could have coffee and donuts provided to ambulance drivers and paramedics. This might provide them an incentive to bring patients to the ANH emergency room. After all, for each patient brought into the emergency room we make about $40 on an average revenue of $100.

Some department managers who did not have product managers were upset because they believed that departments with product managers were getting more attention and were also being allotted bigger shares of the marketing budget.

Pricing

ANH's charges for inpatients were typically divided into a daily room-and-board fee and a fixed fee each time an ancillary service was used by the patient. The impact of ANH's fee structure on its financial performance was directly affected by the mix of patients. For inpatients covered under any cost-based reimbursement program, the fee set had little impact on the revenue-generating ability. For self-paying and privately insured consumers, adjustments to the rate structure could produce meaningful changes in revenues and profits.

The continuing implementation of Medicare's Prospective Payment System (PPS) for hospital inpatient services was having a strong effect on hospitals. Under PPS, which became effective on January 1, 1984, payments to hospitals for inpatient services were set in advance by the U.S. Health Care Financing Administration through a system in which a price was fixed for each of 467 different diagnostic-related groups (DRGs). Several DRGs belonged to each of the "products" at ANH. To be more in line with the new reimbursement scheme, ANH changed its pricing policy from cost-plus to product-based. In addition, price competition was becoming very intense (see *Table C*). ANH management was unsure about the appropriate course of action. As Hillestad said, "We pondered over whether we should continue to price our open heart surgery at $22,000 and watch competitors [who charged $15,000] gain market share but lose money, or whether we should match the $15,000 price to retain our market share."

Outpatients tended to be more profitable than inpatients because third-party payors reimbursed the hospital for outpatient services on a fee-for-service rather than a cost basis. On an average, the revenue from an outpatient was $200 and the contribution was $85, compared with $6,000 and $700 respectively for an inpatient.

Another area of concern was pricing to HMOs. HMOs controlled access to over 40% of the market, and the average number of HMO patients at ANH had risen from 6% in 1983 to 26% in 1985. To protect its patient base, ANH believed it was necessary to establish contractual relationships with HMOs. However, due to intense competition among Twin Cities hospitals, bidding to HMOs had become very competitive. Besides, margins on HMO business were already lower than on the non-HMO business.

Distribution

ANH executives believed, as did most health care corporate executives, that physicians were an important part of the hospital distribution system. As Hillestad noted:

> Physicians are our retailers and are critical in getting patients to the hospital. Physi-

cians play a dominant role in determining who should be hospitalized and the type of services that the patient should receive. Physicians influence 70% of all personal health care spending. Unfortunately, they view themselves as leaders of the health care team and view business terminology as repugnant. At one meeting, when they [physicians] were referred to as "our customers," two physicians walked out.

Of the 1,125 physicians registered with ANH, approximately 400 were active (an "active" physician being one who brought at least 30 patients a year to the hospital). Most physicians wanted to be active members of a hospital, since this qualified them for policy-making positions, and gave them an opportunity to participate in the hospital's malpractice insurance program. Active physicians accounted for almost 85% of ANH's patients.

ANH management took several steps to support its active physicians. One form of support was the physician-referral system, in which ANH referred patients who did not have a regular physician to one of its physicians. To direct referrals appropriately, ANH needed to evaluate its physicians objectively. Physicians were evaluated by peers, administrators, and patients. Some physicians who received high-quality reviews from their peers for their medical practice were not well received by patients because they did not have the best bedside manners. Such physicians were not ANH's best "retailers" in terms of patient satisfaction and the number of patients they brought to ANH.

ANH also initiated a Medical Staff Development Program; in 1984 it helped five groups of physicians (including 31 independent practitioners in downtown Minneapolis) establish full-service suburban clinics in communities with demonstrated needs for primary-care services. Assistance was provided in terms of market research, office site selection, staff to manage the office, and legal advice. Physicians also

Table C Product Line Pricing

Product	ANH's Cost	ANH's Price	Competitors' Prices
Open-heart surgery	$17,000	$22,000	$15,000
Delivery (1-day)	750	800	na
Delivery (3-day)	1,200	1,400	1,100–1,400
One-day surgery	$150–500	$200–900	$200–900

were provided with innovative solutions to capital financing problems. For example, equipment and ambulatory-care ventures were set up in conjunction with physicians and selected outside investors. More suburban clinics were set up in 1985 through joint ventures with leading Twin Cities physicians.

To strengthen its out-of-town "retail network," ANH took steps to link primary physicians and hospitals in rural areas with tertiary care support, teaching, and consultation whenever they were needed. A 24-hour toll-free phone line was set up in 1985 to link rural physicians and hospitals with ANH's subspecialty physicians.

Communications

Historically, ANH's communications had been directed exclusively at physicians, who were viewed as the ones who brought consumers to the hospital. Since 1982, however, most of ANH's communications were being directed at the end consumer.

In 1982, ANH management took advantage of the hospital's centennial celebration to communicate ANH's name and services to a wider public than had previously been attempted. A wide variety of media (radio, television, newspapers, and billboards) was used to enhance the awareness and image of ANH. Research conducted after the campaign showed a significant increase in ANH's name recognition.

Spurred by this success, ANH management decided in 1983 to launch the first major health care advertising campaign in Minneapolis. The campaign focused on individual "products" such as heart disease, cancer, and prenatal care. Expenditure on communications continued to increase, reaching $405,900 in 1984; all the while, all other departments had budget cuts. Richard Kramer noted, "We need and like to have continuity, hence the regular advertising. It's the reinforcement of repeat messages that impacts consumer behavior."

Specific Programs

Some ANH executives felt that although the 1983 communications program was directed at the end consumer, it did not have a "call-to-action." In addition, they felt that consumers would find it easier to deal with just one tele-

phone number for all concerns, rather than many different numbers for different health inquiries. This led to the creation of "Medformation."

Medformation

Medformation was set up in July 1984 as a community telephone line providing health care information and referrals to various programs, services, and physicians affiliated with ANH. Its objective was to reach consumers directly and to make it easier for them to call ANH for any health need, since the various ANH programs would be consolidated under one system.

Selling Medformation internally had been a very difficult task for the marketing group. Several physicians did not understand or appreciate the benefits of advertising and raised concerns about its high expenditures. They felt that the money could be far better utilized by purchasing new medical equipment. Also, they wondered how the physician referral system would actually work. Many expressed the fear that a few physicians would get most of the referrals while others would get none or, at best, a few. Many physicians were uncomfortable with the perceived loss of control resulting from the hospital trying to bring patients to them instead of the traditional method of physicians getting patients to the hospital. In the words of one physician, "ANH is attempting to increase its control so that it can manipulate the physician."

A major statewide promotional campaign announced Medformation and a single phone number that connected callers to the Medformation staff. Care was taken to make sure that the ads downplayed the link between Medformation and Abbott Northwestern Hospital. Some of the consumers interviewed in a focus group revealed that they were surprised and upset to learn that Medformation was in fact linked with a hospital.

John Penrod, marketing manager responsible for Medformation, had a staff consisting of two information specialists and one registered nurse. Two on-call nurses were available to help out if necessary. Medformation staff were trained to provide the caller with necessary information or to forward the call to the appropriate departmental and medical personnel. Medformation operators were provided with a protocol to follow for each product line or department. After the call, an appropriate follow-up letter and collateral pieces including brochures relating to the appropriate ANH programs were sent to the caller. The fixed cost of Medformation was approximately $175,000.

Early Medformation advertising focused on creating an awareness of Medformation and providing a physician referral service. In addition to all those who called in for a physician referral, almost 10% of consumers who called in regarding cancer, medical information, and "other" information, also requested a physician referral. Hillestad estimated that 70% of consumers who were given a physician referral contacted the physician. Of those who contacted the referred physician, it was believed that approximately 25% would return within a year to the hospital (10% as inpatients, 10% as outpatients, and 5% in the emergency room), and that 20% would return during the following year (5% as inpatients, 10% as outpatients, and 5% in the emergency room).

In 1985 the focus of Medformation was extended to cover various other ANH programs such as weight loss, stress management, natural fitness, heart seminars, and quit-smoking. Many who called regarding these programs actually attended the programs. For example, almost 60% of those who called regarding weight loss and quit-smoking attended these programs. The fee was $100–200 and gave ANH a contribution of approximately 60%. In many of these programs, participants were told that they should check with their physicians before adopting the recommended approach. Participants who indicated that they did not have a physician (approximately 10%) were referred to one of ANH's physicians.

Medformation was advertised in the two leading local newspapers; 90% of the insertions were quarter-page ads on weekdays, and cost $700 per insertion (see *Exhibit 5*). The rest were full-page ads in the Sunday edition and cost $7,000 per insertion. Hillestad believed that the higher response to the Sunday ads justified the higher cost. In 1985 a total of 28,667 Medformation calls were received, with the heaviest response on the day of the ad insertion, only slightly lower response on the following day, followed by a sharp drop. (*Exhibit 6* shows a breakdown of the Medformation ads and calls

received in 1985.) The overall response to Medformation ads in terms of telephone calls had far exceeded management's expectations.

Commenting on Medformation, Penrod noted that "Medformation has been a phenomenal success. We have had a big increase in calls, and our research has shown a sharp improvement in consumer perception [see *Exhibit 7*]. We are delighted with this." Hillestad and Penrod were contemplating extending Medformation to cover outbound telemarketing as well (i.e., to have Medformation operators call people at their homes to promote specific programs), but were not sure how effective this would be. Hillestad felt that first they needed to evaluate in a better way the effectiveness of the existing Medformation programs (i.e., inbound) before pushing for extension to outbound.

Hillestad was surprised when on December 20, 1985, he received a call from the marketing director of a New York hospital who wanted to buy the 36 ads used by ANH for $100,000. He also was willing to pay ANH an additional $20,000 to learn which one of the two Medformation cancer ads worked better. Hillestad turned down that offer, but began seriously contemplating putting together a package of the ads, including information on the ads' relative effectiveness, and selling the package to hospitals on a national basis.

ANH management also considered licensing Medformation to hospitals in the nonmetro areas of Minnesota and western Wisconsin. Under this arrangement, ANH would license the Medformation name and telephone number to a hospital in exchange for some predetermined minimum number of referrals of complicated illnesses.

WomenCare

WomenCare was a program developed by ANH, who recognized that women had a variety of specialized health care needs that went beyond obstetrics/gynecology services. The program provided a total range of services for women seeking wellness, fitness, weight control, aging, and behavioral and reproductive guidance. It encouraged women to play a more active role in their health care by becoming better informed through WomenCare seminars and classes.

WomenCare was inaugurated on March 25, 1985, by Women's Day—a day-long event that focused on the special health care needs of women. The response was outstanding; over 2,500 women attended, paying $100 each. Throughout the year, WomenCare continued to provide the community with timely seminars on various subjects. It also helped develop breast cancer diagnostic and osteoporosis prevention programs. During the year there were 12 such programs and the average attendance was 120 people. The fee for these programs ranged from $100 to $200 each, and the contribution was 60%.

ANH management was surprised at the response that WomenCare programs had received. For example, a weight loss program for women, advertised under WomenCare, filled up much faster than a general weight loss program—despite the fact that over 80% of those who attended the general weight loss program were women and that the fee was $120 compared with $100 for the general class. (*Exhibit 8* shows an ad used for WomenCare.)

Other Programs

To meet the needs of a society that had become far more fitness oriented, ANH offered a number of other programs—community courses in weight loss, quit-smoking, and stress management. Each course was presented by trained professionals who emphasized behavior modification.

Keeping elderly people independent was another important part of LifeSpan's philosophy of care. In October 1985 ANH organized "Seniors' Day"—a free event which included sessions on topics such as facing the crisis of illness, managing urinary incontinence, and staying in charge of life. Over 450 people attended. Wellness programs for the elderly on topics such as diabetes, medication, and exercise were offered as well.

Current Situation

In 1986 ANH's communications strategies were to broaden reach for maximum penetration of health care buyers, enlarge and reinforce the centers of excellence among consumers and physicians, and integrate the Medformation

and WomenCare programs more fully with the Abbott Northwestern campaign. Projected media advertising expenditures, summarized in *Exhibit 9*, emphasized television and newspapers with support from radio and posters. The mix for television advertising was the same for all "products"—40% prime time, 30% news, 20% fringe, and 10% daytime.

For Medformation, television would be used in addition to newspapers. In South Minneapolis, to increase emphasis, eight outdoor posters per month would be used for four months. It was estimated that over the four-month period, approximately 74% of adults in South Minneapolis would be exposed to the posters an average of 15 times each.

In order to increase consumer reach and build awareness of the WomenCare program, a broader range of media was planned. In addition to quarter-page newspaper ads, outdoor posters would be used to carry a WomenCare-image program, and 60-second radio spots would promote special events such as Women's Day, Spring Seminar, and Fall Seminar.

Advertising for tertiary care was aimed at adults aged 18 and above. A multimedia campaign using television and newspapers was planned. Television would be used for a total of 14 weeks with 80 GRPs per week.[4] Newspapers would carry 17 full-page ads.

The Decision

Steve Hillestad had a little over 16 hours to think about the next morning's presentation to the ANH board. As he scanned his papers, he focused on two main issues. First, he was convinced that marketing contributed significantly to LifeSpan's 1985 performance. Sales and market share had increased and consumer perceptions of ANH had improved. Hillestad wondered how he could measure the sales response to ANH's marketing activities—especially Medformation—in a manner he and the board would find credible. Second, if the budget was approved, he wondered how he might justify the allocation of resources to the different products and programs.

---

4. Gross Rating Points (GRPs): a combined measure of reach (number of people exposed) and frequency (number of exposures per person reached) for advertising weight.

Exhibit 1 National Health Care Expenses and Gross National Product

	Gross National Product ($ billions)	*National Health Expenditure*	
		($ billions)	*(% of GNP)*
1955	$ 400.0	$ 17.7	4.4%
1965	705.1	41.9	5.9
1970	1,015.5	75.0	7.4
1975	1,598.4	132.7	8.3
1980	2,731.9	248.1	9.1
1981	3,052.6	287.0	9.4
1982	3,166.0	323.6	10.2
1983	3,401.6	357.2	10.5
1984	3,774.7	390.2	10.3
1985	$3,988.5	$425.0	10.7%

Source: Office of Statistics and Data Management, Health Care Financing Administration

Exhibit 2 Health Care Expenditures

I. Financing of Personal Health Care, 1950–1985 (%)

	Public				*Total*	*Patient*	
		State and			*Third*	*Direct*	
Year	*Federal*	*Local*	*Total*	*Private*	*Party*	*Payments*	*Total*
1950	10.4%	12.0%	22.4%	12.1%	34.5%	65.5%	100%
1955	10.5	12.5	23.0	18.9	41.9	58.1	100
1960	9.3	12.5	21.8	23.4	45.2	54.8	100
1965	10.1	11.9	22.0	26.4	48.4	51.6	100
1970	22.2	12.1	34.3	25.2	59.5	40.5	100
1975	26.8	12.7	39.5	28.0	67.5	32.5	100
1980	28.5	11.0	39.5	31.9	71.4	28.6	100
1985	30.3%	9.4%	39.7%	31.9%	71.6%	28.4%	100%

II. Sources of Funds in 1985 ($ billions)

	Total Personal Health Care	*Hospital Care*	*Physicians' Services*	*Dentists' Services*	*Other Professional Services*	*Drugs and Sundries*	*Eyeglasses and Appliances*	*Nursing Home Care*	*Other Health Care*
Total (in billions)	$371.4	$166.7	$82.8	$27.1	$12.6	$28.5	$7.5	$35.2	$11.0
Direct patient payments	105.6	15.5	21.8	17.3	6.0	21.8	5.1	18.1	–
Third parties	265.8	151.2	61.0	9.8	6.6	6.7	2.4	17.1	11.0
Private health insurance	113.5	59.3	36.9	9.2	2.9	4.0	0.9	0.3	–
Other private sources	4.9	2.1	0.0	–	0.1	–	–	0.3	2.4
Government	147.4	89.8	24.1	0.6	3.6	2.7	1.5	16.5	8.6
Federal	112.6	71.6	19.7	0.3	2.8	1.4	1.3	9.4	6.0
Medicare	70.5	48.5	17.1	–	2.0	–	1.2	0.6	1.1
Medicaid	21.9	8.1	1.9	0.3	0.7	1.3	–	8.1	1.5
Other programs	20.2	15.0	0.7	0.0	0.1	0.1	0.1	0.7	3.4
State and local	34.9	18.2	4.4	0.3	0.8	1.3	0.2	7.1	2.6
Medicaid	17.9	6.8	1.5	0.2	0.6	1.0	–	6.6	1.2
Other programs	$ 17.0	$ 11.4	$ 2.9	$ 0.1	$ 0.2	$ 0.3	$0.2	$ 0.5	$ 1.4

Source: Office of Statistics and Data Management, Health Care Financing Administration

Exhibit 3 Income Statement and Change in Operating Fund Equity ($000)

	1985	1984	1983
Total net revenue	211,457	149,941	135,316
Operating expenses			
Salaries	118,083	103,352	92,650
Supplies and other expenses	68,071	28,716	28,121
Depreciation	12,118	8,087	7,177
Interest	6,973	5,523	4,850
Total operating expense	205,245	145,678	132,798
Operating margin	6,212	4,263	2,518
Total other revenue (expense)	3,588	3,583	2,336
Net income (loss)	$9,800	$7,846	$4,854
Operating fund equity at beginning of year	56,232	47,323	42,154
Transfers from restricted funds for purchase of plant assets	0	0	315
Fund equity of new affiliates	19,691	1,063	0
Operating fund equity at end of year	85,723	56,232	47,323

Source: LifeSpan, Inc.

Exhibit 4 Health Care Industry in Minneapolis

	Number of Staffed Beds[a]	Bed Occupancy	Market Shares (M.S.)[b]		(expected)
			1984	1985	1986
Abbott Northwestern	705	71.2	17.2%	18.8%	20.5
South Parkway	372	71.1	12.2	12.7	12.7
Presbyterian	333	68.3	13.8	13.3	12.7
Lawrence Memorial	506	57.3	12.1	11.6	11.1
Glenbrook General	396	55.6	10.8	10.2	10.9
Glenbrook Memorial	488	68.2	7.5	7.6	8.3
Glenbrook Wilson	103	47.8	–	1.9	1.9
St. Agnes	376	71.6	8.2	5.5	4.5
Trinity	223	62.6	6.9	7.4	6.5
Mt. Carmel	160	59.8	6.4	6.0	6.2
Emerson	259	60.7	4.9	5.0	4.7

Source: Metropolitan Health Board (January–June 1985)

a. A staffed bed is one that is operational and available for use by patients.
b. M.S.: Medical Surgical.

Exhibit 5 Quarter-Page Newspaper Ad

If you really want to quit smoking, before you pick up your next cigarette, pick up the phone and call Medformation.

Find out about the Quit Smoking Program that works. It has an 80% success rate for those difficult first 2 months.

It's a professional program—developed by Abbott Northwestern Hospital, and led by psychologists and other health professionals. Best of all, the program takes only 3 weeks to complete.

The next classes begin *January 15th* at Northland Executive Center in Bloomington and *February 5th* at Abbott Northwestern.

For more information on becoming a non-smoker, or for the answer to any health question, call Medformation.

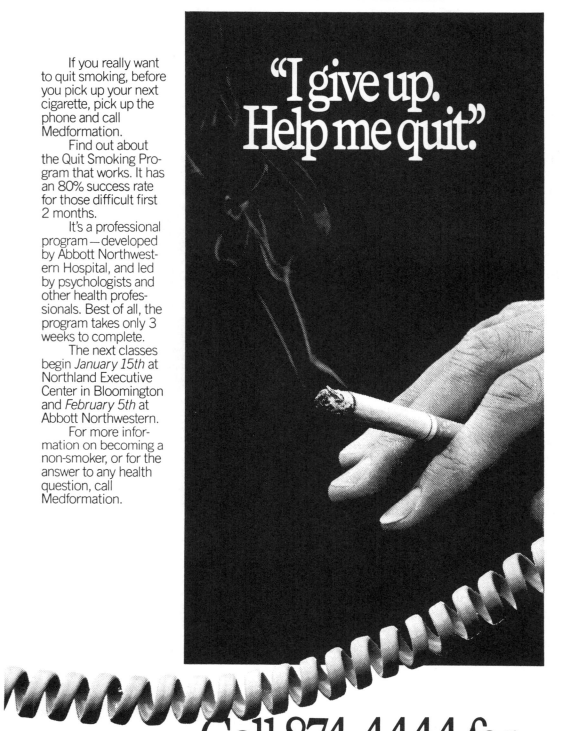

"I give up. Help me quit."

Call 874-4444 for Medformation.™

One of the loving arms of Abbott Northwestern Hospital.

Exhibit 6 Medformation Ads and Responses, 1985

	Weight Loss		Quit Smoking		Physician Referral		Cancer		Medical Information		Others		Total	
	Ads	Calls	Ads	Calls	Ads	Calls	Ads	Calls	Ads	Calls	Ads	Calls	Ads	Calls
January	3	113	4	124	5	119	—	0	—	205	12	1,965	24	2,526
February	2	98	3	118	3	126	—	0	—	181	10	1,745	18	2,268
March	3	147	—	18	2	163	—	0	—	176	10	1,667	15	2,171
April	3	115	3	123	6	261	7	240	—	229	4	1,829	23	2,797
May	—	19	1	53	5	202	2	81	4	256	8	1,767	20	2,378
June	—	33	1	44	6	195	2	61	4	235	12	1,577	25	2,145
July	2	66	2	49	7	265	3	1,087	1	257	4	1,444	19	3,168
August	1	46	2	53	2	218	2	1,414	—	250	5	1,378	12	3,359
September	1	26	2	21	6	220	—	57	—	260	6	1,379	15	1,963
October	—	6	2	25	5	263	—	31	3	344	4	1,393	14	2,062
November	—	9	2	21	3	160	—	3	3	240	6	1,253	14	1,686
December	—	15	—	6	2	146	—	0	—	197	4	1,780	6	2,144
Total	15	693	22	655	52	2,338	16	2,974	15	2,830	85	19,177	205	28,667

Source: LifeSpan, Inc.

Exhibit 7   Consumer Perception of Which Hospital Provides the Best Medical Care, 1984 and 1985 (%)

	Serious Heart Problems		Stroke		Severe Pregnancy Problems		Chemical Dependency		Emergency	
	1984	1985	1984	1985	1984	1985	1984	1985	1984	1985
Abbott Northwestern	13.7[a]	26.1	12.0	15.7	13.7	10.9	5.6	7.0	4.7	5.7
South Parkway	3.0	6.1	4.7	5.7	2.1	3.5	0.4	0.9	7.3	12.2
Presbyterian	3.8	2.2	4.3	3.0	3.8	3.0	0.9	1.3	6.0	6.5
Lawrence Memorial	4.7	4.8	5.1	3.0	1.7	0.0	3.4	2.2	9.0	11.3
Glenbrook General	3.4	1.7	6.0	3.0	4.3	2.6	0.9	0.4	11.5	8.7
Glenbrook Memorial	0.4	0.4	0.4	0.0	0.4	0.0	0.9	0.9	0.4	0.0
Glenbrook Wilson	1.3	0.4	0.9	0.4	1.7	0.4	0.4	0.4	0.9	0.4
St. Agnes	0.4	2.2	1.3	2.6	5.1	3.5	42.5	38.8	0.0	0.0
University of Minnesota	28.2	26.0	16.7	12.6	9.8	7.0	3.0	0.9	2.1	2.2
Others	10.7	7.7	7.7	4.8	8.2	3.9	16.3	13.8	31.7	25.2
All the same	1.7	0.4	0.9	3.9	1.2	2.6	1.3	1.3	1.7	2.6
Don't know	28.7	22.0	40.0	45.3	48.0	62.6	24.4	32.1	24.7	25.2
Total	100.0	100.0	100.0	100.0	100.0	100.0	100.0	100.0	100.0	100.0

Source: LifeSpan, Inc.

a. 13.7% of consumers surveyed perceived that Abbott Northwestern Hospital provided the best medical care for serious heart problems.

Exhibit 8   Ad for WomenCare Health Care Program

WEIGHT CONTROL: IT'S A JOB WHERE WOMEN HAVE TO WORK HARDER THAN MEN.

It's something women have suspected for a long time. But, until recently, no one really understood why women have a more difficult time losing and keeping weight off.

There is a physiological reason. Most women have a higher percentage of body fat while most men have more muscles. Since fat is metabolically less active than muscle, women end up burning fewer calories.

WomenCare's Lifestyle Weight Loss program focuses on these differences. This is a women's weight loss program. It's not a diet. It's a program that gives you the facts, motivation and the emotional support you need to help you control your weight...for good. There are Fitness Specialists who work with you to develop an exercise program that will reduce body fat and increase muscle mass, the key to burning more calories. How successful is this program? The average weight loss is more than 20 lbs. And, it's weight most of the people keep off for years.

For more information call Medformation 874-4444.

WOMENCARE^{SM}

of Abbott Northwestern Hospital

©1985 LifeSpan, Inc.

Exhibit 9 Media Split of Communications Budget

		1985			1986		
		Prod.	*Media*	*Total*	*Prod.*	*Media*	*Total*
Medformation	TV	–	–	–	79,000	278,600	357,600
	Newspaper	24,000	270,000	294,000	9,500	98,100	107,600
	Posters	–	–	–	16,500	60,500	77,000
		24,000	270,000	294,000	105,000	437,200	542,200
Tertiary Care	TV	64,000	164,000	228,000	108,000	217,350	325,350
	Newspaper	–	–	–	33,600	131,650	165,250
		64,000	164,000	228,000	141,600	349,000	490,600
WomenCare	TV	–	–	–	30,000	57,850	87,850
	Newspaper	35,000	131,400	166,400	9,600	64,850	74,450
	Posters	–	–	–	5,000	10,400	15,400
	Radio	–	–	–	4,500	34,900	39,400
		35,000	131,400	166,400	49,100	168,000	217,100
Trade	Magazine	10,400	17,700	28,100	–	–	–
Total	TV	64,000	164,100	228,100	217,000	553,800	770,800
	Radio	–	–	–	4,500	34,900	39,400
	Newspaper	59,000	401,400	460,400	52,700	294,600	347,300
	Posters	–	–	–	21,500	70,900	92,400
	Magazine	10,400	17,700	28,100	–	–	–
		133,400	583,200	716,600	295,700	954,200	1,249,900

Source: LifeSpan, Inc.

Hurricane Island
Outward Bound School

*Bruce H. Clark, Associate for Case Development, prepared this case under the supervision of Professor **Thomas V. Bonoma** as the basis for class discussion rather than to illustrate either effective or ineffective handling of an administrative situation.*

Tell yourself, while 50 feet above a quarry on a one-foot-long, one-inch-wide cliff, being held up by a single rope, that you're not scared, but rather having fun. Capability becomes a state of mind, depending on how focused and committed you are. These are not challenges of you conquering the cliff, but of trust conquering fear. Do you trust the person holding your safety line? Or, rather, do you trust yourself?

—Student

I learned that I am a strong person, that even when I'm almost dead sure I can't do something, I can. Now I'm ready to hold out my hand—like my instructors held out their hands—and pull up someone who needs help. Ready to give my friend who is discouraged a hug. Ready to recognize the people I can rely on and those I can't.

—Student

To serve, to strive, and not to yield.

—Outward Bound motto

P hilip Chin sketched out ideas in a notebook as the small commuter plane he had ridden from Boston approached Owls Head Airport. Behind Owls Head lay the town of Rockland, Maine (population 8,000), home to the headquarters of the Hurricane Island Outward Bound School (Hurricane), where Chin was director of marketing.

Hurricane was one of five U.S. schools in the Outward Bound movement. Outward Bound had pioneered a rigorous form of "experiential" education that placed groups of students in wilderness settings to develop self-confidence, teamwork, and respect for the environment.

In early October 1986, the summer crowds in Penobscot Bay were largely gone; the quiet waters below Chin's plane sported only a few fishing boats at anchor. Soon the fall weather would settle in, closing Owls Head two days out of three and thus requiring a two-hour drive to Portland for reliable air service. Now, operationally, the school was slowing down, while administratively the nonprofit organization's pace was quickening. The school was well into its 1987 planning process.

Chin had been at Hurricane for only eight months. He had been brought to Maine from New York City especially for his marketing experience. A Wharton MBA, he had worked in marketing management at General Foods, Doubleday Book Clubs, and PepsiCo. He had spent the last five years as a new-venture and marketing consultant. Except for the controller, Joe Adams, Chin was the only senior manager at Hurricane who had not risen from the course development and instruction side of the school.

As director of marketing, Chin was responsible for the organization's 1987 marketing plan. The 1987 plan would be his first for Hurricane. Aside from choosing the most productive tactics on which to spend a very limited marketing budget, Chin had to be certain that any marketing initiative would accurately reflect the unique character and concerns of Hurricane Island Outward Bound.

Outward Bound History

The first Outward Bound school was established by Kurt Hahn in 1941. Originally the headmaster of a German boarding school, Hahn was jailed in 1934 for his outspoken criticism of Adolph Hitler. He escaped to Scotland and continued his work in education, developing a system of interrelated athletic and educational standards for teenage boys. This system became the foundation for the first Outward Bound course and school, in Wales. During and after World War II, the Outward Bound concept spread rapidly; in 1986, there were more than 30 chartered Outward Bound schools around the world.

The first U.S. Outward Bound school was chartered in 1962 in Colorado, followed immediately by the Voyageur school in Minnesota. Hurricane was founded in 1964. In 1965, these three schools collaborated to found a national coordinating body—Outward Bound, Inc., also known simply as "National." National was a nonprofit institution responsible for chartering new schools and supporting the Outward Bound movement in the United States. While the schools were independently organized and managed, they agreed to abide by certain joint policies established by National. National also conducted fund-raising, publicity, and advertising campaigns for Outward Bound as a whole. To support these activities, each member school paid franchise and marketing fees to National. Franchise fees went toward safety and curriculum work; marketing fees paid for National's marketing campaign, and were based on the level of activity National conducted for each school. Beyond these activities, the confederation of schools was quite loose.

Each school was governed by a board of trustees, similar in function to a board of directors. The schools' trustee chairs comprised National's Outward Bound Executive Committee (OBEX), which ruled on issues of national concern to Outward Bound.

Hurricane Island Outward Bound School

Most of the Outward Bound schools, while offering a variety of courses, specialized in one area. Hurricane Island was the sea school. Founder and school president Peter Willauer's work in education and sailing led him to envision an outdoor classroom on the ocean. While working at a private high school, he began to piece together the philosophy, funding, and board members for Hurricane. After enlisting volunteers to construct the Hurricane Island site in the summer of 1964, Willauer enrolled and graduated the school's first group of students in 1965.

The early years of the school were lean. In the mid-1980s, Vice President for Development Pen Williamson recalled "a little summer sailing school" struggling for existence in Boston. In 1971, the school moved to new headquarters in Rockland. Over the next decade, Hurricane expanded dramatically, both in facilities and in number of staff and students. It was not until the 1980s, however, that rapid growth seemingly began to outstrip the ability of the organization to manage it. (See *Exhibit 1* for a financial summary of Hurricane's performance.)

Through 1985, Hurricane had never broken even on an operating basis. Instead, the organization relied on contributions to make up the difference between tuition revenues and expenses. In the early 1980s, the trustees became concerned as the organization accumulated a series of large operating deficits. Peter Willauer seemed particularly stretched in his dual role as chief executive officer and chief fund-raiser. Hank Taft, formerly president of National, noted that burnout from this dual role was common for school directors; Willauer was the only school founder in the country who was still running his school.

Like most of the Outward Bound schools, Hurricane had a very active group of trustees. Thirty-six men and women sat on a half-dozen committees, which met monthly to monitor and aid the school's management. Most trustees were successful businesspeople, and all had been on at least one Hurricane course.

In late summer 1985, management and the trustees agreed on a new organizational structure, giving Willauer some relief on the operating side of the organization. They created the office of the vice president to take over day-to-day operating responsibilities. Vice presidents Bob Weiler and George Armstrong shared these tasks, freeing Willauer to focus on strategic direction and fund-raising. (See *Exhibit 2* for Hurricane's organization chart.)

In 1985, the operating deficit became smaller, and 1986 found the school in the midst of its busiest year ever. By year's end, some 3,700 students would spend over 70,000 student program days (SPD)[1] in over 50 courses at any of 13 sites in Maine, Florida, New York, New Hampshire, and Maryland. Controller Joe Adams predicted that in 1986, the school would break even for the first time, and accumulate record revenues of just over $5 million. Still, finances were a high management priority. The school required a sound financial base to continue its growth.

---

1. One student program day: one student in a course for one day.

Course Offerings

The mission of Hurricane Island Outward Bound is providing safe, challenging, educational experiences in a wilderness setting, carefully structured to improve self-esteem, self-reliance, concern for others, and care for the environment.

—*Mission Statement*

The school's offerings were divided into two segments: (1) special programs, administered by vice president George Armstrong, and (2) public courses, directed by vice president Bob Weiler. Special programs were courses that the school ran by contract for specific groups, often through government agencies. Among the populations served in this manner were Vietnam veterans, emotionally and developmentally handicapped youth, juvenile delinquents, and substance abusers. In 1985, special programs accounted for 23% of Hurricane's students, 32% of student program days, and 33% of tuition revenues.

The remainder of the school's students enrolled in public courses. The marketing department worked almost exclusively with public courses (special programs were more the result of contract negotiations). The public courses were divided into four major segments based on location and activity: Maine Sea, Florida Sea, Winter Land, and Summer Land. (See *Exhibit 3* for descriptions of the four segments, *Exhibit 4* for recent attendance trends, and *Exhibit 5* for financial information by course.)

Course length ranged from 3 to 101 days. All courses were carefully constructed to provide challenges while ensuring safety. Both the course directors and an active Trustee Safety Committee rigorously monitored course activities and instructors. In addition, the school required U.S. Coast Guard certification for all sailing instructors, and land instructors were certified by the state of Maine as "Maine Guides." As a result, the school had never had a fatality despite the often strenuous nature of course activities.

In each course, participants were organized into "watches" of up to 12 students and one or two instructors. The watch was the basic unit of instruction; watch members performed most of their activities as a group. In the early part of a course, instructors concentrated on teaching the skills necessary for course activities; they assumed no prior experience. Once student skills were adequate, the instructors began allowing the group to perform activities with less direct supervision, intervening only in the event of trouble. The climax of most courses was Solo, when the watch broke up and individuals spent anywhere from several hours to three days alone in the wilderness, except for daily visits from an instructor.

Although learning wilderness survival skills was an important part of each course, more important was learning to work with a group under often trying circumstances and gaining self-confidence and the ability to trust fellow watch members. For this reason, the school had lately begun running short courses for groups of managers who desired this kind of experience. The courses, called the Professional Development Program (PDP), were very successful—158 executives attended in 1985—leading to expanded activities in 1986. Hurricane's marketing department was responsible for PDP in addition to regular public courses.

Marketing at Hurricane

For a long time, marketing consisted of opening our doors at the beginning of the summer and closing them at the end. More people came every year. Then in 1979 that didn't work anymore; our enrollment dropped. And 1980 was the same.
—*Bob Weiler, Vice President*

Marketing did not exist as a formal function at Hurricane before 1980. The school's major promotion tool then was group presentations: instructors and managers went out to schools and other institutions to talk about the Outward Bound experience. In most cases, Hurricane arranged presentations reactively. A request for a presentation would come in, and whoever wanted to go and give the talk would do so.

One result of the late 1970s' enrollment dip was the upgrading of the marketing function. In 1981, Hurricane hired Ted Rodman as the school's first marketing director. The Trustee Marketing Committee advocated and won a marketing budget equal to 10% of projected public course revenues. (The committee felt this percentage was an average figure for the business world.) The budget included salaries for the marketing and public relations departments, the National marketing fee, and funds for marketing and public relations (PR) campaigns.

Rodman had previously operated his own direct-mail and graphic design firm, and he transferred the skills he had developed there to Hurricane. He championed what he called "volume marketing," which consisted of major direct-mail campaigns whose yields could be accurately predicted. He concentrated on new advertising creative work, market segmentation, and positioning.

The primary direct-mail piece for marketing was the school course catalog. Produced once every two years, it was a glossy, 24-page, full-color magazine describing the school and the various programs it offered. Prospective students could get more information by writing the school or calling its toll-free number. In either case, they received an application and course schedule, which provided additional details about the courses and their exact dates. Students then applied for specific courses on specific dates, listed alternate preferences, and enclosed a nonrefundable $25 application fee. Upon receipt of the application, the admissions department sent the student an enrollment package that included comprehensive information on clothing, travel, and any other requirements for each course. The package also included a 4-page medical form. All students were required to have a physical exam before being accepted in a course.

The admissions department encouraged students to return the enrollment forms as quickly as possible. Along with the completed forms, students sent a nonrefundable $100 enrollment fee. This fee reserved a spot for the student in a specific course. Tuition was due in full 60 days before the beginning of the course, or with the enrollment fee if the student was applying later. If a course was oversubscribed, the admissions department placed students on a waiting list. If a student was not admitted to the course by two weeks before the course's beginning, he or she was given the option of getting a tuition refund or having the money credited to a future course. Noting the length of the admission process, Chin remarked, "Enrollment is not an impulse buy."

Supplementing the Hurricane catalog was the National course catalog, which described all five schools' offerings, organized by activity. Inquiries to National were routed to the appropriate school.

In 1984 and 1985, Ted Rodman, controller Joe Adams, and the Marketing Committee began a re-evaluation of the school's pricing. As Adams put it, "We know we can always sell a course if the price is low enough. Can we sell it at a price where we cover our costs?" Public course tuition in 1986 ranged from $400 to $3,800 per student, depending on the length and nature of the course. Approximately 20% of students received substantial support from Hurricane's financial aid program as part of the school's commitment to serving the underprivileged. Marketing allocated financial aid to help support appropriate levels of female and minority participation in Outward Bound.

Marketing under Ted Rodman received mixed reviews from other Outward Bound managers. Public course enrollment did recover strongly in the 1980s, and the curriculum shifted to a more profitable mix of courses. Others also appreciated Rodman's feel for visuals; his catalogs featured stunning photography. They further credited him with developing an accurate forecasting system for overall public course enrollment.

Still, some staff members were uneasy with the idea of "marketing" the school. Most people who worked for Outward Bound did so because they were dedicated to the concepts behind and experiences offered in the courses. Those who ran the courses feared that marketing would "tell them what to do," or distort the concepts. When formal marketing first came to Hurricane, director of staffing Tino O'Brien recalled, "We spent a good deal of time educating our marketers in the reality of what Outward Bound was."

In September 1985, Rodman left to become marketing director for a local ski area. Vice president George Armstrong took over his duties until Philip Chin arrived in February of 1986.

1986 Marketing Efforts

The 1986 marketing plan was based on four strategic initiatives: (1) segmenting markets, (2) developing new pricing, (3) changing the course mix, and (4) assigning financial aid dollars to low-demand areas.

Hurricane made a concerted effort to segment the markets it served and assign priorities to the segments. Analysis of historic enrollment patterns revealed that some parts of the population dominated the school's student body. Given management beliefs that Hurricane's market penetration was low in all areas, the school de-

cided to target those groups with which it had had the most success in the past.

Demographically, the organization identified 14- to 19-year-olds as its primary target, with 20- to 35-year-olds next. Geographically, the school gave first priority to the northeastern United States, which it defined as the six New England states and New York. Second priority went to the mid-Atlantic states (New Jersey, Pennsylvania, Delaware, and Maryland), plus Florida. In addition to these segments, the marketing department identified six buying groups within the demographic and geographic markets whom it felt the school could successfully address: (1) high school and college students, (2) "juniors" (ages 14 and 15), (3) municipal and agency contacts (for special programs), (4) young professionals, (5) corporations, and (6) Hurricane course alumni.

The school also developed a differential pricing scheme, both to maximize revenue and to smooth demand. Hurricane raised prices on introductory and adult courses, but tried to keep prices competitive on "mature" courses like Maine Sea. The school lowered prices on certain off-peak courses (September through May) to encourage enrollment at those times, although tuition differences between identical courses rarely exceeded 15%. (See *Exhibit 6* for an example of a differential pricing schedule.)

Hurricane continued to examine the profitability and popularity of its courses, shifting the mix to build more revenue and better utilize existing facilities. In many cases this involved shortening less profitable courses or reducing the number of times they were offered. This increased capacity for other, more profitable courses.

Finally, the school used its scholarship program to support Maine Sea and to build off-season demand. Hurricane targeted scholarship-subsidized groups for such efforts, as this was more manageable than attempting to coordinate individual-aid programs.

Tactically, these strategic moves were translated into a number of marketing initiatives over the course of the year, including experimenting with two new sales tools. The first was a direct sales recruiter, who gave presentations to educational institutions, civic groups, trade associations, and business groups. The school especially hoped to increase high school student enrollments, and supported the recruiter, a former course director for Hurricane, with a direct-mail campaign to principals of public and private high schools.

The marketing department's second innovation was a telemarketing campaign aimed toward prospective students who had applied but not yet enrolled. Members of the admissions department staff called these students to discuss the Outward Bound experience as part of a larger effort to improve the school's response to inquiries about courses.

Following the 1985 PDP experience, Hurricane expanded its effort to reach corporations. Chin and Bob Weiler made most of the sales calls, as both had had experience working in major corporations. By summer's end, Hurricane had completed contracts with the Gillette Company, Citicorp, Corning Glass, MCI, Xerox, and General Electric, among others.

The school also continued its advertising and direct-mail effort in 1986, mailing over 35,000 pieces in four major campaigns and a series of smaller efforts, which included the high school mailing mentioned earlier.

1987 Considerations

Nobody's in this to make money. Everybody's involved in a tremendous educational process. Beyond that, you want to run it well.
—Hank Taft, *former president, National; former Marketing Committee chair, Hurricane*

The overall goals for the school were continued growth and financial stability. With those guidelines in mind and a very limited budget, Chin had to develop and support marketing tactics that would help the school realize two strategic objectives: (1) maintain school leadership within the Outward Bound system, and (2) build off-season business.

Maintaining school leadership. Defining Outward Bound's competition was extraordinarily difficult because of the diverse markets the school served. For juniors, the competition could be summer camp. Vacations, summer jobs, and other wilderness experience organizations beckoned college students. Corporate training was a fragmented, high-growth industry that was becoming more competitive.

The one constant in all of these markets was the presence of the other Outward Bound schools in the United States. Although National's policies restrained cutthroat competition on territory and advertising, there was a usually friendly rivalry among the five schools. Hurricane was the largest of the five in terms of SPDs, while Colorado enrolled the most students. Between them, the two schools controlled approximately 70% of the system's business. Leadership in the system was a source of pride to staff members, and the school strove to maintain it.

Building off-season business. In talking with managers, it was apparent that marketing's most important objective was to build off-season business. Each year, Hurricane served well over half of its students in June, July, and August. Marketing Committee chair Bill End noted, "Selling the summer is not the trick for marketing. You could probably do nothing and sell out this period." Building business in the "shoulders" around the peak season, however, seemed to be where marketing could truly add value.

The dramatic seasonality of Hurricane's student population affected every aspect of the school's operations. The biggest problem was staffing the courses. Tino O'Brien, in an office wallpapered with huge charts depicting staffing requirements for every course at the school, spoke with feeling: "It's a totally untenable, high-risk situation with staffing. We need fully trained, fully committed staff for two months." The school's inability to offer year-round positions to instructors hamstrung recruiting efforts. "It affects both quality and safety," added O'Brien. George Armstrong agreed. He noted that over half the school's expenses were labor-related, and that simply hiring people for the summer and then laying them off in the fall was not viable because the immediate labor supply was tight.

Results in this area had been unsatisfactory. Off-season pricing and skewing scholarship funds to off-peak courses had proven unable to offset the fact that most juniors, high school students, and college students were simply unable to attend courses during the academic year. And Hurricane's Florida base was too small to provide a winter counterweight to courses based in the Northeast.

Marketing Options

The 1987 marketing expense allocation was $308,000. Of this, $125,000 was dedicated to payroll for current staff; $40,000 covered the Outward Bound National marketing fee; $39,000 was for other marketing programs, including advertising and the school's direct-mail campaign; $15,000 was for public relations, trade shows, and other sales promotions; and $35,000 was for two new staff positions, an assistant marketing manager and a new public relations/production coordinator. This left $54,000 for discretionary 1987 marketing programs. Chin already had a number of proposals on which he could spend the money.

1. Expand "Alumni in Marketing" network. Chin thought the "Alumni in Marketing" network (AIM) might prove the most cost-effective and least controversial of any of the proposals he was considering. More than 25,000 people had taken Hurricane courses in the last 20 years, and the school had a solid alumni mailing list that it used for fund-raising and public relations activities. Managers throughout Hurricane were enthusiastic about the network in principle, but were uncertain about how to use the alumni resource.

Chin identified two ways alumni could help marketing. The first was to identify interested groups and individuals to whom the school could direct its efforts. Alumni often had access to schools, professional associations, and other institutions through which they assembled audiences for group presentations. The second way alumni could help was to take part in the presentations by doing publicity, helping with logistics, and providing testimonials.

Experiments with alumni volunteers in 1986 had been very successful. Charlie Reade, the direct sales recruiter, had coordinated alumni efforts in the course of making his presentations. Two direct-mail campaigns for leads had been successful enough to warrant repeating them in 1987. But Chin was uncertain how enthusiastically he should push this network, as he had no clear idea of how many alumni would want to volunteer. If too few were interested, the effort in reaching them might be wasted. If too many were interested, administering the network would rapidly become complex. The latter situation seemed more likely than the former. If AIM took off, Chin might have to hire someone to manage it, which he calculated would cost at least $20,000 per year. Even with a manager dedicated to the network, coordination of effort among marketing, sales, and hundreds of alumni would be a substantial task. If volunteers were overutilized, they might tire or reduce donations on the grounds that they were already giving their time. If they were underutilized, they might lose enthusiasm for the network or even the school. Chin felt that careful management of both operations and volunteers' expectations would be critical.

If successful, the AIM network could be a great asset to all phases of marketing. In the future, selected alumni might be able to make their own presentations under Hurricane supervision. Some managers estimated that over half of all public course inquiries came from word of mouth; getting alumni talking about and working for Hurricane in a new way could boost these referral enrollments. And well-managed participation would be bound to generate renewed enthusiasm for the school, perhaps adding to the donor base and generating repeat business.

Unfortunately, Chin foresaw problems in tracing revenues generated by AIM. Like public relations, the benefits generated through AIM would mostly be intangible: better organization for presentations, more word-of-mouth advertising, greater enthusiasm.

Given the response to 1986 tests, Chin felt that expanding a network of volunteers would require hiring a manager over the course of the year. He did not want to cut into Charlie Reade's valuable sales time with extensive administrative duties. Assuming they hired someone in spring 1987, the cost would be about $15,000 for the 1987 budget.

2. Build corporate Professional Development Program (PDP). "PDP raises emotions at the school," Chin commented. "It raises concern with the program [course development] people. It raises joy with Joe Adams."

In the early PDP work Hurricane had done, the school had presented itself as an alternative to traditional in-house training. The goal was to put managers together under adverse conditions and watch them respond. The PDP course focused on leadership, team building, stress management, communication, and goal setting. Usually, the Outward Bound experience was mixed with a more traditional training presentation. For example, General Electric's group came to Rockland for a seminar and a three-day course before reporting to GE's New York training center for four weeks of in-house work.

The 1986 experience with PDP had been very positive. Although there was no formal feedback mechanism to collect information from the companies involved, informal follow-up elicited numerous positive comments. Responses from human resource professionals at the companies suggested that managerial participants showed a greater sense of confidence, were better at meeting deadlines, and had stronger presentation and communication skills than they had had in the past.

In addition to being beneficial to the participants, the program could be extraordinarily profitable for the school. Hurricane could charge corporate clients $200 per SPD, while the overall goal for the school was $75 per SPD. (Adams estimated that the direct cost to Hurricane of one SPD was $45. The remaining $30 in the goal covered fixed overhead.) Also, corporations were more likely to fill off-season courses because executives often took vacations in the summer.

Finally, Chin felt there was a good moral justification for expanding PDP. "Businesspeople need to learn compassion. We hide behind titles and systems rather than confronting emotional and moral issues." Chin noted feedback that suggested the experience of seeing peers perform beyond their limits was transferred back to the workplace. Managers became more open and able to cope with the emotional side of life. Chin felt that such managers would be stronger assets not only to their companies, but also to their communities.

Other Hurricane managers had mixed feelings about the program. Vice president George Armstrong listed three criteria he considered when looking at new course proposals:

> First, does it fit what the organization is all about? Second, does it make money? Third, does it fit the schedule? If we can develop a three-day managers' course that meets those goals, I say let's do as many as we can.

Some felt that PDP was precisely *not* what the organization was all about. Former Marketing Committee chair Hank Taft remarked, "I think we owe it to the underprivileged to serve them, even though managers can benefit."

Tino O'Brien noted that staffing such courses was sometimes difficult. "We have a lot of young, idealistic instructors, and it's hard to get them excited about serving rich people." Still, he continued, "the objection to them is mostly theoretical. Once the instructors get out with them on a course, they usually enjoy it." Per-

sonally, Tino said, he felt the school should run some PDP courses as long as PDP did not drive the organization. He added dryly, "Executives are people, too."

In general, Chin felt, the school needed to strike a balance on PDP. The school could not go very heavily into corporate programs without endangering its donor base. Most managers believed that donors might contribute less to Hurricane if the school seemed to be moving away from its mission to serve youth and the underprivileged.[2] Also, PDP courses were not as operationally flexible as the average Hurricane offering. Once established, schedules could not be changed; groups of managers could not be shifted to different dates or courses. Chin recalled the time when a late-summer demand surge had hit the school, and Hurricane had to scramble to serve all of its students, particularly the corporate clients. He remembered painfully, "There were situations this summer where we mobilized an extra effort to serve the people who paid."

Chin thought the best way to expand PDP was to hire a recruiter specifically for the program. "In the past, we have been reactive. We want to put resources to our opportunities." Chin envisioned a coordinated marketing approach, beginning with a PDP-specific brochure. The brochure would be mailed to the vice presidents of human resources at *Fortune* 500 companies and other identified prospects in the Northeast, and followed up first by phone and then in person by the PDP recruiter.

The mailing alone would cost about $1,000; adding a PDP recruiter would cost as much as $30,000 once travel and other expenses were factored in. In return, Chin hoped to realize about $200,000 in gross revenue. In any case, it did not seem feasible for him and Bob Weiler to continue making these sales calls as the complexity of other parts of their jobs grew, so he would have to develop a staffing solution anyway.

3. Expand direct sales recruitment. In 1986, Hurricane's sales force consisted of two ex-instructors: Charlie Reade, who recruited for public courses, and Holly Miller, who was in charge of special programs. Previously, instructors and managers had gone out on an ad hoc basis, but

---

2. In 1985, donors provided $732,000 in contributions for operations and $956,000 in contributions for property, plant, equipment, and other capital items.

the school felt that it would benefit from a more systematic approach to direct recruitment. Reade and Miller had begun full-time organized recruiting in 1986, with much success. The school projected that recruiting would generate 17% of 1986 applications and 20% of 1986 enrollments. Demand for group presentations was rising. The school estimated that it would make over 50 presentations in the first three months of 1987.

Many managers considered face-to-face presentations the most effective way for the school to approach prospective students. Presentations had changed with the advent of full-time recruiters. Chin explained that the biggest change management had made was to encourage recruiters to ask for applications or a contract on the spot, whereas in the past they had merely given the informational presentation and asked people to call if they were interested. Chin felt "asking for the order" had made a great difference in the success of the recruiters, but it had been controversial. Recruiters were unaccustomed to that style. Chin remarked, "It began to smack of commercialism to some people. That worried them."

Rather than add more full-time recruiters, Chin was considering expanding the use of "sub-recruiters." Sub-recruiters would address specific segments, such as high school students. They would work under short-term contracts with specific performance objectives like the number of presentations made or the number of organizations contacted. Hurricane managers hoped that they might be able to provide off-season work to course instructors by making them sub-recruiters; another leadership school put all its instructors "on the road" every fall. Hurricane's sub-recruiters would work under the supervision of the full-time recruiters. Chin estimated that adding two sub-recruiters would cost $9,000 in 1987.

4. Build telemarketing capabilities. In 1986, the admissions department experimented with calling prospective students after they had applied but before they had enrolled. Students seemed to enjoy speaking with someone from the school, especially given the high levels of anxiety some had about course activities. Chin and others believed that students who were contacted would be more likely to enroll, although tracking on the initial experiment had been inadequate to determine this conclusively.

Unfortunately, the admissions department could not provide full-time telemarketers. Chin believed that hiring good telemarketers for Hurricane would be a tough job. Candidates needed to have both good selling skills and sufficient program knowledge to answer student's questions.

One alternative to full-time telemarketing would be an extended test. Chin envisioned calling 500 to 1,000 prospective students who had applied but not yet enrolled. By setting up a careful response-tracking system, the school could determine whether a further investment was warranted. It was difficult to determine the cost of all this. Even using part-time people to start, payroll and phone costs would escalate rapidly. Chin had tentatively allocated $6,000 for an extended test in 1987.

Alternatives: Pricing and the Course Mix

Given the amount of money Chin had available, he could not fund all four of the programs outlined above. One way of getting around this problem was to find ways to make the school's courses more profitable, thus providing more funds for marketing programs.

In addition to the differential pricing schedules developed in 1985 and 1986, the school's prices in general had increased at a pace of about 15% per year for the last two years. Raising prices again had been discussed in 1987 planning meetings. Joe Adams was in favor of another price increase; the school average was still below his goal of $75 per SPD. Others were not so sure. Hurricane had reached what Chin called "the $2,000 barrier" on a number of popular courses. He was uneasy about raising prices any higher for these courses. It was unclear how much selective or general price increases would affect demand, or what they might do to marketing's overall contribution to profit.

Another way to raise course profitability would be to alter the course mix further. The effect would be easier to trace, though implementation would be more difficult. Course mix was the area in which course managers and the marketing department were most likely to clash. While it was relatively easy to expand activities in a profitable course, it was much more difficult to cut back on an unprofitable one. Because of the school's nonprofit mission, many managers believed firmly that profitability was not a valid criterion for judging the worth of a course. Courses were more likely to be eliminated for safety reasons or for lack of students. In addition, many courses had been championed by individuals who were dedicated to the segments their courses served. The Vietnam veterans' course in the special programs area, for example, had been created, funded, and marketed primarily through the efforts of an ex-Green Beret colonel. Further, certain courses were strongly identified with the organization as a whole. The Maine Sea courses, for example, were part of the school's history and original mission. Despite the significant overhead expense of maintaining the 18 large boats used in them, there was no question that Maine Sea would continue to be integral to Hurricane's operations.

Evaluating Marketing Tactics

Three numbers appeared at the head of virtually every planning document for marketing at the school: the number of students served, the number of SPDs, and total revenue. Different interested parties, however, placed different emphases on these numbers. On one side, the "business-oriented" managers and many of the trustees were most concerned with the revenues that public courses generated. The financial crisis of the early 1980s had convinced them, above all, that the school had to break even on its operating revenues and expenses. Two of their long-term goals were to reduce the school's debt burden and to purchase certain properties critical to its operations; therefore a surplus of revenues over expenses would be even better.

On the other side, many of the "course-oriented" managers and donors were more concerned with serving as many deserving students as possible. They tended to focus on number of students and SPDs. For them, marketing's job was to "fill the courses." Beyond students and SPDs, these people watched such measures as the proportion of students receiving financial aid, and the demographic characteristics of students, including age, sex, and race. While they knew that obtaining funds was important, they were worried that marketing and finance concerns might drive the organization away from its original mission of serving youth and the disadvantaged. Growth seemed far more worthwhile than debt reduction.

Each of the four marketing initiatives proposed had strengths and weaknesses relative to the tension between financial concerns and service concerns. Direct sales and telemarketing, for example, were targeted approaches that allowed the school to solicit populations with desirable demographic traits, such as minority groups. They could also be used to concentrate on filling specific courses. AIM was less controllable and measurable—who the tactic reached depended on which alumni volunteered and what their contacts were. PDP was focused and profitable, but some felt it was aimed at the wrong target market.

Beyond all this, Chin was concerned about how accurately the school would be able to link results to *any* initiative. Despite the admissions department's heroic effort to organize student data, Hurricane often had no idea why a given student enrolled. (See *Exhibit 7* for a rough forecast of 1986 results by marketing tactic.) Chin was dedicated to developing better marketing information systems at the school (which was one reason he wanted an assistant marketing manager aboard), but this would require changing procedures in marketing and admissions, and he was not sure what the financial or organizational costs of these changes would be.

Finally, there were the three marketing objectives staring at him from the front page of his notebook. With all the other plan goals, these were the real ones: delivering 2,700 students, 47,800 SPDs, and—perhaps most important—$3.4 million in revenues while staying within his budget and balancing the interests of management, donors, trustees, instruction staff, and, ultimately, the students.

On the one hand, Chin felt the school was slowly becoming more "businesslike" due to the demands of growth. On the other hand, as Hank Taft had remarked before he retired in September, "Nobody's in this to make money." Changing the way Outward Bound concepts were marketed could change other things about the organization as well. Chin wondered if there were other ways to reach his goals that he had missed. As his plane landed at Owls Head, he snapped his notebook shut, but the questions remained.

Exhibit 1 Statement of Activity, 1982–1985 ($000)

	1982	*1983*	*1984*	*1985*
Support and revenue				
Tuition				
Public courses	$1,563	$2,013	$2,445	$2,672
Special programs	485	744	944	1,284
Subtotal	2,048	2,757	3,389	3,956
Outside support				
Operating contributions	418	883	789	732
Support from National	0	68	85	66
Other	169	191	256	200
Subtotal	587	1,142	1,130	998
Total support and revenue	2,635	3,899	4,519	4,954
Expenses				
Cost of sales				
Public courses	1,442	1,851	2,264	2,395
Special programs	425	644	793	1,054
Depreciation	95	138	73	84
Subtotal	1,962	2,633	3,130	3,533
Operating expenses				
Administration	421	543	639	697
Marketing	346	319	293	319
Development	131	135	188	173
Student aid	333	467	486	323
Depreciation	49	51	63	71
Other	104	81	37	0
Subtotal	1,384	1,596	1,706	1,583
Total expenses	3,346	4,229	4,836	5,116
Operating surplus (deficit)	(711)	(330)	(317)	(162)
Net capital additions[a]	1,028	177	60	962
Excess (deficiency) to funds	317	(153)	(257)	800
Fund balances end of year	2,148	1,995	1,738	2,538
Balance sheet items				
Total assets	3,522	3,650	3,635	3,981
Total liabilities	1,374	1,655	1,897	1,443

Source: Hurricane Island Outward Bound School

a. Includes capital contributions, gain (loss) on sale of property and equipment, and net investment activity.

Exhibit 2 Organization Chart

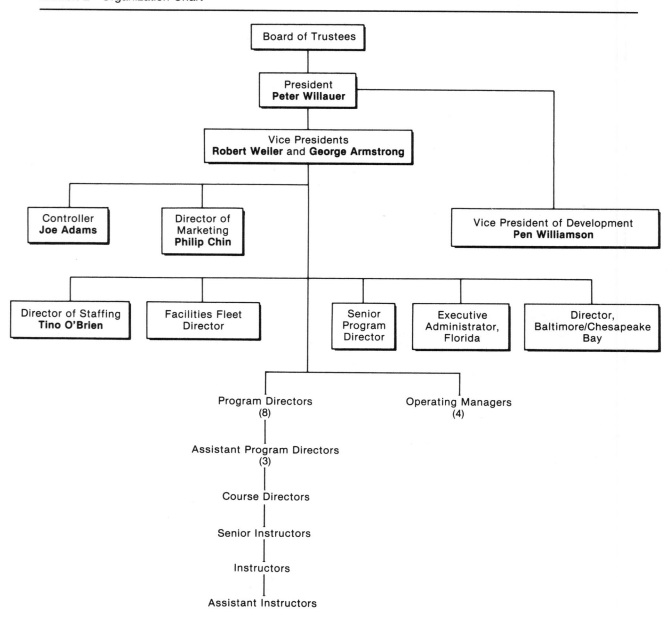

Source: Hurricane Island Outward Bound School

Exhibit 3   Course Descriptions

I. Public Courses

Maine Sea Program

Sailing courses run from May through September. A 30-foot open pulling boat becomes the base for lessons in seamanship, navigation, sailing, rowing, ecology, and survival on land and sea. Includes segments on rock climbing and the Hurricane Island ropes course. Based in Penobscot Bay, Maine.

Florida Sea Program

Sailing courses run from November through April. Content similar to Maine Sea, but conducted in the tropical wilderness of the Florida Keys. Includes extensive swimming and snorkeling to explore the ecology of the Keys. Based in the Great Heron Wildlife Preserve, Florida.

Summer Land Program

Canoeing, backpacking, white water rafting, bicycling, and "multi-element" courses run from May through September. Most courses include rock climbing, wilderness camping, and expedition-planning skills. Based in Maine and New York.

Winter Land Program

Winter mountaineering courses run from December through March. Activities include cross-country skiing, snowshoeing, backpacking, and winter camping. Based in Maine and New Hampshire.

II. Special Programs and Populations

Ongoing programs have been developed for a wide range of audiences, including Vietnam veterans, substance abusers, troubled youth, schools, and corporations. These customized programs use many of the facilities and activities of the public courses.

Source: Hurricane Island Outward Bound School

Exhibit 4 Attendance by Course Area, 1981–1985

	1981		1982		1983		1984		1985	
	Students	*SPDs*[a]	*Students*	*SPDs*	*Students*	*SPDs*	*Students*	*SPDs*	*Students*	*SPDs*
Public Courses										
Maine Sea program	1,016	18,432	938	16,849	1,091	19,439	1,208	21,409	1,120	18,088
Florida Sea program	183	2,095	249	3,097	230	3,287	275	4,315	289	4,658
Winter Land program	120	1,017	244	2,711	231	1,970	184	1,612	190	1,611
Summer Land program	157	2,771	289	4,304	372	6,141	441	5,599	645	8,700
Other	92	1,343	236	5,724	319	7,824	366	8,056	363	8,169
Subtotal public courses	1,568	25,658	1,956	32,685	2,243	38,661	2,474	40,991	2,607	41,226
Special Programs	474	8,686	726	13,060	1,596	15,134	1,264	16,525	760	19,137
Total enrollment	2,042	34,344	2,682	45,745	3,839	53,795	3,738	57,516	3,367	60,363

Source: Hurricane Island Outward Bound School

a. Student program days

Exhibit 5 Projected Performance by Course, 1986

Course	Student Capacity	SPD Capacity	Tuition	Students	SPD	Revenue
Maine Sea						
HI 26–day	100	2,600	$1,600	64	1,664	$102,400
HI 22–day	596	13,112	1,225/1,425	386	8,492	541,650
HI 11–day	240	2,640	900	152	1,672	136,800
HI 6–day	120	720	600	57	342	34,200
Sea Kayak 7–day	40	280	700	36	252	25,200
Sea Kayak 14–day	20	280	1,000	18	252	18,000
Contracts/Groups	90	990	809	85	935	68,765
Subtotal	1,206	20,622		798	13,609	$927,015
Florida Sea						
FL College 22–day	10	220	$1,200	8	176	$9,600
FL 22–day	10	220	1,200	8	176	9,600
FL 14–day	180	2,520	1,000	104	1,456	104,000
FL 8–day	200	1,600	800	72	576	57,600
Contracts/Groups	20	160	500	18	144	9,000
Subtotal	420	4,720		210	2,528	$189,800
Summer Land						
Maine Chall. 26–day	192	4,992	$1,600	128	3,328	$204,800
Long jrs. 28–day	144	4,032	1,700/1,800	126	3,528	223,400
Juniors 22–day	72	1,584	1,300	66	1,452	85,800
Rafting 6–day	105	630	600	90	540	54,000
Summerland 22–day	120	2,640	1,300	92	2,024	119,600
Summerland 9–day	160	1,440	800	105	945	84,000
Cycling 22–day	40	880	1,300	16	352	20,800
Cycling 9–day	100	900	800	46	414	36,800
Dynamy 22–day	48	1,056	700	42	924	29,400
Contracts/Groups	36	288	500	32	256	16,000
Subtotal	1,017	18,442		743	13,763	$874,600
Winter Land						
Winter College 22–day	12	264	$1,000	8	176	$8,000
Winter 22–day	12	264	1,000	6	132	6,000
Winter 9–day	60	540	800	24	216	19,200
Winter 6–day	100	600	600	34	204	20,400
Gould 8–day	84	672	400	72	576	28,800
Subtotal	268	2,340		144	1,304	$82,400
Managers						
Career Dev 4–day	96	384	$500	80	320	$40,000
Maine Sea 8–day	116	928	950	84	672	79,800
Land 6–day	20	120	750	16	96	12,000
Contracts/Groups	60	360	1,200	50	300	60,000
Subtotal	292	1,792		230	1,388	$191,800
Other						
Summer 64–day	24	1,536	$3,200	20	1,280	$64,000
Florida 78–day	24	1,872	3,800	16	1,248	60,800
Florida 80–day	24	1,920	3,800	17	1,360	64,600
Jrs. 15–day	180	2,700	900/950	162	2,430	150,400
Maine directive	154	4,312	1,800	127	3,556	228,600
Florida directive	110	3,080	1,800	82	2,296	147,600
Instructor training	36	3,612	3,800	21	2,107	79,800
Subtotal	552	19,032		445	14,277	$795,800
Public Course Total	3,755	66,948		2,570	46,869	$3,061,415

Source: Hurricane Island Outward Bound School

Exhibit 6 1986 Pricing, 22–Day Maine Sea Course

Starting Date	Ending Date	Tuition	Student Capacity	Actual Students
5/16/86	6/6/86	$1,225	72	12
5/26/86	6/16/86	1,225	72	12
6/12/86	7/3/86	1,425	72	48
6/14/86	7/5/86	1,425	48	46
7/9/86	7/30/86	1,425	48	46
7/11/86	8/1/86	1,425	72	70
8/5/86	8/26/86	1,425	68	64
8/8/86	8/29/86	1,425	72	70
9/5/86	9/26/86	1,225	72	18

Source: Hurricane Island Outward Bound School

Exhibit 7 Projected Results by Marketing Tactic, 1986

	National Marketing[a]	Direct Sales	Direct Mail	Other/ Unknown	Total
Applications[b]	1,100	600	340	1,500	3,540
Conversion rate	60%	85%	75%	75%	72%
Students enrolled	660	510	256	1,125	2,551
Revenues	$792,000	$612,000	$307,200	$1,350,000	$3,061,200
Direct cost	$39,000	$68,500	$26,250	na	$295,000

Source: Hurricane Island Outward Bound School

a. Inquiries about Hurricane courses generated by National (Outward Bound, Inc.) marketing.

b. Approximately 1 of every 15 inquiries about all Outward Bound courses generated by National eventually converted to applications. Approximately 1 of every 8 inquiries Hurricane generated internally converted to applications. Hurricane received about 27% of all applications generated by National.

Questionnaire on Assessing

Marketing Performance

QUESTIONNAIRE ON ASSESSING MARKETING PERFORMANCE

Please answer the questions posed below as best you can. Don't hesitate to write notes, ignore our classification schemes, or do whatever else you need to inform us accurately of your own and your firm's practices.

About Programs. A marketing program is a targeted attempt to bring together the smaller elements of the marketing job (selling, advertising, pricing, etc.) in the service of a brand or to better target a key market segment. For example, the marketing of a computer, with associated pricing, advertising, and distribution components, is a marketing program. So is a key account management program.

I. Programs

What are one or two major marketing programs your firm is pursuing, and for which you have some knowledge or direct management responsibility? The programs you choose should represent products or services that are currently available to customers. If you have no special programs, just list the overall marketing effort as "Program A." If you do have separate programs, it would be most helpful to us if you picked one program you thought was highly successful, and one not so successful. However, if that's difficult for you, any one or two marketing programs are fine.

Program A	Program B
Name: _____	Name: _____
Description: _____	Description: _____
_____	_____
_____	_____
_____	_____
_____	_____
_____	_____

All our questions about your programs refer to the last full fiscal year. If this is not the base you use, please indicate the relevant time frame:

Basis for my answers: (please check one)

___ LAST FULL FY   ___ OTHER (PLEASE SPECIFY)_____

_____

Rev. 4.3, 5/88, © T.V. Bonoma, B.H. Clark   - 1 -

High-Performance Marketing Survey

RES

1. How would you describe the success of the program(s) you have chosen? Please tell us as well the reasons for your judgment.

Program level of success was   (Please check the relevant blanks)

		Program A	Program B
1 VERY GOOD		1 ___	1 ___
2 GOOD		2 ___	2 ___
3 NEITHER GOOD NOR POOR		3 ___	3 ___
4 POOR		4 ___	4 ___
5 VERY POOR		5 ___	5 ___

Reasons for your judgment_____

_____

_____

_____

RES

2. To top management of your organization, how high a priority was successful execution of this program?

		Program A	Program B
1 VERY HIGH PRIORITY		1 ___	1 ___
2 HIGH PRIORITY		2 ___	2 ___
3 NEITHER HIGH NOR LOW PRIORITY		3 ___	3 ___
4 LOW PRIORITY		4 ___	4 ___
5 VERY LOW PRIORITY		5 ___	5 ___

II. Program Results

SAT

1. How satisfied have you been with the performance of these marketing programs? Please tell us as well the reasons for your judgment.

I HAVE BEEN		Program A	Program B
1 EXTREMELY SATISFIED		1 ___	1 ___
2 VERY SATISFIED		2 ___	2 ___
3 SATISFIED		3 ___	3 ___
4 MODERATELY UNSATISFIED		4 ___	4 ___
5 EXTREMELY UNSATISFIED		5 ___	5 ___

Reasons for your judgment_____

_____

_____

_____

Rev. 4.3, 5/88, ©T.V. Bonoma, B.H. Clark   - 2 -

High-Performance Marketing Survey

RES

2. How would you describe the results of the two programs? Please tell us as well the reasons for your judgment.

PROGRAM RESULTS WERE		Program A	Program B
1 VERY GOOD	1 ___	1 ___
2 GOOD	2 ___	2 ___
3 NEITHER GOOD NOR POOR	3 ___	3 ___
4 POOR	4 ___	4 ___
5 VERY POOR	5 ___	5 ___

BASIS FOR JUDGMENT   Program A   Program B
(Check all that apply)

1 MARKET SHARE	1 ___	1 ___
2 SALES	2 ___	2 ___
3 PROFIT	3 ___	3 ___
4 RETURN (ON ASSETS, INVESTMENT, ETC.)	4 ___	4 ___
5 NUMBER OF CUSTOMERS SERVED	5 ___	5 ___
6 OTHER (PLEASE SPECIFY):	6 ___	6 ___

_____

_____

_____

EXP

3. Overall, how high were your expectations for these programs at the beginning of the last fiscal year or the base you identified above?

MY EXPECTATIONS WERE	Program A	Program B
1 VERY HIGH	1 ___	1 ___
2 HIGH	2 ___	2 ___
3 NEITHER HIGH NOR LOW	3 ___	3 ___
4 LOW	4 ___	4 ___
5 VERY LOW	5 ___	5 ___

RES/EXP

4. Would you say that the program's results were better or worse than you expected?

RESULTS WERE	Program A	Program B
1 MUCH BETTER THAN EXPECTED	1 ___	1 ___
2 BETTER THAN EXPECTED	2 ___	2 ___
3 ABOUT WHAT WAS EXPECTED	3 ___	3 ___
4 WORSE THAN EXPECTED	4 ___	4 ___
5 MUCH WORSE THAN EXPECTED	5 ___	5 ___

RES/EXP

5. Would you say that the program's results were better or worse than any formal marketing plan led you to expect?

RESULTS WERE	Program A	Program B
1 MUCH BETTER THAN EXPECTED	1 ___	1 ___
2 BETTER THAN EXPECTED	2 ___	2 ___
3 ABOUT WHAT WAS EXPECTED	3 ___	3 ___
4 WORSE THAN EXPECTED	4 ___	4 ___
5 MUCH WORSE THAN EXPECTED	5 ___	5 ___

High-Performance Marketing Survey

Please make any comments you'd like about how you judged the programs' results:

_____

_____

_____

_____

_____

III. Effort Expended

1. Overall, how much effort would you say management who executed the program expended to produce the results you rated above? Please compare yourself to what you think might be found at your best competitor.

In Terms of Time. . .

		Program A	Program B
1 MUCH MORE TIME THAN BEST COMPETITOR	1 ___	1 ___
2 MORE TIME THAN BEST COMPETITOR	2 ___	2 ___
3 ABOUT EQUAL TIME	3 ___	3 ___
4 LESS TIME THAN BEST COMPETITOR	4 ___	4 ___
5 MUCH LESS TIME THAN BEST COMPETITOR	5 ___	5 ___

In Terms of Money Relative to Sales. . .

		Program A	Program B
1 MUCH MORE MONEY THAN BEST COMPETITOR	1 ___	1 ___
2 MORE MONEY THAN BEST COMPETITOR	2 ___	2 ___
3 ABOUT EQUAL MONEY	3 ___	3 ___
4 LESS MONEY THAN BEST COMPETITOR	4 ___	4 ___
5 MUCH MORE MONEY THAN BEST COMPETITOR	5 ___	5 ___

In Terms of People. . .

		Program A	Program B
1 MANY MORE PEOPLE THAN BEST COMPETITOR	1 ___	1 ___
2 MORE PEOPLE THAN BEST COMPETITOR	2 ___	2 ___
3 ABOUT EQUAL PEOPLE	3 ___	3 ___
4 FEWER PEOPLE THAN BEST COMPETITOR	4 ___	4 ___
5 MANY FEWER PEOPLE THAN BEST COMPETITOR	5 ___	5 ___

High-Performance Marketing Survey

SKL/STR

2. Would you say that Programs A and B required a great deal of managerial "exception-handling" and special intervention, or were they routine, where many of the firm's established marketing procedures and systems operated normally?

2a   Please compare yourself to what you think is "normal" for your organization on other programs.

		Program A	Program B
1 MUCH MORE INTERVENTION THAN NORMAL	1 ___	1 ___
2 MORE INTERVENTION THAN NORMAL	2 ___	2 ___
3 ABOUT NORMAL INTERVENTION	3 ___	3 ___
4 LESS INTERVENTION THAN NORMAL	4 ___	4 ___
5 MUCH LESS INTERVENTION THAN NORMAL	5 ___	5 ___

2b   Now compare yourself to what you think might be found at your best existing competitor.

		Program A	Program B
1 MUCH MORE INTERVENTION THAN BEST COMP.	1 ___	1 ___
2 MORE INTERVENTION THAN BEST COMPETITOR	2 ___	2 ___
3 ABOUT EQUAL INTERVENTION	3 ___	3 ___
4 LESS INTERVENTION THAN BEST COMPETITOR	4 ___	4 ___
5 MUCH LESS INTERVENTION THAN BEST COMP.	5 ___	5 ___

2c *compare competitive IS*

SKL

3. How much skill did the marketing managers responsible for this program have to exercise to implement it?

		Program A	Program B
1 MUCH MORE SKILL THAN NORMAL	1 ___	1 ___
2 MORE SKILL THAN NORMAL	2 ___	2 ___
3 ABOUT NORMAL SKILL	3 ___	3 ___
4 LESS SKILL THAN NORMAL	4 ___	4 ___
5 MUCH LESS SKILL THAN NORMAL	5 ___	5 ___

		Program A	Program B
1 MUCH MORE SKILL THAN BEST COMPETITOR	1 ___	1 ___
2 MORE SKILL THAN BEST COMPETITOR	2 ___	2 ___
3 ABOUT EQUAL SKILL	3 ___	3 ___
4 LESS SKILL THAN BEST COMPETITOR	4 ___	4 ___
5 MUCH LESS SKILL THAN BEST COMPETITOR	5 ___	5 ___

STR

4. How strongly did your organization's standard marketing procedures and systems support the program?

		Program A	Program B
1 VERY STRONGLY	1 ___	1 ___
2 STRONGLY	2 ___	2 ___
3 NEITHER STRONG NOR WEAK	3 ___	3 ___
4 WEAKLY	4 ___	4 ___
5 VERY WEAKLY	5 ___	5 ___

5. Info Sys
6. ES

Rev. 4.3, 5/88, ©T.V. Bonoma, B.H. Clark   - 5 -

Please make any comments you'd like about how you judged the effort expended on the programs:

_____

_____

_____

_____

IV. External Factors

QCR

1. While the program was being executed, what would you say was the quality of the <u>competition's responses</u>? Here we mean all competition, not just your best competitor.

		Program A	Program B
1 NO RESPONSE	1 ___	1 ___
2 MUCH STRONGER RESPONSE THAN NORMAL	2 ___	2 ___
3 STRONGER RESPONSE THAN NORMAL	3 ___	3 ___
4 ABOUT NORMAL RESPONSE	4 ___	4 ___
5 WEAKER RESPONSE THAN NORMAL	5 ___	5 ___
6 MUCH WEAKER RESPONSE THAN NORMAL	6 ___	6 ___

And did management responsible for executing the program, to your knowledge, expect this level of response to occur?

	Program A	Program B
1 COMPLETELY UNEXPECTED	1 ___	1 ___
2 A PARTIAL SURPRISE	2 ___	2 ___
3 NO SURPRISE AT ALL	3 ___	3 ___

PTR

2. Regarding how the distribution channels supported the program, what would you say?

	Program A	Program B
1 WE DISTRIBUTE DIRECTLY	1 ___	1 ___
2 MUCH LESS SUPPORT THAN NORMAL	2 ___	2 ___
3 LESS SUPPORT THAN NORMAL	3 ___	3 ___
4 ABOUT NORMAL SUPPORT	4 ___	4 ___
5 MORE SUPPORT THAN NORMAL	5 ___	5 ___
6 MUCH MORE SUPPORT THAN NORMAL	6 ___	6 ___

ENV

3. Relative to your expectations, how much did the external environment (regulations, consumer buying patterns, other "uncontrollables") help or hurt the program during the period about which we are talking?

	Program A	Program B
1 HURT MUCH MORE THAN EXPECTED	1 ___	1 ___
2 HURT MORE THAN EXPECTED	2 ___	2 ___
3 HELPED AS EXPECTED	3 ___	3 ___
4 HELPED MORE THAN EXPECTED	4 ___	4 ___
5 HELPED MUCH MORE THAN EXPECTED	5 ___	5 ___

High-Performance Marketing Survey

Please make any comments you'd like about how you judged the impact of competition, distribution channels, and the environment:

_____

_____

_____

_____

_____

V. About Your Programs   (Please check the relevant blanks)

1. What we do: (Check all that apply)

	Program A	Program B
CONSUMER PRODUCTS MANUFACTURING		
1 DURABLE PRODUCT	1 ___	1 ___
2 NONDURABLE PRODUCT	2 ___	2 ___
INDUSTRIAL PRODUCTS MANUFACTURING		
3 DURABLE PRODUCT	3 ___	3 ___
4 NONDURABLE PRODUCT	4 ___	4 ___
5 RAW OR SEMIFINISHED PRODUCT	5 ___	5 ___
SERVICES		
6 CONSUMER SERVICES	6 ___	6 ___
7 INDUSTRIAL SERVICES	7 ___	7 ___
8 RETAIL OR WHOLESALE DISTRIBUTION	8 ___	8 ___

2. Current market position:

	Program A	Program B
1 4TH PLACE OR LOWER IN MARKET SHARE	1 ___	1 ___
2 2ND OR 3RD PLACE IN MARKET SHARE	2 ___	2 ___
3 1ST PLACE IN MARKET SHARE	3 ___	3 ___

3. The top three companies in this program's industry control what percentage of the market (in sales)?

	Program A	Program B
1 LESS THAN 10%	1 ___	1 ___
2 10-25%	2 ___	2 ___
3 26-60%	3 ___	3 ___
4 GREATER THAN 60%	4 ___	4 ___

4. Time since program introduction:

	Program A	Program B
1 LESS THAN ONE YEAR	1 ___	1 ___
2 ONE YEAR OR MORE	2 ___	2 ___

5. Sales growth:

		Program A	Program B
1 SALES DECLINING		1 ____	1 ____
2 SALES GROWING 0-15%/YEAR		2 ____	2 ____
3 SALES GROWING MORE THAN 15%/YEAR		3 ____	3 ____

6. Dollar sales:

	Program A	Program B
1 LESS THAN $500,000	1 ____	1 ____
2 $500,000-999,000	2 ____	2 ____
3 $1-5 MILLION	3 ____	3 ____
4 $6-10 MILLION	4 ____	4 ____
5 $11-25 MILLION	5 ____	5 ____
6 $26-50 MILLION	6 ____	6 ____
7 $51-100 MILLION	7 ____	7 ____
8 GREATER THAN $100 MILLION	8 ____	8 ____

7. Percent of division or business unit sales:

	Program A	Program B
1 LESS THAN 4% OF TOTAL SALES	1 ____	1 ____
2 4-10%	2 ____	2 ____
3 11-20%	3 ____	3 ____
4 21-30%	4 ____	4 ____
5 31-40%	5 ____	5 ____
6 41-50%	6 ____	6 ____
7 51-60%	7 ____	7 ____
8 GREATER THAN 60%	8 ____	8 ____

8. Percent overall selling and marketing expenses
   to sales for program:

	Program A	Program B
1 LESS THAN 6% OF TOTAL SALES	1 ____	1 ____
2 6-10%	2 ____	2 ____
3 11-15%	3 ____	3 ____
4 16-20%	4 ____	4 ____
5 21-30%	5 ____	5 ____
6 31-40%	6 ____	6 ____
7 GREATER THAN 40%	7 ____	7 ____

8. Product/Service is distributed

	Program A	Program B
1 DIRECTLY, BY YOUR COMPANY	1 ____	1 ____
2 EXCLUSIVELY, THROUGH A SINGLE OUTLET	2 ____	2 ____
3 SELECTIVELY, THROUGH SOME OUTLETS	3 ____	3 ____
4 INTENSIVELY, THROUGH MANY OUTLETS	4 ____	4 ____

High-Performance Marketing Survey

VI. About You and Your Company

1. What are the three most important factors you consider in evaluating how good a marketing program is?

MOST IMPORTANT_____

2ND IN IMPORTANCE_____

3RD IN IMPORTANCE_____

2. Do you use different factors to judge new programs versus established ones?
   __ YES __ NO. If yes, how do the factors differ?

_____

_____

_____

_____

In the following questions, we want to know about your division, Strategic Business Unit (SBU), or reporting unit, not the total corporation of which your unit may be a part.

3. Total number of products/services   _____

4. Total sales last year $_____ (MILLIONS)

5. Total operating earnings last year $_____ (MILLIONS)

6. Length of time in business   _____ (YEARS)

7. Orientation of top management (check all that apply)
   ___ R&D
   ___ FINANCE
   ___ PRODUCTION
   ___ MARKETING
   ___ SALES
   ___ ENGINEERING
   ___ OTHER (PLEASE SPECIFY):
       _____
       _____

8. Total selling and marketing expenses
   as a percentage of sales   _____%

9. Info System installed - last

High-Performance Marketing Survey

Here, we mean you personally, the one who is filling this out.

9. I am   ___ MALE   ___ FEMALE

10. My age is: _____ YEARS

11. I hold the following highest
    degree (please check one)   ___ JUNIOR HIGH SCHOOL
                                 ___ HIGH SCHOOL
                                 ___ UNDERGRADUATE COLLEGE
                                 ___ MASTER'S
                                 ___ M.D.
                                 ___ PH.D.
                                 ___ OTHER (PLEASE SPECIFY):
                                 _____
                                 _____

12. I have worked for my current organization _____ years.

13. I have worked in my current industry _____ years.

(In the next question, please fill in all the blanks relevant to you.)

14. I have worked in marketing for _____ years, general management for

    _____ years, selling for _____ years, and another function,

    _____, for _____ years.

15. My job title is:

    _____

Please give us any additional comments you think we should have:

_____

_____

_____

_____

_____

_____

Thank you very much for your cooperation. Please return the survey in the
enclosed postage-paid envelope. To obtain results of this survey, see page 11.

High-Performance Marketing Survey

IF YOU WOULD LIKE A COMPLETE RESEARCH REPORT FROM A NATIONAL SAMPLE OF COMPANIES RESPONDING TO THIS QUESTIONNAIRE, PLUS AN OCCASIONAL SERIES OF WORKING PAPERS ON HOW TO IMPROVE MARKETING PERFORMANCE, PLEASE FILL IN YOUR NAME AND ADDRESS BELOW, OR ELSE STAPLE A BUSINESS CARD TO THIS PAGE.

IF YOU WOULD BE WILLING TO BE INTERVIEWED AT GREATER LENGTH BY PHONE SHOULD OUR STUDY REQUIRE IT, PLEASE FILL IN YOUR PHONE NUMBER BELOW.

I would like to receive a summary report of your findings when they are completed. I understand this will not contain my own or anyone else's individual responses, but only aggregates of the data.

Name:_____

Title:_____   You can just

Company:_____   staple your

Division:_____   business card

Address:_____   here instead,

_____   if you like.

City, State, Zip:_____

I would like to get some of your work on improving marketing performance.

___ **YES**   ___ NO

I would be willing to talk with you further by phone.

___ **YES**   ___ NO

My phone number is (_____)_____
                      area
                      code

Note: If you're concerned about confidentiality, detach this page from the questionnaire and send it back in a separate envelope from the one we've provided for returning the survey. The return address is:

Marketing Performance Assessment Project
Morgan Hall, Room 145
Harvard Business School
Boston, MA 02163
ATTN: Professor Bonoma

If you have comments or questions concerning this research project, don't hesitate to write us as well. Thanks again for your help.

Rev. 4.3, 5/88, ©T.V. Bonoma, B.H. Clark   - 11 -

References and an Annotated Bibliography on Marketing Performance and Productivity

Appendix C
References and Bibliography

Abell, D. F., and J. S. Hammond. 1979. *Strategic Market Planning: Problems and Analytical Approaches*. Englewood Cliffs, N.J.: Prentice-Hall.

Although almost ten years old, this book remains an excellent review of the strategic planning process for marketing. Includes detailed discussions of the PIMS and Boston Consulting Group strategy models.

Ackoff, R. L., and J. R. Emshoff. 1985. "Advertising Research at Anheuser-Busch, Inc. (1963–68)." In B. M. Enis and K. K. Cox, eds., *Marketing Classics: A Selection of Influential Articles*, pp. 458–470. Boston: Allyn & Bacon.

Describes a five-year series of experiments the authors conducted with Anheuser-Busch. Experiments reduced, increased, or maintained advertising expenditures in selected markets and monitored results.

Alderson, W. 1959. "New Concepts for Measuring Productivity in Marketing." In Bureau of Economic and Business Research (symposium), *Productivity in Marketing: Its Measurement and Change*, pp. 3–11. Urbana: University of Illinois.

Anderson, E., and B. A. Weitz. 1986. "Make-or-Buy Decisions: Vertical Integration and Marketing Productivity." *Sloan Management Review* 27:3 (Spring), pp. 3–19.

Discusses vertical integration decisions in the context of transaction cost economics. (See text for a detailed review.)

Andrews, K. R. 1980. *The Concept of Corporate Strategy*. 2nd ed. Homewood, Ill.: Richard D. Irwin.

General management book on strategic planning. Not marketing-specific, but still worthwhile.

Anthony, R. N., and J. Dearden. 1980. *Management Control Systems*. 4th ed. Homewood, Ill.: Richard D. Irwin.

Management accounting and control text.

Armitage, H. M. 1984. "The Use of Management Accounting Techniques to Improve Productivity Analysis in Distribution Operations." *International Journal of Physical Distribution and Materials Management* 14:1 (January), pp. 41–51.

Outlines a methodology for measuring productivity changes in distribution. Distinguishes between efficiency of given work methods and effectiveness of alternative work methods.

Bagozzi, R. P. 1982. *Causal Models in Marketing*. New York: Wiley.

A ground-breaking book on applying sophisticated methods for determining cause-and-effect to marketing problems.

Band, W. A. 1983. "How to Improve Your Marketing Productivity." *Sales and Marketing Management in Canada* (May), pp. 18–20.

Short piece on Sevin-style marketing productivity analysis.

Barger, H. 1951. *The Transportation Industries, 1899–1946: A Study of Output, Employment, and Productivity*. New York: National Bureau of Economic Research.

———. 1955. *Distribution's Place in the American Economy Since 1869*. Princeton: Princeton University Press.

   Seminal study of distribution costs in United States. (See text for a detailed review.)

Barger, H., and H. H. Landsberg. 1942. *American Agriculture, 1899–1939: A Study of Output, Employment, and Productivity*. New York: National Bureau of Economic Research.

Barger, H., and S. H. Schurr. 1944. *The Mining Industries, 1899–1939: A Study of Output, Employment, and Productivity*. New York: National Bureau of Economic Research.

Beckman, T. N. 1957. "The Value Added Concept as a Measurement of Output." *Advanced Management* 22:4 (April), pp. 6–9.

   Beckman's advocacy piece on value-added measures. (See text for a detailed review.)

———. 1959. "Productivity in Wholesaling—Measurement and Change." In Bureau of Economic and Business Research (symposium), *Productivity in Marketing: Its Measurement and Change*, pp. 80–104. Urbana: University of Illinois.

   Industry-level analysis of merchant wholesalers. Considers the disparity between required data and information available from business records.

———. 1961. "Measuring Productivity in Marketing." In *1960 Proceedings of the Business and Economic Section of the American Statistical Association*. Washington: American Statistical Association.

   Examines wholesale and retail productivity on a macroeconomic level, using both labor and capital as inputs. (See text for a detailed review.)

———. 1965. "Marketing Productivity—Appraisal and Challenge." In J. L. Heskett, ed., *Productivity in Marketing: Papers of the Theodore N. Beckman Symposium on Marketing Productivity*, pp. 59–72. Columbus: College of Commerce and Administration, Ohio State University.

Beckman, T.N., and R. D. Buzzell. 1958. "Productivity: Facts and Fiction." *Business Horizons* 1:1 (Winter), pp. 24–38.

   Clear survey of the key concepts in productivity measurement. Not marketing-specific.

Beik, L. L., and S. L. Buzby. 1973. "Profitability Analysis by Market Segments." *Journal of Marketing* 37:3 (July), pp. 48–53.

   Champions profitability analysis by customer segment.

Berkowitz, L. 1969. "Social Motivation." In G. Lindzey and E. Aronson, eds., *The Handbook of Social Psychology*, Vol. 3, pp. 50–135. Englewood Cliffs, N.J.: Addison-Wesley.

   A classic review article based on the social psychology of expectation, social motives, and other factors.

Bilon, R. L. 1979. "Measuring Sales Productivity." *Retail Control* (National Retail Merchants Association) 47:6 (February), pp. 35–42.

   A review of productivity measures for retail sales clerks, focusing on sales, transaction costs, and payroll costs.

Boehm, B. W. 1978. *Characteristics of Software Quality*. New York: Elsevier North Holland.

Bonoma, T. V. 1981. "Market Success Can Breed 'Marketing Inertia'." *Harvard Business Review* 59:5 (September–October), pp. 115–121.

   Managers are frequently reluctant to tamper with marketing strategies that have been successful in the past, even when market conditions have changed. The inability of management to adapt to market changes, "marketing inertia," is caused by rigidity in values.

———. 1984. *Managing Marketing: Text and Cases*. New York: Free Press.

   Graduate textbook dealing with the problems of marketing implementation. Includes both text and case studies.

———. 1985a. *The Marketing Edge: Making Strategies Work*. New York: Free Press.

   Reports findings of Bonoma's six-year marketing implementation research project in managerial form. (See text for a detailed review.)

———. 1985b. "Case Research in Marketing: Opportunities, Problems, and a Process." *Journal of Marketing Research* 22:2 (May), pp. 199–208.

   Argues that the trade-off between needs for data integrity and currency or generalizability in research requires that marketing use a broad set of methods. Describes case research as one alternative method that offers much to marketing.

———. 1986. "Marketing Subversives." *Harvard Business Review* 64:6 (November–December), pp. 113–118.

> Describes the tension between management skills and corporate structures that characterizes many marketing organizations. Contends that the best managers are the ones who have the skills to "subvert the system" to achieve objectives. (See text for a detailed review.)

Bonoma, T. V., and V. L. Crittenden. 1988. "Toward a Model of Marketing Implementation." *Sloan Management Review* 29:2 (Winter), pp. 7–14.

> A managerial treatment of the authors' work in marketing implementation. Proposes a model of implementation practice. (See text for a detailed review.)

Bonoma, T. V., V. L. Crittenden, and R. J. Dolan. Forthcoming. "Can We Have Rigor and Relevance in Pricing Research?" In T. Devinney, ed., *Issues in Pricing Research*. Lexington, Mass.: Lexington Books.

> Based on detailed interviews examining the pricing process in four diverse firms, the authors suggest a research agenda to close the current gap between rigorous academic research and relevant management practice.

Borden, N. 1964. "The Concept of the Marketing Mix." *Journal of Advertising Research* 4:20 (June), pp. 2–7.

> Borden's classic statement of his elegant conception of the marketing mix.

Bower, J. L. 1983. *The Two Faces of Management*. Boston: Houghton-Mifflin.

> Discusses general management in political and corporate environments.

Browne, W. G., and E. D. Reiten. 1978. "Auditing Distribution Channels: A Case Study from the Forest Products Industry." *Journal of Marketing* 42:3 (July), pp. 38–41.

> Distribution channel audit for a timber company.

Bucklin, L. P. 1978. *Productivity in Marketing*. Chicago: American Marketing Association.

> A thoughtful exposition of the theoretical issues in marketing productivity analysis, analyzing both macroeconomic and microeconomic productivity. (See text for a detailed review.)

———. 1981. "Advertising Productivity." *Advertising Age* 52:16 (April 13), pp. S-1, S-12.

> Discusses interpretation of productivity measures, noting the total factor versus labor productivity argument and the effects of qualitative differences on inputs.

———. 1983. "Capital Productivity in Retailing." In D. A. Gautschi, ed., *Productivity and Efficiency in Distribution Systems*, pp. 63–73. New York: American Elsevier.

Burstiner, I. 1974. "Improving the Productivity of a Telephone Sales Force." *Management Review* 63:11 (November), pp. 26–33.

> Illustrates an efficiency improvement program for a land-sale telemarketing effort.

Buzzell, R. D., and M. J. Chussil. 1985. "Managing for Tomorrow." *Sloan Management Review* 26:4 (Summer), pp. 3–14.

> Calculates management performance by comparing discounted cash flows of actual business to potential identified by "twins" in the PIMS database. Very ingenious. (See text for a detailed review.)

Buzzell, R. D., and B. T. Gale. 1987. *The PIMS Principles: Linking Strategy to Performance*. New York: Free Press.

> Puts forth lessons learned from the fifteen years of the PIMS research project. An important work on a major strategic model.

Buzzell, R. D., B. T. Gale, and R. G. M. Sultan. 1975. "Market Share—A Key to Profitability." *Harvard Business Review* 53:1 (January–February), pp. 97–106.

> Major PIMS-based article reporting findings that increases in share of market served correlate with increases in ROI. Discusses possible explanations of this and other findings.

Buzzell, R. D., R. E. M. Nourse, J. B. Matthews, Jr., and T. Levitt. 1972. *Marketing: A Contemporary Analysis*. 2nd ed. New York: McGraw-Hill.

> General marketing text. Chapter 26 is a thorough exposition on performance measurement systems within marketing organizations.

Campbell, J. P. 1976. "Contributions Research Can Make in Understanding Organizational Effectiveness." In S. L. Spray, ed., *Organizational Effectiveness: Theory-Research-Utilization*, pp. 29–45. Kent, Ohio: Kent State University Press.

> Review of the theoretical construct of "organizational effectiveness" from the perspective of a "differential, measurement-oriented psychologist" (p. 29). Table 2 lists

thirty different possible indices of organizational effectiveness.

Campbell, R. H. 1973. "Conducting a Marketing Audit." *The Magazine of Bank Administration* 49:11 (November), p. 78.

Outlines a general four-step approach to conducting a marketing audit. Not limited to banking.

Capella, L. M., and W. S. Sekely. 1978. "The Marketing Audit: Methods, Problems and Perspectives." *Akron Business and Economic Review* 9:3 (Fall), pp. 37–41.

Reports results of a mail survey querying marketing executives about their experiences with marketing audits. Discusses methods and problems revealed by the survey.

Christopher, W. F. 1984. "Marketing Achievement Reporting: A Profitability Approach." In S. J. Shapiro and V. H. Kirpalani, eds. *Marketing Effectiveness: Insights from Accounting and Finance*, pp. 79–100. Boston: Allyn & Bacon.

Excellent article discussing not only profitability but business definition, goal setting, appropriate levels of feedback within an organization, and control measures.

Cook, J. 1985. "Conducting an Audit of the Sales Organization." In E. E. Bobrow and L. Wizenberg, eds., *Sales Manager's Handbook*, pp. 467–476. Homewood, Ill.: Dow Jones–Irwin.

Good overview of sales force audits. Outlines who should be responsible for the various steps in an audit and typical audit topics. Offers a good list of reasons *not* to perform an audit.

Corey, E. R. 1985. "Marketing Audit Outline." Personal communication.

Outline of audit for major chemical products concern. Especially good questions on analyzing management attitudes and orientations.

Corey, E. R., and S. Star. 1971. *Organizational Strategy: A Marketing Approach*. Boston: Division of Research, Harvard Business School.

A path-breaking casebook, with accompanying text, on marketing organization structures.

Corr, A. V. 1976. "A Cost-Effectiveness Approach to Marketing Outlays." *Management Accounting* 57:7 (January), pp. 33–36.

Defines cost-effectiveness as the amount of profit added divided by the amount spent on any given action. Similar to Feder's (1965) treatment of opportunity rates.

Coughlan, A. T., and M. T. Flaherty. 1983. "Measuring the International Marketing Productivity of U.S. Semiconductor Companies." In D. A. Gautschi, ed., *Productivity and Efficiency in Distribution Systems*, pp. 123–149. New York: American Elsevier.

Develops two models of international marketing productivity in semiconductor companies. Flaherty proposes a structural model of the way a variety of factors affect market share in a country over time, including technological level; share of local engineers, sales-, and service-people; and local content of products. Coughlan's model addresses the direct/indirect sale issue by examining region, type of equipment, experience, sales training, customer training, and service.

Cox, R., C. S. Goodman, and T. C. Fichandler. 1965. *Distribution in a High-Level Economy*. Englewood Cliffs, N.J.: Prentice-Hall.

Major analysis of marketing and distribution in the United States. Examines quantitative and qualitative effects of marketing on economy and society. Discusses the structure of the distribution system and its activities. (See text for a detailed review.)

Cronin, J. J., Jr., and S. J. Skinner. 1984. "Marketing Outcomes, Financial Conditions, and Retail Profit Performance." *Journal of Retailing* 60:4 (Winter), pp. 9–22.

Examines data from thirty-five supermarket chains to discover relationships among various marketing outcomes (including market share, sales volume, gross margin, sales per employee, sales per square foot, and inventory turns) and financial conditions of the chains (liquidity and leverage) as they affect profit. The authors conclude that retailers should strive to reduce all types of debt.

Deal, T. E., and A. A. Kennedy. 1982. *Corporate Cultures: The Rites and Rituals of Corporate Life*. Reading, Mass.: Addison-Wesley.

A very popular book on this topic. Says culture is a function of a firm's myths (stories) and heroes, plus symbols.

Dean, J. 1959. "Marketing Productivity and Profitability." In Bureau of Business and Economic Research (symposium), *Productivity in Marketing: Its Measurement and Change*, pp. 53–65. Urbana, Ill.: University of Illinois.

Argues that physical productivity measurement has little use in marketing. Instead discusses "economic efficiency" of marketing, which is equated with profit.

Denison, E. 1967. *Why Growth Rates Differ.* Washington: Brookings Institution.

A massive study of national income growth in nine Western industrialized nations between 1950 and 1962. Tries to discern the impact of a variety of inputs on the differences in growth rates among these countries.

Dhalla, N. K. 1977. "Increase Your Marketing Productivity." *Canadian Business* 50:3 (March), pp. 68–74.

Advocates use of experimentation in marketing to discover how sales and profits are affected by variation in marketing efforts. Outlines a procedure for conducting experiments.

Donath, B. 1982. "Measuring Bang in the Marketing Buck: How General Electric Predicts Marketing Productivity." *Industrial Marketing* 67:7 (July), pp. 60–64.

Describes GE's PIMS-based, twenty-five-factor model to predict market share results of advertising and sales promotion efforts. Factors affecting share are classified in three categories: market structure, seller decisions, and marketing performance.

Drucker, P. 1974. *Management: Tasks, Responsibilities, Practices.* New York: Harper and Row.

Drucker's classic general management text.

———. 1985. "How to Measure White-Collar Productivity." *The Wall Street Journal* (November 26), p. 30.

Op-ed piece on white-collar productivity, using auto industries as an example. Suggests four measures: output per white-collar employee, length of time to bring a product or service to market, number of new products introduced in a period, and numbers of support staff and, especially, levels of management, for a given output. Not marketing-specific.

———. 1986. "If Earnings Aren't the Dial to Read." *The Wall Street Journal* (October 30), p. 32.

Op-ed article on business performance measurement. (See text for a detailed review.)

Druckman, D. (ed.). 1977. *Negotiations: Social-Psychological Perspectives.* Beverly Hills, Calif.: Sage.

On the social psychology of negotiating. See especially the Tedeschi and Bonoma chapter on coercion and aggression in bargaining.

Dubinsky, A. J., and R. W. Hansen. 1982. "Improving Marketing Productivity: The 80/20 Rule Revisited." *California Management Review* 25:1 (Fall), pp. 96–105.

Claims that this common phenomenon (that 20 percent of a firm's customers typically generate 80 percent of its sales and profits—a phenomenon the authors confirm with a survey) indicates slack marketing productivity. Prescribes strategic remedies to this problem, and discusses the organizational prerequisites to taking action against the 80/20 rule. Illustrates a useful "Marketing Assessment Grid," which plots profit potential versus current profit performance.

Dunne, P. M., and H. I. Wolk. 1977. "Marketing Cost Analysis: A Modularized Contribution Approach." *Journal of Marketing* 41:3 (July), pp. 83–94.

Presents a method for breaking down marketing costs and revenues into measurable segments. Uses the concept of controllable and uncontrollable costs in combination with fixed and variable costs. Diagrammatically breaks income statement into modules by order size, product, and market.

Engel, J. F., R. D. Blackwell, and P. W. Miniard. 1986. *Consumer Behavior.* 5th ed. Chicago: Dryden.

Consumer behavior textbook.

Enis, B. M., and K. K. Cox (eds.). 1985. *Marketing Classics: A Selection of Influential Articles.* Boston: Allyn & Bacon.

A compendium of classic marketing articles on a wide variety of topics.

Etgar, M. 1976. "Effects of Administrative Control on Efficiency of Vertical Marketing Systems." *Journal of Marketing Research* 13:1 (February), pp. 12–24.

Conducts a multivariate analysis to compare two systems of distributing insurance: company-owned versus independent agencies.

Etzel, M. J., and J. M. Ivancevich. 1974. "Management by Objectives in Marketing: Philosophy, Process, and Problems." *Journal of Marketing* 38:4 (October), pp. 47–55.

Very good review of MBO results and tenets as they might apply to marketing. Discusses objectives, timing, participation, and motivation factors as well as general process.

Feder, R. A. 1965. "How to Measure Marketing Performance." *Harvard Business Review* 43:3 (May–June), pp. 132–142.

Develops a system to allow assessment of the effect of marketing expenditures on profits. (See text for a detailed review.)

Ferber, R. C. 1979. "Measuring the Marketing Buck." *Industrial Marketing* 64:11 (November), pp. 60–65.

Advocates multivariate analysis as a solution to complex business problems. Illustrates the analytic process with a sales force audit. Explains how to use the resulting regression equations.

Fisk, G. 1967. *Marketing Systems: An Introductory Analysis.* New York: Harper and Row.

Text on marketing systems. Chapter 23 provides an intriguing perspective on the "social efficiency" of marketing. Distinguishes between "social efficiency," what is best for society, and "acquisitive efficiency," what is best for business.

Freud, S. 1950. *The Interpretation of Dreams.* Trans. by A. Brill. New York: Modern Library.

The classic book on dreams as a window to the unconscious psyche.

Gallup, G. 1966. "Measuring Advertising Sales Effectiveness: The Problem and the Prognosis." In E. Konrad and R. Erickson, eds., *Marketing Research: A Management Overview*, pp. 145–151. New York: American Management Association.

Proposes methods for getting at advertising's role in sales. Key to the methods is the playback notion, whereby the customer is interviewed in depth with only the advertiser's name and the product as recall aids. Separates effectiveness from sales response.

Garvin, D. A. 1984. "Japanese Quality Management." *The Columbia Journal of World Business* 29:3 (Fall), pp. 3–12.

Compares air conditioner manufacturing facilities in the United States and Japan to uncover the reasons for higher product quality in Japan.

Gautschi, D. A. (ed.). 1983. *Productivity and Efficiency in Distribution Systems.* New York: American Elsevier.

Collection of articles on distributive productivity.

George, K. D. 1966. *Productivity in Distribution.* London: Cambridge University Press.

Studies the productivity of retailing in 160 British towns. (See text for a detailed review.)

Gergen, K. J. 1969. *The Psychology of Behavior Exchange.* Reading, Mass.: Addison-Wesley.

Looks at human behavior in groups from an exchange theory point of view.

Gilbert, T. H. 1978. *Human Competence.* New York: McGraw-Hill.

Fascinating book on "competence engineering." Argues convincingly that any type of performance can be measured, and then improved. Uses extensive examples from business and education. (See text for a detailed review.)

Ginter, P. M., and J. M. Starling. 1979. "A Two-fold Analysis of Comparative Advertising Effectiveness." *Akron Business and Economic Review* 10:1 (Spring), pp. 12–18.

Analyzes the effectiveness of advertising that compares one product with another. Claims there are two relevant measures of advertising effectiveness: advertising's effect on sales and profits, and advertising's effect on consumer dispositions.

Gleason, J. M., and D. T. Barnum. 1982. "Toward Valid Measures of Public Sector Productivity: Performance Measures in Urban Transit." *Management Science* 28:4 (April), pp. 379–386.

Examines efficiency and effectiveness measures for public transit.

Goodman, P. S., and J. M. Pennings (eds.). 1977. *New Perspectives on Organizational Effectiveness.* San Francisco: Jossey-Bass.

Gathers articles on organizational effectiveness from an organization studies perspective. Good overview of this area.

Goodman, S. R. 1967. "Improved Marketing Analysis of Profitability, Relevant Costs, and Life Cycles." *Financial Executive* 35:6 (June), pp. 28–34.

Explores product profitability analysis in terms of relevant costs and product life cycle. Suggests weighting profit by cost of capital to adjust for risk. (See text for a detailed review.)

———. 1970. *Techniques of Profitability Analysis.* New York: Wiley-Interscience.

Along with Sevin (1965), this book is one of the classics on ratio analysis and product profitability. Includes many useful charts and forms to help companies incorporate profitability analysis into their control systems. (See text for a detailed review.)

———. 1972. *The Marketing Controller*. New York: AMR International.

Goodman's full exposition of his marketing controller concept. Argues that having a financial analyst dedicated to a marketing department can provide quantitative expertise and guidance while helping marketers understand financial dictates. (See text for a detailed review.)

Gross, I. 1981. "Advertising Productivity." *Advertising Age* 52:16 (April 13), pp. S-1, S-12.

States that simple ratios are insufficient to measure productivity in marketing due to mediating factors such as external events. Notes that it is "usually impossible" to relate sales or earnings to a specific activity, such as advertising, but that through experimentation the manager may be able to relate *changes* in activity to *changes* in results.

———. 1984. "Marketing Productivity Measurement: A Conceptual Framework." Unpublished. Media: Institute for the Study of Business Markets, Pennsylvania State University.

Develops a concise theoretical model of marketing productivity. (See text for a detailed review.)

Hall, W. P. 1975. "Improving Sales Force Productivity." *Business Horizons* 18:4 (August), pp. 32–42.

Good article discussing methods of improving sales force productivity, defined as profit improvement.

Hammond, K. 1966. *The Psychology of Egon Brunswik*. New York: Appleton-Century-Crofts.

A collection of Brunswik's most famous lectures, including material on his "lens model."

Harper, P. C. 1981. "Advertising Productivity." *Advertising Age* 52:16 (April 13), pp. S-1, S-12.

An unusual view of advertising productivity from the chairman of the Needham, Harper & Steers agency in New York.

Hawkins, D. I., R. J. Best, and K. A. Coney. 1986. *Consumer Behavior: Implications for Marketing Strategy*. Plano, Tex.: Business Publications.

Consumer behavior textbook. Chapter 19 discusses post-purchase processes and consumer satisfaction.

Hayes, P. J., W. W. White, and L. Williams. 1984. "Yours for Greater Productivity." *The Discount Merchandiser* 24:7 (July), pp. 94–99.

Trade magazine article explaining productivity improvements and measurements used by three discount chains. Hayes offers a thorough discussion of gross margin ROI. Williams provides a notion of departmental "yield," a combination of gross margin, space utilization, location, and inventory turns.

Henderson, B. D. 1973. "The Experience Curve Revisited: IV. The Growth Share Matrix of the Product Portfolio." Boston: Boston Consulting Group, Perspectives No. 135.

One of the original expositions of the Boston Consulting Group's growth-share matrix.

Heskett, J. L. (ed.). 1965. *Productivity in Marketing: Papers of the Theodore N. Beckman Symposium on Marketing Productivity*. Columbus: College of Commerce and Administration, Ohio State University.

Collection of articles on marketing productivity written in honor of T. N. Beckman.

Hill, G. V. 1978. "Evaluating Profitability by Customer." *Marketing* (U.K.) (November), pp. 33–38.

Excellent piece on customer account profitability.

Homans, R. E., and B. M. Enis. 1973. "A Guide for Appraising Marketing Activities." *Business Horizons* 16:5 (October), pp. 20–30.

Intriguing summary of marketing's role in society. Argues that in appraising marketing one must weigh direct and indirect costs. Sees society as a third participant in any exchange between producer and consumer.

Hovland, C. I., I. L. Janis, and H. H. Kelley. 1953. *Communication and Persuasion: Psychological Studies of Opinion Change*. New Haven: Yale University Press.

Classic social psychology book on attitude change.

Hulbert, J. M., and N. E. Toy. 1977. "A Strategic Framework for Marketing Control." *Journal of Marketing* 41:2 (April), pp. 12–20.

Emphasizes controlling the marketing function by measuring actual performance variances relative to marketing plans. Innovative and illuminating. (See text for a detailed review.)

Jackson, D. W., and L. L. Ostrom. 1980. "Grouping Segments for Profitability Analyses." *MSU Business Topics* 28 (April), pp. 39–44.

Brief but thorough review of segmenting quantitative results for profitability analysis.

Kahn, R. L. 1977. "Organizational Effectiveness: An Overview." In P. S. Goodman and J. M. Pennings, eds., *New Perspectives on Organizational Effectiveness*, pp. 235–248. San Francisco: Jossey-Bass.

Summary article of collection. Reviews six themes in organizational effectiveness work: conceptual utility, multiple outcomes, definition versus prediction, problems with outcomes, organizational level for analysis, and measurement.

Kanter, R. M., and D. V. Summers. 1987. "Doing Well While Doing Good: Dilemmas of Performance Measurement in Nonprofit Organizations and the Need for a Multiple-Constituency Approach." In W. W. Powell, ed., *The Nonprofit Sector: A Research Handbook*, pp. 154–166. New Haven: Yale University Press.

Excellent overview of the problems of performance appraisal in nonprofit organizations. Reviews much of the recent sociological and psychological literature in organizational effectiveness measurement. Well worth reading from a for-profit standpoint as well.

Kendrick, J. W. 1961. *Productivity Trends in the United States*. Princeton: Princeton University Press.

Major work evaluating productivity from the 1930s to the 1950s in multiple U.S. industries, including retailing and wholesaling.

———. 1973. *Postwar Productivity Trends in the United States, 1948–1969*. New York: Columbia University Press.

Extends Kendrick's 1961 work through the 1960s, using improved data sources to revise earlier estimates.

Kling, N. D. 1985. "The Marketing Audit: An Extension of the Marketing Control Process." *Managerial Finance* (U.K.) 11:1, pp. 23–26.

Excellent brief overview of the marketing audit literature.

Kotler, P. 1984. *Marketing Management: Analysis, Planning, and Control*. 5th ed. Englewood Cliffs, N.J.: Prentice-Hall.

Top-flight graduate-level marketing textbook.

Kotler, P., W. Gregor, and W. Rodgers. 1977. "The Marketing Audit Comes of Age." *Sloan Management Review* 18:2 (Winter), pp. 25–43.

Thorough, rigorous presentation of information about the marketing audit. Covers the audit process in detail, and includes a sample audit outline.

LaForge, R. W., D. W. Cravens, and C. E. Young. 1985. "Improving Salesforce Productivity." *Business Horizons* 28:5 (September–October), pp. 50–59.

Explains an intriguing application of strategic portfolio analysis to sales force deployment. Rather than examining the strength of position and market growth of a strategic business unit, the authors apply strength of position and "account opportunity" to sales territories.

Lavidge, R. J., and G. A. Steiner. 1961. "A Model for Predictive Measures of Advertising Effectiveness." *Journal of Marketing* 25:6 (October), pp. 59–62.

Outlines a three-part model of consumer attitudes toward purchasing a given item. Argues that the object of advertising is to discover the key attitude stage for a product or service and develop advertising to address that attitudinal stage.

Lewin, A. Y., and J. W. Minton. 1986. "Determining Organizational Effectiveness: Another Look, and an Agenda for Research." *Management Science* 32:5 (May), pp. 514–538.

A thorough review of theories of organizational effectiveness, with an exposition on applying data envelopment analysis (DEA), a quantitative analysis technique, to measurement of effectiveness. Good bibliography and mathematical appendix on DEA.

Lewin, K. 1951. *Field Theory in Social Science*. New York: Harper & Row.

Brilliant book by a famous psychologist applying field theory to topics as diverse as physics and interpersonal relations.

Little, J. D. C. 1981. "Advertising Productivity." *Advertising Age* 52:16 (April 13), pp. S-1, S-12.

Calls productivity a combination of efficiency and effectiveness. Defines efficiency as the amount of work managers accomplish per unit of resource employed, and effectiveness as improved "decision quality." Advocates computerized decision support systems.

Locke, E. A. 1976. "The Nature and Causes of Job Satisfaction." In M. D. Dunnette, ed., *Handbook of Industrial and Organizational Psychology*, pp. 1297–1350. Chicago: Rand-McNally.

A review of what is known about satisfaction, morale, turnover, and other variables.

Mahajan, V., P. Varadarajan, and R. A. Kerin. 1987. "Metamorphosis in Strategic Market Planning." In G. L. Frazier and J. Sheth, eds., *Contemporary Views on Marketing Practice*. Lexington, Mass.: Lexington Books.

Excellent overview of recent theoretical and empirical work in strategic planning for marketing.

McGuire, W. J. 1969. "The Nature of Attitudes and Attitude Change." In G. Lindzey and E. Aronson, eds., *The Handbook of Social Psychology*, Vol. 3, pp. 136–314. Englewood Cliffs, N.J.: Addison-Wesley.

The definitive statement summarizing what is known about attitudes and changing them.

McNiven, M. 1980. "Plan for More Productive Advertising." *Harvard Business Review* 58:2 (March–April), pp. 130–136.

Criticizes traditional advertising planning measures such as "percentage of sales" or "percentage increase over last year." Recommends instead that businesses discover their "advertising elasticity" by regression of historical data, modeling, and field experiments. Elasticity can then be used to optimize advertising spending.

Mehrotra, S. 1984. "How to Measure Marketing Productivity." *Journal of Advertising Research* 24:3 (June–July), pp. 9–15.

Argues that traditional measures of marketing productivity, such as share and profits, are too short-term oriented and do not address the true purpose of marketing. Instead, claims that the best long-term measure of productivity is "consumer franchise." Describes General Electric's method of assessing this variable. (See text for a detailed review.)

Miller, E. C. 1967. *Objectives and Standards of Performance in Marketing Management* (Research Study No. 85). New York: American Management Association.

A collection of forms for setting and meeting objectives, gathered from nine companies. Includes other advice on the topic as well.

Mischel, W. 1974. "Processes in Delay of Gratification." In L. Berkowitz, ed., *Advances in Experimental Social Psychology*, Vol. 7, pp. 249–293. New York: Academic Press.

Summary of work, mostly with children, investigating how and when they learn to delay rewards they have coming to them.

Mossman, F. H., P. M. Fischer, and W. J. E. Crissy. 1974. "New Approaches to Analyzing Marketing Profitability." *Journal of Marketing* 38:2 (April), pp. 43–48.

Proposes the use of a modular database to help companies allocate marketing costs to segments. The authors advocate a residual income approach to calculating net segment margin, thereby accounting for the capital invested in the segment.

Oxenfeldt, A. R. 1959. "How to Use Market-Share Measurement." *Harvard Business Review* 37:1 (January–February), pp. 59–68.

Cogent indictment of the way market share measurements are used in business.

Pirsig, R. 1974. *Zen and the Art of Motorcycle Maintenance*. New York: Bantam Books.

A combination of philosophical essays, journal entries, and autobiography centering around an intellectual quest to understand the concept of "quality." (See text for a detailed review.)

Porter, M. E. 1980. *Competitive Strategy: Techniques for Analyzing Industries and Competitors*. New York: Free Press.

Seminal work on analysis of strategic forces that affect industries and individual companies.

Raisbeck, G. 1979. "How the Choice of Measures of Effectiveness Constrains Operational Analysis." *Interfaces* 9:4 (August), pp. 85–93.

An informal, telling article on mistakes the author has made in selecting measures of effectiveness. Discusses desirable qualities in effectiveness measures.

Ramond, C. K. 1959. "The Measurement of Advertising Productivity." In Bureau of Economic and Business Research (symposium), *Productivity in Marketing: Its Measurement and Change*, pp. 114–131. Urbana, Ill.: University of Illinois.

A treatise on S-O-R psychology in business and advertising management.

Rayburn, L. G. 1973. "Analysis of Current Marketing Cost Methods." *CPA Journal* 43:11 (November), pp. 985–991.

Presents qualitative findings of a survey on marketing cost methods, using the issues raised to examine some of the major points of contention in marketing cost analysis.

Roethlisberger, F. J., and W. J. Dickson. 1934. *Management and the Worker*. Boston: Bureau of Business Research, Harvard University.

The discovery and description of the original Hawthorne effect work. This work is usually misinterpreted to mean that no matter how an investigator pays attention to research subjects, their productivity goes up. It is worth reading the original.

Roseman, E. 1979. "An Audit Can Make the Accurate Difference." *Product Marketing* 8:8 (August), pp. 24–25.

Effectively highlights the grossly inaccurate management assumptions that a marketing audit can reveal. Uses composite example of audits at several pharmaceutical companies.

Ruekert, R. W., O. C. Walker, Jr., and K. J. Roering. 1985. "The Organization of Marketing Activities: A Contingency Theory of Structure and Performance." *Journal of Marketing* 49:1 (Winter), pp. 13–25.

Combines economics and marketing viewpoints to develop a contingency theory for organizing marketing activities. Compares internal to external organization of a task, and centralized-formalized to decentralized-specialized organization of a task. (See text for a detailed review.)

Schoeffler, S., R. D. Buzzell, and D. F. Heany. 1974. "Impact of Strategic Planning on Profit Performance." *Harvard Business Review* 52:2 (March–April), pp. 137–145.

Early report on findings of the profit impact of marketing strategies (PIMS) database. (See text for a review of PIMS.)

Schudson, M. 1984. *Advertising, the Uneasy Persuasion: Its Dubious Impact on American Society*. New York: Basic Books.

Provocative review of advertising's role in the United States, examining both social and economic impacts.

Sevin, C. H. 1965. *Marketing Productivity Analysis*. New York: McGraw-Hill.

A classic of ratio analysis. Defines marketing productivity as sales or profit per unit of effort. Particularly concerned with quantitative factors affecting productivity. (See text for a detailed review.)

Shapiro, B. P. 1977. *Sales Program Management: Formulation and Implementation*. New York: McGraw-Hill.

Text and cases focusing on the many tasks of sales managers, including recruitment, training, organization, compensation, account management, and deployment of sales forces.

Shapiro, S. J., and V. H. Kirpalani (eds.). 1984. *Marketing Effectiveness: Insights from Accounting and Finance*. Boston: Allyn & Bacon.

Collection of classic articles providing advice for marketers based on research and techniques from accounting and finance.

Sherlock, J. F. 1983. "Market Audits Can Give a Competitive Edge." *Fundraising Management* 14:4 (June), pp. 75, 79.

Explains the use of traditional marketing audits in a hospital setting.

Simon, H. A., and A. C. Stedry. 1969. "Psychology and Economics." In G. Lindzey and E. Aronson, eds., *The Handbook of Social Psychology*, Vol. 5, Chapter 40. Englewood Cliffs, N.J.: Addison-Wesley.

Looks at the fascinating conjunction of two very different ways of looking at human behavior.

Spray, S. L. (ed.). 1976. *Organizational Effectiveness: Theory-Research-Utilization*. Kent, Ohio: Kent State University Press.

Collection of articles addressing organizational effectiveness issues from sociological and psychological viewpoints.

Starbuck, W. H. 1983. "Organizations as Action Generators." *American Sociological Review* 48:1 (February), pp. 91–102.

Thoughtful sociological work discussing the common phenomenon of organizations adopting systematized behaviors ("behavior programs") that quickly become nonadaptive as the environment changes. Claims that organizations then create problems, successes, threats, and opportunities to justify their actions.

Stefflre, V. 1985. *Developing and Implementing Marketing Strategies*. New York: Praeger.

Work on implementation that is especially strong on the intra-organizational obstacles to effective marketing actions.

Steiner, R. L. 1978. "Marketing Productivity in Consumer Goods Industries—A Vertical Perspective." *Journal of Marketing* 42:1 (January), pp. 60–70.

Argues that the proper measure of productivity is not manufacturer productivity but vertical industry productivity, due to the importance of wholesale and retail distribution. Uses examples from the toy and women's outerwear industries.

Takeuchi, H., and W. J. Salmon. 1985. "A New Data Management System for Food Retailers: Departmental ROI." Unpublished. Boston: Division of Research, Harvard Business School.

Develops a "refined measure" of departmental return on investment (DROI) for food retailers. Uses a six-month study of fourteen departments within four food chain stores to illustrate. Ranking by DROI dramatically changed the perceived success of a product line compared to rankings based on gross margin.

Tedeschi, J. T., B. R. Schlenker, and T. V. Bonoma. 1973. *Conflict, Power, and Games*. Chicago: Aldine.

Presents a unified theory of conflict and conflict management.

Thomas, M. J. 1984. "The Meaning of Marketing Productivity Analysis." *Marketing Intelligence and Planning* (U.K.) 2:2, pp. 13–28.

Thorough review of various methods of analyzing marketing productivity. Defines productivity as a product of how efficiently a company can apply its marketing mix to target segments. Extensive ratio analysis.

Tosdal, H. R. 1959. "Productivity in Sales Management." In Bureau of Economic and Business Research (symposium), *Productivity in Marketing: Its Measurement and Change*, pp. 132–151. Urbana, Ill.: University of Illinois.

Twentieth Century Fund, Committee on Distribution. 1939. *Does Distribution Cost Too Much?* New York: The Twentieth Century Fund.

Landmark study on the role of distribution and marketing in the American economy. (See text for a detailed review.)

Tye, W. B. 1983. "Fundamental Elements of a Marketing Audit for a More Competitive Motor Carrier Industry." *Transportation Journal* 22:13 (Spring), pp. 5–22.

Proposes a marketing audit outline for the trucking industry that seems applicable to other industries as well. Pays particular attention to the information flows within a company.

Waterman, R. H., T. J. Peters, and R. Julien. 1980. "Structure Is Not Organization." *Business Horizons* 23:3 (June), pp. 14–26.

Description of the McKinsey Seven-S model of corporate strategy and culture.

Webster, F. E., Jr. 1981. "Top Management Concerns about Marketing: Issues for the 1980's." *Journal of Marketing* 45:3 (Summer), pp. 9–16.

Reports results of in-depth interviews on marketing with top executives of thirty companies, identifying issues for concern and/or study.

Weitz, B. A. 1981. "Effectiveness in Sales Interactions." *Journal of Marketing* 45:1 (Winter), pp. 85–103.

Reviews research in the area of salesperson effectiveness, and proposes a contingency model of sales effectiveness.

Williamson, O. 1975. *Markets and Hierarchies: Analysis and Antitrust Implications*. New York: Free Press.

Williamson's book on transaction cost economics.

Wind, Y., and R. N. Cardozo. 1974. "Industrial Marketing Segmentation." *Industrial Marketing Management* 3:3 (March), pp. 153–166.

Proposes a two-stage model of market segmentation. The first stage (macro) segments markets based on characteristics of buyer organizations, while the second stage (micro) segments markets based on characteristics of key decision-making units. Also reports findings of interviews concerning industrial marketers' use of segmentation.

Wintrobe, R., and A. Breton. 1986. "Organizational Structure and Productivity." *American Economic Review* 76:3 (June), pp. 530–538.

Intriguing economic analysis proposing that output is not only a function of capital and labor inputs, but also vertical and horizontal networks of "trust" within the organization.

Zabriskie, N. B., and J. Browning. 1979. "Measuring Industrial Salespeople's Short-Term Productivity." *Industrial Marketing Management* 8:2 (April), pp. 167–171.

Reports results of interviews with five firms in each of three industries to examine the way companies measure sales force productivity. Classifies selling behaviors into sales seeking, market intelligence, goodwill, and channel assistance. (See text for a detailed review.)

INDEX

Aaker, David A. "Multivariate Analysis in Mktg:
(1971)   Theory & Application"   CA: Wadsworth Pub
Dewey HF 5415. A22C